# INFORMATION TECHNOLOGIES IN MEDICINE

# INFORMATION TECHNOLOGIES IN MEDICINE

## VOLUME II: REHABILITATION AND TREATMENT

Edited by

**Metin Akay**
Dartmouth College

**Andy Marsh**
National Technical University of Athens

A WILEY-INTERSCIENCE PUBLICATION

**JOHN WILEY & SONS, INC.**

New York · Chichester · Weinheim · Brisbane · Singapore · Toronto

This book is printed on acid-free paper.☉

Copyright © 2001 by John Wiley & Sons, Inc. All rights reserved.

Published simultaneously in Canada.

For ordering and customer service, call 1-800-CALL-WILEY.

*Library of Congress Cataloging in Publication Data is available.*

Akay, Metin
  Information Technologies in Medicine, Volume II: Rehabitation and Treatment, edited by
    Akay, Metin and Marsh, Andy.

ISBN 0-471-41492-1

Printed in the United States of America.

10 9 8 7 6 5 4 3 2 1

# ■ CONTRIBUTORS

**Luciano Beolchi**, European Commission DGXIII-C4, Office BU29-3/68, Rue de la Loi 200 B-1049, Brussels, Belgium
luciano.beolchi@BXL.DB13.cec.be

**Alberto Bianchi**, LBHL, 50A-1148, 1 Cyclotron Road, University of California, Berkeley, CA 94720
asarti@math.lbl.gov

**Curtis Boswell**, Jet Propulsion Laboratory, California Institute of Technology, 4800 Oak Grove Drive, Pasadena, CA 91109

**Hari Das**, Jet Propulsion Laboratory, California Institute of Technology, 4800 Oak Grove Drive, Pasadena, CA 91109

**Mark Draper**, Human Interface Technology Laboratory, Box 352142, University of Washington, Seattle, WA 98195-2142

**Thomas A. Furness, III**, Human Interface Technology Laboratory, Box 352142, University of Washington, Seattle, WA 98195-2142

**Roberto Gori**, LBHL, 50A-1148, 1 Cyclotron Road, University of California, Berkeley, CA 94720
asarti@math.lbl.gov

**Qinglian Guo**, Department of Information Science, Faculty of Science, University of Tokyo, 7-3-1 Hongo, Bunkyo-ku, Tokyo 113-0033, Japan

**Walter J. Greenleaf**, Greenleaf Medical Systems, 2248 Park Boulevard, Palo Alto, CA 94306
walter@greenleafmed.com

**Claudio Lamberti**, LBHL, 50A-1148, 1 Cyclotron Road, University of California, Berkeley, CA 94720
asarti@math.lbl.gov

**Zsolt Lorant**, 9904 Carlyle Way W Apt. #446, Mobile, AL 36609

**Claudio Marchetti**, LBHL, 50A-1148, 1 Cyclotron Road, University of California, Berkeley, CA 94720
asarti@math.lbl.gov

**Katsunobu Muroi**, Mitsubishi Electric Corporation, Tsukaguchi-Honmachi, Amagasaki, Hyogo, JAPAN

**Tim Ohm**, Jet Propulsion Laboratory, California Institute of Technology, 4800 Oak Grove Drive, Pasadena, CA 91109

**Mieko Ohsuga**, Mitsubishi Electric Corporation, Tsukaguchi-Honmachi, Amagasaki, Hyogo, JAPAN

**Guiseppe Riva**, Instituto Auxologico Italiano, Applied Technology for Neuro-Psychology, Verbania, Italy

**Guillermo Rodriguez**, Jet Propulsion Laboratory, California Institute of Technology, 4800 Oak Grove Drive, Pasadena, CA 91109

**Alessandro Sarti**, LBHL, 50A-1148, 1 Cyclotron Road, University of California, Berkeley, CA 94720
asarti@math.lbl.gov

**Rob Steele**, Jet Propulsion Laboratory, California Institute of Technology, 4800 Oak Grove Drive, Pasadena, CA 91109

**Robert John Stone**, Virtual Presence Ltd., Chester House, 79 Dane Road, Sale, Cheshire, M33 7BP UK
r.stone@vrsolns.co.uk

**Erik Viirre**, 3081 Nute Way, San Diego, CA 92117

**Jihong Wang**, Department of Radiology, University of Texas Southwestern Medical School, Dallas, TX 75235-9071
wang@phyics.swmed.edu

**Brenda K. Wiederhold**, Center for Advanced Multimedia Psychotherapy, CSPP Research and Service Foundation, 6160 Cornerstone Court East, San Diego, CA 92121
brendaweid@aol.com

**Mark D. Wiederhold**, Department of Internal Medicine, Scripps Clinic Medical Group, 1200 Prospect Street, Suite 400, La Jolla, CA 92037
mark_weiderhold@cpqm.caic.com

# CONTENTS

For many patients, the real world is too risky or disconcerting for them to move around in. The agoraphobic patient has a fear of open or public places and so may become housebound. The psychiatric technique of desensitization has been in use for a number of years. The patient is asked to imagine the things that are most disturbing and gradually their fears are controlled. Now a virtual environment can be created for treatment of these patients. They can gradually experience their feared objects in a manner with complete control. Similarly, people who need rehabilitation from weakness or loss of body function or control can have a custom environment created for them that will represent an appropriate challenge to help them recover.

Delivery of medical care has be progressively hampered by the lack of ability to provide specialized information uniformly to all people. Specialists tend to be located in university, urban centers that are distant from many patients and their primary care physicians. With the explosion of understanding of many diseases, the primary care physician will need more and more access to agents able to understand and synthesize information about patients.

Beyond telemedicine, telesurgery has been touted as a means of getting surgeon to a remote location and allowing him to operate on his patient. Since there are many surgeons, this application of telepresence will only be useful in places that doctors are not willing to go, such as the battlefield. However, there are remote locations that no surgeon is currently able to go; microscopic sites inside the body. Surgeons now manipulate blood vessels inside the eye or bones in the middle ear. However, at current size, even when viewed through the best microscope, the VRT can also be used in the areas of physical disabilities. Virtual environments can be created for the treatment of the patients with the motor disturbances such as parases. The speech disabilities can be assisted by simply using the data gloves which translate the gestures into spoken words.

In this volume, we will discuss the use of information technologies in in the rehabilitation, treatment of physical disabilities in details and the delivery of health care using the information technologies.

The first chapter by W. J. Greenleaf summarizes the current status of the virtual reality technologies and discusses the use of these technologies in neuro/ orthopedic rehabilitation as well as the new systems under development.

The second chapter by B. K. Wiederhold and M. D. Wiederhold gives the use of virtual reality technologies for the treatment of many anxiety disorders including fear of heights, flying, spiders, driving, social phobia, and the possibility of using these technologies for the treatment of acute stress disorders and generalized anxiety disorders.

The third chapter by L. Beolchi and G. Riva gives an indepth summary of virtual reality technologoies and their applications in health care as well as the healt care market analysis.

The fourth chapter by Das et al. presents the recenty developed RAM tele-robot system and its demonstration of a simulated microsurgery procedure performed at the JPL.

The fifth chapter by Viirre et al. discusses motion sickness caused by the virtual reality technology and the application of VR for vestibular patients.

The sixth chapter by Guo et al. introduces a telemedicine diagnosis support systems based on the computer graphics and multimedia technologies.

The seventh chapter by J. Wang presents the implementation of a picture-achieving and comunication system (PACS) and teleradiology system by emphasing the practical issues in the implementation of a clinical PACS.

The eighth chapter by Stone discusses the adoptation of virtual reality technologies in medicine and other sectors and presents a case study of one surgical training system.

The last chapter by Sarti et al. discusses a simulation method that allows one to deal with extremely complex anatomical geometrics and gives a detailed comparison between virtual and real surgical opertions performed on patients.

We thank the authors for their valuable contributions to this volume and George Telecki, the Executive Editor and Shirley Thomas, Senior Associate Managing Editor of John Wiley & Sons, Inc. for their valuable support and encouragement througout the preparation of this volume.

METIN AKAY

*This work was partially supported by a USA NSF grant (IEEE EMBS Workshop on Virtual Reality in Medicine, BES – 9725881) made to Professor Metin Akay.*

# INFORMATION TECHNOLOGIES IN MEDICINE

# PART I

# TREATMENT

# CHAPTER 1

# Neuro/Orthopedic Rehabilitation and Disability Solutions Using Virtual Reality Technology

WALTER J. GREENLEAF, Ph.D.

Greenleaf Medical Systems
Palo Alto, California

Virtual reality (VR) is an emerging technology that allows individuals to experience three-dimensional (3-D) visual, auditory, and tactile environments. Highly specialized sensors and interface devices allow the individual to become

*Information Technologies in Medicine, Volume II: Rehabilitation and Treatment,* Edited by
Metin Akay and Andy Marsh.
ISBN 0-471-41492-1 © 2001 John Wiley & Sons, Inc.

immersed and to navigate and interact with objects in a computer-generated environment. Most people associate VR with video games; however, researchers and clinicians in the medical community are becoming increasingly aware of its potential benefits for people with disabilities and for individuals recovering from injuries.

## 1.1   VR ENVIRONMENTS AND INTERFACES

The computer-generated environment, or virtual world, consists of a 3-D graphics program that relies on a spatially organized, object-oriented database in which each object in the database represents an object in the virtual world (Fig. 1.1). A separate modeling program is used to create the individual objects for the virtual world. For greater realism, these modeling programs apply state-of-the-art computer-graphics techniques, such as texture mapping and shading, to all of the objects of the scene. The object database is manipulated using a real-time dynamics controller that specifies how objects behave within the world according to user-specified constraints and according to natural laws, such as gravity, inertia, and material properties. These laws are application specific. The dynamics controller also tracks the position and orientation of the user's head and hand.

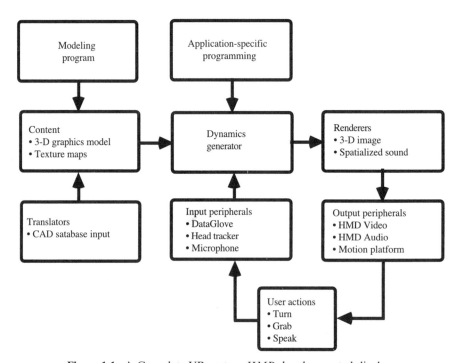

**Figure 1.1.** A Complete VR system *HMD*, head-mounted display.

Common computer input devices, such as a mouse and a keyboard, do not provide a sense of immersion in a virtual world. To create a VR experience, the conventional computer interface is replaced by one that is more natural and intuitive for interaction within complex 3-D environments. The need for improved human–computer interaction with virtual environments (VEs) has motivated the development of a new generation of interface hardware. To date, the most common 3-D input devices used in VR applications are head-mounted displays (HMDs) and instrumented clothing (gloves and suits). VEs may also be created through circuambiant projections (1), 3-D spatialized sound (2), haptic feedback, and motion effectors.

### 1.1.1  Head-Mounted Display

The best-known tool for data output in VR is the head-mounted display. It supports first-person immersion by generating a wide field of view image for each eye, often in true 3-D. Most lower-cost HMDs ($1000 range) use liquid crystal displays (LCDs) others use small cathode ray tubes (CRTs). The more expensive HMDs ($60,000 and up) use optical fibers to pipe the images from non-HMDs. An HMD requires a position tracker in addition to the helmet. Alternatively, the binocular display can be mounted on an armature for support and tracking (a Boom display) (3).

### 1.1.2  Instrumented Clothing

Among the most popular and widely available input devices for VR are hand-tracking technologies. Such glove-based input devices let VR users apply their manual dexterity to the VR activity. Hand-tracking gloves currently in use include Sayre Glove, MIT LED Glove, Digital Data-Entry Glove, DataGlove, Dexterous HandMaster, Power Glove, CyberGlove, and Space Glove (4). This chapter describes two prototype clinical and rehabilitation applications using instrumented clothing technology (Fig. 1.2).

Originally developed by VPL Research, the DataGlove is a thin cloth glove with engraved optical fibers running along the surface of each digit that loop back to a light-processing box. The optical fibers that cross each joint are treated to increase the refractive surface area of that segment of the fiber over the joint. Each optical fiber originates at, and returns to, a light-processing box. In the light-processing box, light-emitting diodes send photons along the fibers to the photo detector. When the joints of the hand bend, the optical fibers bend so that the photons refract out of the fiber, thus attenuating the signal that passes through the fibers. The transmitted signal is proportional to the amount of flexion of a single joint and is recorded as such.

Because the attenuation of light along each optical fiber is interpreted as a measurement of joint flexion, the set of joint measurements can be thought of as a hand gesture. To provide feedback to the user, most VR applications render a graphic representation of the hand moving in real time; this representation

**Figure 1.2.** The WristSystem, based on the VR DataGlove.

shadows the movements of the hand in the DataGlove and replicates even the most subtle actions.

To determine the orientation and the position of the hand in 3-D space, the glove relies on a spatial tracking system. Tracking systems usually rely on electromagnetic, ultrasonic, or infrared sensors to determine the position and orientation of a the glove in relation to the signal source. Typically, the source is placed at a desired point of reference and the sensor is mounted on the dorsum of the glove.

The DataSuit is a custom-tailored body suit fitted with the same sophisticated fiberoptic sensors found in the DataGlove. The sensors are able to track the full range of motion of the person wearing the DataGlove or DataSuit as he or she bends, moves, grasps, or waves. Missing from the instrumented clothing is haptic feedback, which provides touch and force-feedback information to the VR participant.

### 1.1.3  3-D Spatialized Sound

The impression of immersion within a VE is greatly enhanced by inclusion of 3-D spatialized sound (5). Stereo-pan effects alone are inadequate because they tend to sound as if they are originating inside the head. Research into 3-D audio has shown the importance of modeling the head and pinna and using this model as part of the 3-D sound generation. A head-related transfer function

(HRTF) can be used to generate the proper acoustics. A number of problems remain, such as the cone of confusion, wherein sounds behind the head are perceived to be in front of the head.

### 1.1.4   Other VR Interfaces

Senses of balance and motion can be generated in a VR system by a motion platform. These have been used in flight simulators to provide motion cues that the mind integrates with other cues to perceive motion. Haptics is the generation of touch and force-feedback information. Most systems to date have focused on force feedback and kinesthetic senses, although some prototype systems exist that generate tactile stimulation. Many of the haptic systems thus far are exoskeletons used for position sensing as well as for providing resistance to movement or active force application.

Some preliminary work has been conducted on generating the sense of temperature in VR. Small electrical heat pumps have been developed that produce sensations of heat and cold as part of the simulated environment.

### 1.2   DIVERSITY OF VR APPLICATIONS

VR has been researched for decades in government laboratories and universities, but because of the enormous computing power demands and associated high costs, applications have been slow to migrate from the research world to other areas. Recent improvements in the price:performance ratio of graphic computer systems have made VR technology more affordable and thus used more commonly in a wider range of applications. In fact, there is even a strong "garage VR" movement—groups of interested parties sharing information on how to build extremely low cost VR systems using inexpensive off-the-shelf components (6). These homemade systems are often inefficient, uncomfortable to use (sometimes painful), and slow; but they exist as a strong testament to a fervent interest in VR technology.

Current VR applications are diverse and represent dramatic improvements over conventional visualization and planning techniques:

- **Public entertainment.** VR is arguably the most important current trend in public entertainment, with ventures ranging from shopping mall game simulators to low-cost VR games for the home.
- **Computer-aided design (CAD).** Using VR to create virtual prototypes in software allows engineers to test potential products in the design phase, even collaboratively over computer networks, without investing time or money for conventional hard models.
- **Military.** Using VR, the military's solitary cab-based systems have evolved into extensive networked simulations involving a variety of equipment and situations. Extensive battle simulations can now be created that net-

work tanks, ships, soldiers, and fighters all into the same shared training experience.

- **Architecture and construction.** VR allows architects and engineers and their clients to walk through structural blueprints. Designs may be understood more clearly by clients who often have difficulty comprehending even conventional cardboard models. The city of Atlanta credits its VR model for winning the site of the 1996 Olympics, and San Diego used a VR model of a planned convention center addition to compete for (and obtain) the 1996 Republican Party convention.

- **Financial visualization.** By allowing navigation through an abstract world of data, VR helps users rapidly visualize large amounts of complex financial market data and thus supports faster decision making.

VR is commonly associated with exotic fully immersive applications because of the overdramatized media coverage of helmets, body suits, entertainment simulators, and the like. As important are the window-into-world applications by which the user or operator is allowed to interact effectively with virtual data, either locally or remotely.

## 1.3 CURRENT STATUS OF VR TECHNOLOGY

The commercial market for VR, although taking advantage of advances in VR technology at large, is nonetheless contending with the lack of integrated systems and the lack of reliable equipment suppliers. Typically, researchers buy peripherals and software from separate companies and configure their own systems. Companies that can offer integrated systems for commercial applications are expected to fill this gap over the next few years. Concurrently, the nature of the commercial VR medical market is expected to change as the prices of today's expensive, high-performance graphics systems decrease dramatically. High-resolution display systems will also significantly drop in cost as the VR display business can piggyback on HDTV projection and home-entertainment technologies.

Technical advances have occurred in networking applications, which include improved visual photo realism, decreased tracker latency through predictive algorithms, and variable resolution image generators. Work to improve database access methods is under way. Important hardware advances include eye gear with an increased field of view, wireless communications, lighted and smaller devices, and improved tracking systems.

## 1.4 VR-BASED MEDICAL APPLICATIONS IN DEVELOPMENT

The first wave of VR development efforts in the medical community addressed seven key categories:

Surgical training and surgical planning.

Medical education, modeling, and nonsurgical training.

Anatomically keyed displays with real-time data fusion.

Telesurgery and telemedicine.

Patient testing and behavioral intervention.

Rehabilitation, functional movement analysis, and motion/ergonomic studies.

Disability solutions.

The potential of VR through education and information dissemination indicates there will be few areas of medicine not taking advantage of this improved computer interface. However, the latent potential of VR lies in its capacity to be used to manipulate and combine heterogeneous datasets from many sources. This feature is most significant and likely to transform the traditional applications environment in the near future.

### 1.4.1   Surgical Training and Planning

Various projects are under way to use VR and imaging technology to plan, simulate, and customize invasive (an minimally invasive) surgical procedures. Ranging from advanced imaging technologies for endoscopic surgery to routine hip replacements, these new developments will have a tremendous effect on improving surgical morbidity and mortality. According to Merril (7), studies show that doctors are more likely to make errors when performing their first few to several dozen diagnostic and therapeutic surgical procedures then when performing later procedures. Merril claims that operative risk could be substantially reduced by the development of a simulator that would allow transference of skills from the simulation to the actual point of patient contact. With surgical modeling, we would generally expect a much higher degree of precision, reliability, and safety, in addition to cost efficiency.

Several VR-based systems currently under development allow real-time tracking of surgical instrumentation and simultaneous display and manipulation of 3-D anatomy corresponding to the simulated procedure (8, 9). Using this design, surgeons can practice procedures and experience the possible complications and variations in anatomy encountered during surgery. Necessary software tools have been developed to enable the creation of virtual tissues that reflect the physical characteristics of physiologic tissues. This technology operates in real-time using 3-D graphics, on a high-speed computer platform.

### 1.4.2   Medical Education, Modeling, and Nonsurgical Training

Researchers at the University of California at San Diego are exploring the value of hybridizing elements of VR, multimedia (MM), and communications technologies into a unified educational paradigm (10). The goal is to develop powerful tools that extend the flexibility and effectiveness of medical teaching and promote lifelong learning. To this end, they have undertaken a multiyear initiative, named the VR-MM Synthesis Project. Based on instructional design and user need (rather than technology per se), they plan to link the computers of the Data Communications Gateway, the Electronic Medical Record System, and the Simulation Environment. This system supports medical students, surgical residents, and clinical faculty and runs applications ranging from full surgical simulation to basic anatomic exploration and review, all via a common interface. The plan also supports integration of learning and telecommunications resources (such as interactive MM libraries, on-line textbooks, databases of medical literature, decision support systems, email, and access to electronic medical records).

### 1.4.3   Anatomically Keyed Displays with Real-Time Data Fusion

An anatomically keyed display with real-time data fusion is currently in use at the New York University Medical Center's Department of Neurosurgery. The system allows both preoperative planning and real-time tumor visualization (11, 12). The technology offers the opportunity for a surgeon to plan and rehearse a surgical approach to a deep-seated, centrally located brain tumor before doing of the actual procedure. The imaging method (volumetric stereotaxis) gathers, stores and reformats imaging-derived, 3-D volumetric information that defines an intracranial lesion (tumor) with respect to the surgical field.

Computer-generated information is displayed during the procedure on computer monitors in the operating room and on a heads-up display mounted on the operating microscope. These images provide surgeons with CT- and MRI-defined maps of the surgical field scaled to actual size and location. This information guides the surgeon in finding and defining the boundaries of brain tumors. The computer-generated images are indexed to the surgical field by means of a robotics-controlled stereotactic frame that positions the patient's tumor within a defined targeting area.

Simulated systems using VR models are also being advocated for other high-risk procedures, such as the alignment of radiation sources to treat cancerous tumors.

### 1.4.4   Telesurgery and Telemedicine

Telepresence is the sister field of VR. Classically defined as the ability to act and interact in an off-site environment by making use of VR technology, telepresence is emerging as an area of development in its own right. Telemedicine (the telepresence of medical experts) is being explored as a way to reduce the cost of medical practice and to bring expertise into remote areas (13, 14).

Telesurgery is a fertile area for development. On the verge of realization, telesurgery (remote surgery) will help resolve issues that can complicate or compromise surgery, including

- A patient that is too ill or injured to be moved for surgery.
- A specialized surgeon located at some distance from the patient who requires specialized intervention.
- Accident victims who need immediate, on-the-scene surgery.
- Soldiers wounded in battle.

The surgeon really does operate—on flesh, not a computer animation. Although the distance aspect of remote surgery is a provocative one, telepresence is proving to be an aid in nonremote surgery as well. It can help surgeons gain dexterity and improve their operative technique, which is expected to be particularly important in endoscopic surgery. For example, suturing and knot tying will be as easy to see in endoscopic surgery as it is in open surgery, because telepresence offers the ability to emulate the look and feel of open surgery.

As initially developed at SRI International (15), telepresence not only offers a compelling sense of reality for the surgeon but also allows him or her to perform the surgery according to the usual methods and procedures. There is nothing new to learn. Hand motions are quick and precise. The visual field, the instrument motion, and the force feedback can all be scaled to make micro-surgery easier than it would be if the surgeon were at the patient's side. While current technology has been implemented in several prototypes, SRI and Tele-surgical Corporation (Redwood City, CA) are collaborating to develop a full comercial system based on this novel concept.

## 1.5  NEUROLOGIC TESTING AND BEHAVIORAL INTERVENTION

For Parkinson disease victims, initiating and sustaining walking becomes progressively difficult. The condition known as akinesia can be mitigated by treatment with drugs such as L-dopa, a precursor of the natural neural transmitter dopamine, but usually not without unwanted side effects. Now, collaborators at the Human Interface Technology Laboratory and the Department of Rehabilitation Medicine at the University of Washington, along with the San Francisco Parkinson's Institute are using virtual imagery to simulate an effect called kinesia paradoxa, or the triggering of normal walking behavior in akinetic Parkinson patients (16).

Using a commercial, field-multiplexed, heads-up video display, the research team has developed an approach that elicits near-normal walking by presenting collimated virtual images of objects and abstract visual cues moving through the patient's visual field at speeds that emulate normal walking. The combination of image collimation and animation speed reinforces the illusion of space-stabilized visual cues at the patient's feet. This novel, VR-assisted technology may also prove to be therapeutically useful for other movement disorders.

Lamson and Meisner (17) investigated the diagnostic and treatment possibilities of VR immersion on anxiety, panic and height phobias. By immersing both patients and controls in computer-generated situations, the researchers were able to expose the subjects to anxiety-provoking situations (such as jumping from a height) in a controlled manner. Experimental results indicate a significant subject habituation and desensitization through this approach, and the approach appears clinically useful.

Pugnetti (18) explored the potential of enhancing the clinical evaluation and management of acquired cognitive impairments in adults. By using a VR-based navigation paradigm, researchers were able to challenge both patients and normal subjects with a complex cognitive activity and simultaneously generate performance data. Behavioral data analysis was then carried out using established scoring criteria.

## 1.6 REHABILITATION, FUNCTIONAL MOVEMENT ANALYSIS, AND ERGONOMIC STUDIES

The field of VR is still at the proof-of-concept stage, yet there is a growing number of potential applications related to motion monitoring, rehabilitation, and ergonomic analysis. I (19) theorized that the rehabilitation process can be enhanced through the use of VR technology.

Evaluation of hand impairment involves detailed physical examination and functional testing of the afflicted person. The physical examination is designed to determine the presence of pain and any loss of strength, sensation, range of motion, and structure. The results are combined to produce a numerical assessment of impairment that is used to evaluate the patient's progress over time, yet examinations and calculations can be time-consuming, expensive, and subject to observer error.

Functional evaluation is usually accomplished by subjective observation of patient performance on standardized tests for motor skills. However, reproducibility of measurements becomes an issue whenever different examiners evaluate the same patient, which makes it difficult to evaluate a patient's progress over time. The more objective assessments of upper extremity motion fall into two categories: visual and effective.

Visual methods involve digitizing and estimating a visual record of the motion: The patient is videotaped performing a task; then the individual frames of the video are digitized and evaluated to quantify the degree of motion of the joint under study. The main limitation of this technique is that the camera can view motion in only two dimensions. To assess movement in the camera's visual plane accurately, the third dimension must be held constant, i.e., the person must move along a known line parallel to the plane of the film in the camera. In most cases, the examiner cannot maintain the correct orientation even for short periods, making this a difficult and cumbersome technique.

Effective methods measure the motion's effect rather than the motion itself. A work simulator is one example of an effective assessment tool. Work simulators measure the force exerted by a subject on a variety of attachments that simulate tools used in the workplace. A major limitation of this approach is that no data are collected on how the person effects the force.

Ideally one would like to collect and compare range of motion data for a joint in several planes simultaneously while specific tasks were being performed by the patient, a measurement that is impossible using a standard goniometer. At one point my group considered using the DataGlove with its multiple sensors as a means of collecting dynamic functional movement data. However, migrating the DataGlove technology from the field of VR to clinical evaluation posed several problems. For example, during manufacture of the DataGlove, the treatment of individual fiberoptic cables was not identical, thus it was impossible to characterize and predict their behavior. Moreover, empirical observations show hysteresis, making repeated measurements irreproducible and making it difficult to determine the accuracy of the measurements. For highly accurate measurements, it is important to have a perfect fit of the glove, because poor placement of the sensitive areas of fibers yields incorrect measurements. Achieving a perfect fit of the DataGlove posed a serious challenge because of the variability of hand shapes and sizes across a given patient population. Moreover, the use of the fiberoptic DataGlove excluded the population of patients with anatomic deformities.

With the goal of obtaining accurate, dynamic range of motion data for the wrist joint, my group investigated other sensor materials and developed the glove-based WristSystem. Fiberoptic sensors were replaced by dual-axis electrogoniometric sensors that could be inserted into machine-washable Lycra gloves that fit different sizes of hands.

WristSystem gloves are currently being used to track flexion, extension, radial, and ulnar deviations of the wrist while patients are performing routine tasks. A portable, lightweight DataRecorder worn in a waist pack permits the patient to be ambulatory while data are being collected at the clinic or work site (Fig. 1.3); no visual observation or supervision is required beyond the initial calibration of the glove sensors. Real-time visual and auditory feedback can also be used to train the patient to avoid high-risk postures in the workplace or at home.

The WristSystem includes Motion Analysis System (MAS) software for the interpretation of the dynamic-movement data collected by the DataRecorder over several minutes or hours. This software offers rapid, quantitative analysis of data that includes the total and percent time the wrist spends at critical angles (minimum, maximum, and mean wrist angles in four directions), the number of repetitions, and the velocity and acceleration. Figure 1.4 shows a sample plot of some of these data. In this example, it can be seen that the patient's right hand was ulnar-deviated >15° for 84% of the time he performed a certain task.

The WristSystem is currently being used by occupational and rehabilitation medicine specialists (MDs, PTs, and OTs), ergonomists, industrial safety managers, biomechanical researchers, and risk management consultants. The ultimate extension of this project is to build an augmented-reality environment for quantitative evaluation of functional tasks. The system will link multiple input

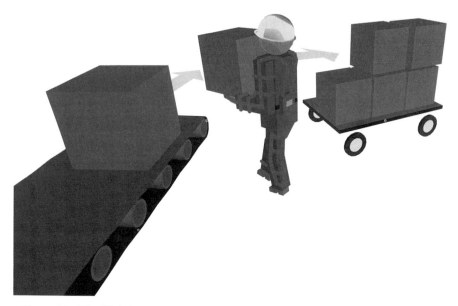

**Figure 1.3.** The WristSystem being used to track functional movement at a job site.

devices or sensors worn by the patient and 3-D modeling software. Therapists will be able to design a virtual world composed of objects traditionally used in functional assessment tests, such as balls, cubes, keys, and pencils. The therapist will be able to record the motion, location, and trajectory of the user's hand that is required to accomplish the motion and any associated hand tremors or

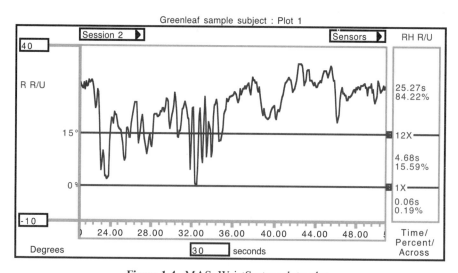

**Figure 1.4.** MAS: WristSystem data plot.

spasms. Once the data are collected, the therapist can use statistical analysis software to interpret them. The clinician can also elect to review the motions by animation of the data and to change the orientation to study the motion from another angle.

Other control devices originally developed for VR are being improved and applied to the field of functional evaluation of movement in a variety of ways. Burdea (20) described a system that would couple a glove with force-feedback devices to rehabilitate a damaged hand or to diagnose a range of hand problems. He describes another system under development that incorporates tactile feedback in a glove to produce feeling in the fingers when virtual objects are "touched."

My research group previously theorized that the rehabilitation process could be enhanced through the use of VR technology (21). Perhaps the most significant advantage is that a single VR-based rehabilitation workstation can be easily customized for individual patient needs. We are currently developing some basic components for a VR-based workstation (Fig. 1.5) that will be used to

- Restructure the rehabilitation process into small, incremental functional steps.

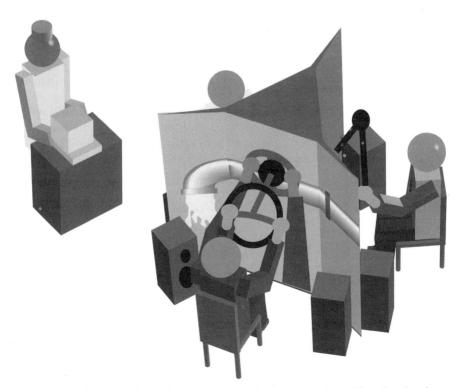

**Figure 1.5.** Virtual reality technology for quanitative evaluation of functional tasks.

- Make the rehabilitation process more realistic and less boring, enhancing patient motivation and recovery of function.
- Facilitate home rehabilitation.
- Provide an objective index of function for activities of daily living and work.

### 1.6.1   The Role of VR in Disability Solutions

One exciting aspect of VR technology is the inherent ability to enable individuals with physical disabilities to accomplish tasks and have experiences that would otherwise be denied them. There are approximately 35 million people in the United States who have physical disabilities that affect their ability to work in certain types of jobs. Computers and VR software can provide increased access to daily activities for people with disabilities. VR technology may provide an adaptable mechanism for harnessing a person's strongest physical ability to operate an input device for a computer program.

A simple glove-based system allows users to record custom-tailored gestures and to map these gestures to actions. These actions can range from a simple command, such as a mouse click on a computer screen, to more complex functions, such as controlling a robotic arm. An application programmer can define the functional relationship between the sensor data and a task with real-time graphical representation on a computer screen. Simple gestures can be translated to a preprogrammed set of instructions for speech or movement.

The prototype GloveTalker is an example of a one-to-one mapping of a gesture to a computer-generated action to provide additional communication skills to people with vocal impairment. The patient is able to speak by signaling the computer with his or her personalized set of gestures while wearing the DataGlove, which recognizes hand positions (gestures) and passes the information to the computer's voice-synthesis system (Fig. 1.6). For example, a patient may map a specific gesture, such as a closed fist, for the phrase "Hello, my name is Susan." The computer has some freedom in interpreting the gesture so that people capable of only relatively gross muscle control may use the system. There is also the possibility of sending the voice output through a telephone system, enabling vocally impaired individuals to communicate verbally over distance.

### 1.7   CONCLUSION

VR tools and techniques are rapidly developing in the scientific, engineering, and medical areas. Although traditionally used as input devices for virtual worlds in the entertainment and defense industry, sensor-loaded gloves may become the clinical tools of choice for measuring, monitoring, and amplifying upper-extremity motion. Although I have identified other potential clinical applications, many technological challenges must be met before such devices can be made available for patient care.

**Figure 1.6.** The GloveTalker: speech communication for the vocally impaired.

Pioneers in the field of medical VR are being encouraged to design sophisticated devices that promote both physical and psychological gains for injured and disabled patients while keeping costs for the devices within an acceptable range for health-care providers and third-party payors. The mandate is complex, but like VR technology itself, the possibilities are promising and exciting.

## REFERENCES

1. C. Cruz-Neira, D. J. Sandin, and T. A. DeFanti. Surround-screen projection-based virtual reality: the design and implementation of the CAVE. Paper presented at Computer Graphics. Anaheim, CA, 1993.
2. M. F. Deering. Explorations of display interfaces for virtual reality. Paper presented at IEEE Virtual Reality Annual International Symposium. New York, 1993.
3. M. T. Bolas. Human factors in the design of an immersive display. IEEE Comput Graph Appl 1994;14:55–59.

4. D. J. Sturman and D. Zeltzer. A survey of glove-based input. IEEE Comput Graph Appl 1994;14:30–39.

5. N. I. Durlach, B. G. Shinn-Cunningham, and R. M. Held. Supernormal auditory localization. I. General background. Presence 1993;2:89–103.

6. L. Jacobs. Garage virtual reality. Indianapolis: Sams, 1994.

7. J. R. Merril. Photorealistic interactive three-dimensional graphics in surgical simulation. Interactive technology and the new paradigm for healthcare. Burke, VA: IOS Press, 1995.

8. D. Hon. Ixion's laparoscopic surgical skills simulator. Paper presented at Medicine Meets Virtual Reality II. San Diego, CA, 1994.

9. K. T. McGovern and L. T. McGovern. Virtual clinic: a virtual reality surgical simulator. Virtual Reality World 1994;2:1994.

10. H. M. Hoffman. Virtual reality and the medical curriculum: integrating extant and emerging technologies. Paper presented at Medicine Meets Virtual Reality II. San Diego, CA, 1994.

11. P. J. Kelly. Quantitative virtual reality surgical simulation, minimally invasive stereotactic neurosurgery and frameless stereotactic technologies. Paper presented at Medicine Meets Virtual Reality II. San Diego, CA, 1994.

12. B. A. Kall, P. J. Kelly, S. O. Stiving, and S. J. Goerss. Integrated multimodality visualization in stereotactic neurologic surgery. Paper presented at Medicine Meets Virtual Reality II. San Diego, CA, 1994.

13. M. Burrow. A telemedicine testbed for developing and evaluating telerobotic tools for rural health care. Paper presented at Medicine Meets Virtual Reality II. San Diego, CA, 1994.

14. J. Rosen. The role of telemedicine and telepresence in reducing health care costs. Paper presented at Medicine Meets Virtual Reality II. San Diego, CA, 1994.

15. R. M. Satava. Robotics, telepresence and virtual reality: a critical analysis of the future of surgery. Minim Invasive Ther 1992;1:357–363.

16. S. Weghorst, J. Prothero, and T. Furness. Virtual images in the treatment of parkinson's disease akinesia. Paper presented at Medicine Meets Virtual Reality II. San Diego, CA, 1994.

17. R. Lamson and M. Meisner. The effects of virtual reality immersion in the treatment of anxiety, panic, & phobia of heights. Virtual reality and persons with disabilities. Paper presented at the 2nd Annual International Conference. San Francisco, CA, June 8–10, 1994.

18. D. V. Pugnetti. Recovery diagnostics and monitoring in virtual environments. Virtual reality in rehabilitation, research, experience and perspectives. Paper presented at the 1st International Congress on Virtual Reality in Rehabilitation. Gubbio, Italy, June 13–18, 1994.

19. W. J. Greenleaf. DataGlove and DataSuit: virtual reality technology applied to the measurement of human movement. Paper presented at Medicine Meets Virtual Reality II. San Diego, CA, 1994.

20. G. Burdea, J. Zhuang, E. Roskos, et al. A portable dextrous master with force feedback. Presence 1992;1:18–28.

21. W. J. Greenleaf and M. A. Tovar. Augmenting reality in rehabilitation medicine. Artif Intel Med 1994;6:289–299.

■■■■■■ **CHAPTER 2**

# The Use of Virtual Reality Technology in the Treatment of Anxiety Disorders

BRENDA K. WIEDERHOLD, M.S., MBA

California School of Professional Psychology
San Diego, California

MARK D. WIEDERHOLD, M.D., Ph.D.

Scripps Clinic Medical Group
La Jolla, California

*Information Technologies in Medicine, Volume II: Rehabilitation and Treatment,* Edited by
Metin Akay and Andy Marsh.
ISBN 0-471-41492-1   © 2001 John Wiley & Sons, Inc.

Approximately 23 million Americans will suffer from an anxiety disorder some time during their life. Anxiety disorders are the most common mental disorders in the United States, the fifth most common diagnosis given to those seen by primary care physicians, and the number one psychiatric diagnosis made by primary-care physicians (1).

In 1990, 147.8 billion mental health dollars were spent in the United States. Of this amount $46.6 billion (32%) was spent on the treatment of anxiety disorders. The cost of treatment of all other mental health disorders was $101.2 billion (2). In a more recent study, the following costs were estimated for anxiety disorders: $15 billion in direct costs, such as medical, administrative, and research costs, and $50 billion in indirect costs, including illness, death, and lost or reduced productivity (3).

Of patients presenting with insomnia, chest pain, or abdominal pain 33% actually had an anxiety disorder, as did 25% percent of those with headache, fatigue, or joint or limb pain (4). Women, individuals under age 45, separated and divorced persons, and those in lower socioeconomic groups suffer the highest incidence of anxiety disorders. Unfortunately, these are often the individuals who can least afford treatment (5).

Anxiety can be seen as a contributory factor in some medical disorders as well. A study of 2,000 men conducted from 1961 to 1993 found a correlation between high anxiety and sudden cardiac death. After correcting for several physical conditions, high anxiety did not raise the risk of fatal or nonfatal heart disease but did increase the chance of a sudden fatal heart attack (three to four times as high as those without anxiety) (6).

As part of the National Health and Nutrition Examination Survey I (NHANES I), 2992 subjects were assessed for anxiety and depression between 1971 and 1975, and follow-ups were conducted between 1982 and 1984, and 1986 and 1987. All subjects were normotensive when the study began. The researchers found that high depression and anxiety scores were independent predictors of hypertension (7). The Normative Aging Study followed 1759 men without coronary heart disease (CHD) from 1975 to 1995. The subjects completed a Worries Scale in 1975. The researchers found that worry doubled myocardial infarction risk and CHD by 1.5 (8).

All anxiety disorders have two common characteristics. First, patients with these disorders usually experience apprehension, worry, and anxiety more intensely and for a longer period of time than the anxiety experienced by the average person in everyday life. Second, patients often develop ritual acts, repetitive thoughts, or avoidance mechanisms as a way to protect themselves from the anxiety.

Anxiety disorders are categorized according to the presence or absence of external stimuli, the cause of the disorder, and the nature of the symptoms. Table 2.1 shows the 12 codable anxiety disorders contained in the *Diagnostic and Statistical Manual of Mental Disorders*, 4th edition (DSM-IV) (9).

Somatic symptoms associated with anxiety disorders may include fatigue, weakness, flushing, chills, insomnia, dizziness, paresthesias, restlessness, pal-

**TABLE 2.1. Codable Anxiety Disorders**[a]

Panic disorder without agoraphobia
Panic disorder with agoraphobia
Agoraphobia without a history of panic disorder
Specific phobias
Social phobia
Obsessive–compulsive disorder
Post-traumatic stress disorder
Acute stress disorder
Generalized anxiety disorder
Anxiety disorder owing to a general medical condition
Substance-induced anxiety disorder
Anxiety disorder not otherwise specified

[a] Adapted from Ref. 9.

pitations, chest pain, rapid heart rate, hyperventilation, choking, dry mouth, nausea, diarrhea, and urinary frequency. Because of this, the average person suffering from an anxiety disorder sees a primary-care physician 10 times before being correctly diagnosed, increasing health-care costs (10).

Since the mid-1980s, surveys have shown a general improvement in primary-care diagnosis of anxiety, but these disorders are still missed one third of the time. Anxiety disorders are thought now to arise from to a combination of genetic vulnerability and environmental factors (4; www.nimh.nih.gov). Early diagnosis is important to prevent secondary problems (such as agoraphobia, depression, or alcoholism) (10).

In a study of nine New England clinics in 1993, the following methods of treatment for anxiety disorders were administered either alone or in combination with another method of treatment: 45% of patients were receiving a behavioral method of treatment (relaxation, exposure, or role play), 42% were receiving a cognitive method of treatment (thought stopping, mental distraction, or recording of thoughts); 93% were receiving medication; 76% were receiving psychodynamic treatment; 45% were receiving family therapy; and 3% were receiving biofeedback therapy. Obsessive–compulsive disorder (OCD) and agoraphobia were the two most common anxiety disorders treated with a behavioral method. Although many studies have shown the efficacy of behavioral methods for the treatment of anxiety disorders, these therapies as a group are still being underused. Anxiety disorders included in the survey were generalized anxiety disorder, social phobia, agoraphobia without a history of panic disorder, and panic disorder with or without agoraphobia. Psychodynamic psychotherapy, which has not been proven efficacious for panic disorder, was the most widely used nonpharmacologic treatment used in this sample (11).

Each major anxiety disorder category is described below and current treatment modalities are evaluated. When viewing mental health disorders and statistics, it is important to remember that *incidence* refers to the number of new cases in a specific time period, whereas *prevalence* refers to the total number of cases at a given time. For instance, lifetime prevalence would mean that a person had the disorder at some point in his or her life but may not have had it at the time of the survey (12).

## 2.1  PANIC DISORDER WITH OR WITHOUT AGORAPHOBIA

Each year, panic disorder (PD) strikes more individuals than does AIDS, epilepsy, or stroke (www.nimh.nih.gov). As noted in the DSM-IV:

> The essential feature of Panic Disorder (PD) is the presence of recurrent, unexpected Panic Attacks followed by at least 1 month of persistent concern about having another Panic Attack, worry about the possible implications or consequences of Panic Attacks, or a significant behavioral change related to the attacks.

Lifetime prevalence of panic disorder (with or without agoraphobia) is 1.5 to 3.5%, with 1-year prevalence estimated at 1 to 2%. In community samples, one third to one have of those with PD also have agoraphobia. Typical age of onset is either in late adolescence or in the mid-30s. It is twice as common in women as in men (9). It has been shown that 2.8 to 5.7% of the population sample used in the ECA study (sponsored by the National Institute of Mental Health) met DSM-IV criteria for agoraphobia, and another 1% met DSM-IV criteria for panic disorder (13).

   Treatment of PD usually involves medication or cognitive-behavioral therapy, sometimes in combination. Cognitive-behavioral therapies may include relaxation, breathing retraining (biofeedback), exposure therapy, and cognitive restructuring. Medications used include benzodiazepines and antidepressants (14).

   Exposure therapies include systematic desensitization, in vivo exposure, and imaginal exposure. Systematic desensitization is a type of exposure therapy that pairs relaxation with imagined scenes depicting situations the client has indicated cause him or her anxiety. In vivo exposure involves exposing the patient to the actual real-life phobic situation. This may be done after teaching the patient anxiety management techniques, (e.g., thought stopping, relaxation, and diaphragmatic breathing), or it may be done without first teaching any of these techniques. Imaginal exposure involves having the patient imagine the phobic situation. The patient first builds a fear hierarchy of more and more anxiety-provoking situations and moves step by step through the hierarchy. When a scene no longer causes anxiety, the next imaginal scene in the hierarchy is attempted, until all scenes can be imagined with no resulting anxiety. Exposure techniques are usually found to be effective, with some improvement being achieved in 70% of cases (15).

   Although cognitive therapy is often incorporated into exposure treatments, some studies have indicated that cognitive therapy adds no significant advantage (16, 17), and in fact was shown to be detrimental in one study (18).

Relaxation procedures, sometimes using biofeedback to aid patient awareness, have been helpful when taught before exposure therapy. Relaxation is then used during exposure therapy as a coping technique (19). Relaxation may include helping the patient to relax muscles using electromyography (EMG) recording. The therapist guides the patient through exercises that allow him or her to experience muscle tension and muscle relaxation. Breathing retraining using biofeedback may also help the patient become aware of slow, diaphragmatic breathing versus fast, chest breathing. During panic attacks, there is a tendency to hyperventilate, actually achieving mild respiratory alkalosis, so providing the patient with breath awareness is a useful adjunct to treatment (20).

## 2.2 AGORAPHOBIA WITHOUT A HISTORY OF PANIC DISORDER

Individuals suffering from agoraphobia have anxiety that focuses on "the occurrence of incapacitating or extremely embarrassing panic-like symptoms or limited-symptom attacks rather than full panic attacks. The patient fears being in places where escape would be difficult or embarrassing" (9). Little is known about the course of this disorder, but evidence suggests that considerable impairment persists for long periods of time without treatment. Lifetime prevalence for agoraphobia has been reported at 6.7% and a 30-day prevalence of 2.3% was found (21).

Exposure therapy, sometimes in combination with medication, breathing retraining (biofeedback), and relaxation techniques are currently acceptable forms of treatment (14). Exposure treatments have not been shown effective for all individuals, however. Some individuals may also not be able to tolerate the side effects associated with pharmacological therapy (14). Because of shortcomings with current available treatments, North's group (22) has begun to experiment with virtual reality (VR) exposure therapy to treat agoraphobia. Because one of the criteria for agoraphobia is anxiety about being in places or situations in which escape might be difficult or embarrassing, and because fears usually involve a cluster of situations rather than just one, several virtual scenarios were used. Scenes included a series of bridges suspended over a canyon, hot-air balloons positioned at different heights, an empty room, a dark barn, a dark barn with a black cat, a covered bridge, an elevator, and a series of balconies. Participants in the first study were 30 undergraduate students presenting with agoraphobia. They were treated individually with eight 15-min sessions (one per week for eight consecutive weeks), using VR exposure. A total of 24 subjects (80%) experienced a 50% decrease in discomfort levels.

The proposed advantages of virtual reality compared to in vivo exposure include the following.

1. No loss of patient confidentiality. The entire treatment is done in the therapist's office. The patient and therapist do not have to venture out

into public and risk exposing the patient to possible embarrassment if he or she would prefer the treatment remain confidential.

2. No safety issues. The patient is in the safety of the therapist's office, and the VR system can be turned off at any time the patient requests. When in real life, there is less control of the exposure scenario.

3. More flexibility of the session. If a patient is scared of only one aspect of exposure, e.g., the actual experience of standing in a grocery checkout line, then this can be practiced over and over in the virtual world. In the real world, a patient may feel conspicuous checking out over and over again at the grocery store.

4. Just unreal enough so that many patients who have resisted therapy owing to in vivo approaches are willing to try it. They know they can stop the virtual experience instead of being trapped in a real-life scenario (23, 24).

5. Less time involved. The clinician does not have to drive to the store, go shopping with the patient, etc. This should prove to be more cost effective, because of the time savings (23, 24).

Despite significant evidence of role impairment in phobias, only 18.6% of those with phobias ever seek professional treatment (25). Without treatment, only 20% of cases will remit. (www.nimh.nih.gov). Perhaps VR therapy may be a therapy more patients are willing to try.

The advantages of virtual reality over imaginal exposure include are as follows.

1. The highly immersive nature of VR. Some patients cannot visualize and, therefore, imaginal exposure doesn't work as well for them. VR should work better for this group of individuals because it provides several sensory modalities.

2. The therapist sees what the patient sees. Emotional processing theory purports that to successfully treat a phobia, the patient's fear structure must be activated and modified (26). With VR, the therapist has a chance to see exactly what stimuli is activating the patient's fear structure and will then be better able to work on reducing the fear.

3. The therapy is more realistic than imaginal for most people, which should allow for less treatment sessions and, therefore, less cost for treatment (23, 24).

## 2.3  SPECIFIC PHOBIAS

The DSM-IV criteria that must be met for a diagnosis of specific phobia are as follows (9):

1. A marked and persistent fear that is excessive, unreasonable, and cued by the presence or anticipation of a specific object or situation.

2. Exposure to the phobic stimulus provokes an anxiety response.
3. The person recognizes that the fear is excessive.
4. The phobic situation is avoided or else endured with intense anxiety.
5. The anxiety response interferes significantly with the person's normal functioning.

Phobias are found to be the most common psychiatric disorder in the community, more common than major depression, alcohol abuse, or alcohol dependence. The 1-year prevalence rate is estimated at 9%, with lifetime prevalence estimated at between 10 and 11.3% (25).

There is a strong familial pattern with phobias; first-degree relatives have a greater likelihood to also have a phobia of the same specific subtype. The strongest risk factor associated with phobias is the presence of another psychiatric disorder, and the most frequent co-occurrence is with panic disorder (25).

Prevalence rates are found to be significantly higher in women, who make up 75 to 90% of those who seek treatment for phobias. Of those with a specific phobia, 83.4% also report having another mental health disorder sometime in their life. Phobias are strongly comorbid with each other, with other anxiety disorders, and with affective disorders (such as mania and depression). Age of onset may be either childhood or in the mid-20s. Specific phobias are negatively related to education but not income and are significantly elevated among Hispanics, among those who are not employed, and among those who live with their parents (21). Only 12.4% of those with a specific phobia ever seek treatment (25).

Those suffering from a specific phobia have anxiety that is provoked by confronting a specific stimulus or anticipating confronting the stimulus. More than 200 phobias have been identified; the DSM-IV subtypes for specific phobias are as follows:

*Animal type.* Generally has a childhood onset; females account for 75 to 90% of those with this subtype.

*Natural environment type.* Includes fear of heights, water, and storms and generally has a childhood onset; females account for 75 to 90% of those with this subtype.

*Blood-injection-injury type.* Includes invasive medical procedures other than just injections and produces a vasovagal response; females account for 55 to 70% of those with this subtype.

*Situational type.* Includes fear of flying, bridges, elevators, driving, and enclosed places; age of onset is either during childhood or in the mid-20s; most frequent subtype seen in adults; females account for 75 to 90% of those with this subtype.

*Other type.* Includes fear of falling down when away from walls, fear of vomiting, contracting an illness, fear of loud sounds, and fear of costumed characters (in children) (9).

In community samples, lifetime prevalence rates range from 10 to 11.3%, with a 1-year prevalence of 9%. Without treatment, only 20% of cases that persist into adulthood will remit (www.nimh.nih.gov).

Exposure therapy, sometimes in combination with relaxation training, is generally used to treat phobias. Medication may also be used as an adjunct (14). VR-graded exposure therapy (VRGET) has been researched most for use in the area of specific phobias. Initial studies show promise for incorporating VRGET into standard treatment protocols.

### 2.3.1    Fear of Heights

The first study by Hodges et al. (27–29) used VR exposure to treat fear of heights. A VR-treatment group and a no-treatment control group were used. A total of 17 subjects were exposed to virtual height situations: a glass elevator, a series of bridges with varying heights and degrees of stability, and a series of balconies with varying heights. Subjective ratings of fear, anxiety, and avoidance decreased significantly for all participants in the VR exposure group after seven 35- to 45-min exposure sessions, but remained unchanged for the control group. Some of those in the treatment group also exposed themselves to real-world height situations although not required to do so, which seems to show that training does carry over to the real world.

The same group (30) performed a case study. The participant showed a reduction in fear, anxiety, and avoidance and was able to put himself into height situations in real life once treatment was completed.

In another study, Lamson (31) exposed 30 participants to simulated height situations. Of these 90% were able to put themselves into height situations in the real world after 1 week of simulation. And 30 months later, 90% were still able to ride in a glass elevator while looking out. This shows that treatment effects are lasting.

To follow-up on these studies, which did not include a group receiving any other treatment, Huang et al. (32) conducted a study to compare in vivo exposure and VR exposure to treat fear of heights. They modeled a virtual world to exactly duplicate a staircase at the University of Michigan. One treatment group was treated using VR exposure and the other group was given in vivo exposure.

### 2.3.2    Fear of Flying

Characterized by an unreasonable or excessive fear cued by flying or the anticipation of flying, fear of flying affects an estimated 10 to 20% of people in the United States (33). Two cases studies using VR exposure to treat fear of flying have appeared in the literature. The first, involved a subject who had not flown for 2 years before treatment (28, 34, 35). She had become progressively more anxious about flying and had finally discontinued flying for business or pleasure. After seven sessions of anxiety-management techniques, such as relaxation skills and thought stopping, and six sessions of VR exposure in a virtual fixed wing aircraft, she was able to fly again with her family on vacation, self-reporting less fear on exposure.

North et al. (36) did a case study with one of the subjects who had been treated for fear of heights in the first VR study. After five VR exposure sessions in a virtual helicopter, he was able to fly with less self-reported anxiety.

Research is now under way at the Center for Advanced Multimedia Psychotherapy in San Diego to look at VRGET vs imaginal exposure to treat fear of flying (23, 24). Real-time physiologic monitoring and feedback are also being incorporated for one group. During the exposure sessions, physiology is monitored for all patients. Based on studies initiated by Jung in 1907, which revealed that skin resistance was a means to objectify emotional tones previously thought to be invisible, skin resistance levels are being fed back to patients as an indicator of arousal and anxiety. Jung found that skin resistance tends to reflect mental events more quickly and with more resolution than other physiological measures (20). Because other VR studies have not reported these physiologic parameters, the San Diego Study is monitoring heart rate, respiration rate, peripheral skin temperature, and brain wave activity. Analysis will reveal whether other physiologic data may be important to note as patients become desensitized to the phobic stimuli. Emotional processing theory indicates that to change a fear structure, it must be activated and information incompatible with the fear must be provided. For instance, if a patient has a fear of flying that centers around crashing and during therapy numerous imagined or in vivo flights are taken with no crashes, the patient's fear structure would be provided with incompatible information that should modify it (26). According to Foa and Kozak (26), there are three indications that emotional processing is occurring: physiologic arousal and self-reported fear during exposure, diminution of fear responses within sessions, and a decline of arousal across sessions (37). This study will examine how physiology, self-report measures, and behavioral indices correlate.

All patients receiving VR treatment will receive two sessions of relaxation training before exposure treatment. The groups receiving VRGET will then be allowed to progress through a series of VR scenarios, including sitting on the plane with the engines on and engines off, taxiing down the runway, taking off, experiencing a smooth flight, experiencing a turbulent flight with thunderstorms, and landing. Exposure will be once per week for 6 weeks. Patients receiving imaginal exposure will be guided by the therapist through visualization of an individualized fear hierarchy, which the patient and therapist have created during an initial two sessions of relaxation training.

### 2.3.3  Fear of Spiders

Carlin et al. (38) completed a case study to treat fear of spiders using both VR and augmented reality. The subject had been phobic for 20 years. Treatment involved exposure to a tarantula and a black widow in the virtual world, then eventually touching a furry toy spider while viewing a corresponding spider in the virtual world. After twelve 1-h sessions, the patient was able to go camping in the woods and successfully encounter a spider in her home. The 1-year follow-up indicated that treatment gains were still intact.

### 2.3.4 Claustrophobia

Bullinger et al. (39) have begun to explore VR for the treatment of claustrophobia, using a head-mounted display (HMD) and a three-dimensional (3-D) joystick. Claustrophobia, which has a lifetime prevalence of 2%, involves fear of enclosed places. During virtual exposure, the patient is allowed to increase or decrease the size of a virtual room, bringing the walls closer and closer as desensitization continues. The patient can at any time go through a virtual door at one end of the virtual room and end the simulation at any time that anxiety becomes too intense. Patients in the initial study received 3 sessions per week for 4 weeks (12 sessions). Initial results show a decrease in overall anxiety scores.

### 2.3.5 Fear of Driving

Berger et al. (40) are currently conducting a study on the treatment of fear of driving. The study compares imaginal exposure therapy and VR exposure treatment. Data collection is in the initial stages. Because a fear of driving may occur as part of a simple phobia or as part of agoraphobia and because driving deficits are often seen after head trauma, stroke, or other physical insult, this area has a wide range of potential applications for VR technology.

## 2.4 SOCIAL PHOBIA

Social phobia has a lifetime prevalence of 13.3% with a 30-day prevalence reported at 4.5%. Of those with social phobia, 59% also have a specific phobia (21). Social phobia may include such things as fear of eating in public, signing checks in front of others, or and public speaking (9).

Those with social phobia show increased risk of alcohol abuse, alcohol dependence, and suicide attempts (41). It is often difficult to arrange in-vivo exposure for social phobia if it involves, for example, confronting authority figures. Treatment must, therefore, resort to imaginal exposure, which has obvious limitations (15). It would be much more powerful to digitize the authority figure's face into the virtual world and allow the patient to do repeated role playing. With intelligent software, perhaps driven by neural networks, the virtual personae of the authority figure could teach social skills and assertion, provide systematic desensitization, and react differently according to how the patient handled himself or herself.

The most common social phobia is a fear of public speaking. It is the third most common psychiatric disorder, and was listed by the *Book of Lists* (42) as the number one fear among Americans (43). At a 1983 American College of Cardiology meeting, 13% of speakers admitted to having used $\beta$-blockers before speaking at the meeting (44). Treatment usually involves cognitive-behavioral therapy, medications, or a combination of the two. Therapy may involve exposure, reframing thoughts about a social scene, social skills training, or relaxation techniques. Medications may include MAO inhibitors or $\beta$-blockers (which are used on the day of performance) (14). In a *Wall Street Journal* article (45), stage fright was said to afflict approximately 20 million people at some point during their lifetime. High blood pressure medications ($\beta$-blockers) such as propranolol have been used for years to stop the physiologic effects of stage fright, such as hand tremors and rapid heart beat, but anti-anxiety drugs and antidepressants are now being explored for treatment. The drawback to antidepressants is that they must be taken daily to work; but some newer short-acting antianxiety drugs can be used as needed. There is no indication that the use of drugs has a lasting affect on curing stage fright; however, thus for many patients a better answer might be behavioral therapy.

North et al. (22) have begun using VR to treat fear of public speaking. Subjects in the initial study were exposed to a virtual audience and experienced many of the same symptoms someone with a fear might experience when in front of a real audience—dry mouth, sweaty palms, and increased heart rate. Self-reported anxiety (SUDs) and scores on the Attitude Toward Public Speaking Questionnaire decreased after treatment.

A concomitant disorder with social phobia is body dysmorphic disorder. If this is present, role playing during therapy appears to increase the chance of successful treatment (41). A good use of VR technology might be to have the patient role-play in a VR environment in which different scenarios can be acted out and then discussed. This may provide a beginning point for meaningful dialogue between therapist and patient.

## 2.5  OBSESSIVE–COMPULSIVE DISORDER

Obsessive–compulsive disorder is characterized by recurrent, intrusive ideas, images, impulses, obsessions. Repetitive behaviors (compulsions) are performed to decrease the discomfort. For example, a person with this disorder may be obsessed with disturbing thoughts or images of germs (an obsession) and may feel the need to wash their hands over and over (a compulsion) to try and prevent thoughts of germs (9).

OCD strikes equal numbers of men and women, afflicting 1 in 50 people, or 5 million Americans (3). As many as 80% of patients with OCD may also have concurrent depression. OCD generally begins when a patient is his or her teens or early adult years and appears to run in families (46).

The most effective behavioral treatment used for OCD is exposure and response prevention. In this treatment, the patient is exposed to situations that

normally cause compulsive behavior. The patient is then prevented from performing the associated ritual. Results from 18 studies conclude 51% of patients
are symptom-free after treatment and another 39% are moderately improved
(47). Two medications used to treat OCD are clomipramine and fluoxetine.
Studies on the medications effectiveness have shown mixed results, but the cer-
tainty is that relapse should be expected when medications are discontinued
(48).

A group in Georgia is now exploring the efficacy of treating OCD with
VRGET (22). Moving in this direction, another study that began in 1994 deals
with a telephone interface for simulated behavior therapy of OCD. The system,
called BT Steps, appears to be helpful in reducing symptoms (49). The program
has nine steps, four that prepare patients, two that set them on a therapeutic
course, and three that continue them through their therapy. The steps involve
education, behavioral assessment, a treatment plan, treatment, and relapse
prevention. It is an interactive voice-response system using a prerecorded voice
that responds to the callers' answers to several questions. Step 7 in the program,
which is the first exposure and ritual prevention session, may be done again and
again to maintain gains. There are 700 frames within the computer-assisted
phone system. The phone system remembers the patient's previous responses
and helps the patient build an exposure and ritual prevention hierarchy. During
the first controlled study, 17 subjects completed at least two sessions using the
system. Of those completing the sessions, a decrease in discomfort of $>50\%$
was obtained; 85% of patients subjectively rated themselves as very much or
much improved (49).

## 2.6   POST-TRAUMATIC STRESS DISORDER

Post-traumatic stress disorder (PTSD) is a heterogeneous disorder that may
occur after exposure to actual or threatened events of death or serious injury to
self or others. Symptoms include dissociation, flashbacks, and increased anxiety
or arousal (9). Antidepressants, anxiety-reducing medications, support from
family and friends, and cognitive-behavioral therapy (with some exposure involved) can help with recovery (14).

Approximately 15.2% of the men and 8.5% of the women stationed in Vietnam were found to be suffering from PTSD 15 or more years after their service.
Because of its varied symptomatology and resistance to treatment, many treatment modalities have been investigated (50). Currently, only 66% of people
with PTSD fully recover (51). Because most studies have used some form of
exposure therapy as part of the treatment regimen, a group led by Hodges is
exploring VRGET at the Atlanta Veteran's Administration Hospital to treat
PTSD. Currently, five case studies are being performed using VRGET. Treatment involves exposing the veterans to virtual Huey helicopters that will fly
them over the jungles of Vietnam. Treatment will involve nine 60-min individual sessions over a period of 5 weeks (52).

VA researchers identified biochemical markers that are associated with PTSD. In addition, they found psychophysiologic instruments to be reliable and valid at discriminating between PTSD and non-PTSD persons. VRGET and physiologic feedback may lead to treatments that will benefit not only veterans but also those suffering from PTSD owing to violent crimes, natural disasters, and terrorism (50).

## 2.7   FUTURE TARGETS FOR VR TREATMENT

### 2.7.1   Acute Stress Disorder

Acute stress disorder (ASD) is diagnosed when someone is exposed to a traumatic event but suffers from 2 days to <4 weeks with symptoms including dissociation, flashbacks, and increased anxiety. If symptoms persist for more than 1 month, the PTSD diagnosis is given (9). Although no VR application is currently available to treat ASD, its use might allow for powerful, immediate treatment of the patient following a stressful event. This might allow the patient to recover from the stressor without developing PTSD.

### 2.7.2   Generalized Anxiety Disorder

Generalized anxiety disorder (GAD) is characterized by worry and excessive anxiety that occur more often than not for a period of 6 months or more. Worry and anxiety are not directed toward one specific event or stimulus but are rather more diffuse and occur about several activities. Because of the anxiety, restlessness, easy fatiguability, irritability, sleep disturbances, concentration difficulties, or muscle tension may occur. GAD often co-occurs with other anxiety disorders, mood disorders such as depression, substance-related disorders, and psychophysiologic disorders often associated with stress such as irritable bowel syndrome and tension headache. There is a 5.1% lifetime prevalence, with most cases beginning between age 15 and 45 (9).

Successful treatments used for GAD include nonbenzodiazepine anxiolytics (e.g., buspirone), benzodiazepines (e.g., xanax and klonopin), relaxation techniques, cognitive-behavioral therapy, and biofeedback (www.nimh.nih.gov). Among anxiety disorders, benzodiazepine drug treatments for GAD have been the most competently and extensively tested. Results of numerous well-controlled, double-blind studies indicate short-term value for using these drugs but no long-term effectiveness. Given the side effects associated with the drugs, such as impaired cognitions and psychological dependence, another form of treatment would be considered preferable (14).

To target somatic components of GAD, biofeedback and relaxation techniques have been investigated. Some studies (53) have shown superiority of EMG biofeedback over relaxation training, but others (54) have shown relaxation training superior to biofeedback. Both, however, have been shown as superior to no treatment (14).

To target cognitive aspects of GAD, cognitive therapy is most often used. Cognitive coping techniques often include cognitive restructuring and distraction to control distressing thoughts. A hierarchy of anxiety-provoking situations may also be used during systematic desensitization to treat GAD (14). Although not currently being treated with VR therapy, this disorder could also very easily lend itself to VR exposure as an adjunct to learning cognitive coping. Because of the importance of treating the cognitive component also in GAD, however, VR alone may not be enough.

### 2.7.3    Anxiety Disorder Owing to a General Medical Condition

According to the DSM-IV, "the essential feature of Anxiety Disorder Due to a General Medical Condition is clinically significant anxiety that is judged to be due to the direct physiological effects of a general medical condition." Many medical conditions may cause anxiety symptoms to manifest. These include cardiac conditions, thyroid conditions, vitamin deficiencies, respiratory conditions, and certain neurologic conditions. Although in most cases, medication must be administered to help resolve the condition; in other cases, such as hyperventilation (a respiratory condition), breathing retraining may help correct the disorder. Anxiety caused by a medical condition or from having been diagnosed with a medical condition does not fall under this category but is likely to fall under adjustment disorder with anxiety, which emphasizes physiologically induced anxiety (9).

### 2.7.4    Substance-Induced Anxiety Disorder

A substance-induced anxiety disorder would be diagnosed if the anxiety was "judged to be due to the direct physiological effects of a substance" (9). The disorder must occur either while a person is under the influence of a substance or withdrawing from a substance. If anxiety continues beyond 4 weeks after discontinuing the substance, another cause for the anxiety must be explored. For instance, if the patient currently has a medical disorder, the actual disorder itself may be causing the anxiety physiologically rather than the substance being used to treat the medical condition (9).

### 2.7.5    Unspecified Anxiety Disorder

Unspecified anxiety disorder is used for patients who have anxiety or a phobic avoidance that does not meet the full criteria for any of the specific anxiety disorders. This might include patients who as a result of a medical condition such as Parkinson disease have developed social phobic symptoms. Also included under this category would be patients who have anxiety and depression but do not meet the full criteria for a mood disorder or another anxiety disorder (9).

## 2.8  CONCLUSION

Initial VR studies have shown VR technology to be effective for the treatment of many anxiety disorders. However, there are some issues that clinicians should think about when considering this treatment.

1. Until recently, the cost of equipment to treat anxiety disorders was approximately $150,000. Now, some systems are available for under $25,000 and run on a personal computer. This cost may still be prohibitive for individual therapists, so a cost-benefit analysis should be considered before purchasing required equipment.
2. Many systems are still difficult to operate; and for mental health professionals who are sometimes themselves a little computer phobic, this can pose a problem. Systems that are more user friendly and require less in-house technical support will appeal to a wider mental health-care market.
3. Some small percentage of the population experiences side effects similar to those experienced in motion sickness, has oculomotor problems, or has VR-triggered migraines. Also, some populations of patients (e.g., schizophrenics who already have a fragmented reality) may not be good candidates for VR therapy, which may cause them to decompensate further. Borderlines, who often have attachment issues, may also not fare well in VR environments, which require less contact with the therapist.
5. Environments are fixed and cannot be modified to fit each client's individual fear and phobia hierarchies.
6. The virtual scenes may not seem real enough to some people. The graphics are still cartoonish, which may not invoke the fear response in some people.
7. No objective measurements of desensitization have been used so far. Only self-report measures and subjective units of distress, which may be subject to social desirability. Patients feels as if they should be getting better, so they report that they are getting better.

Physiologic monitoring, an objective measurement, might be a useful incorporation in the virtual world. Because biofeedback therapy offers a method for the objective quantification of the response of patients during the therapy session, introducing this information into the virtual world may both augment and enhance the capabilities of the therapist in providing more meaningful interventions in a variety of mental health disorders (23, 24).

Biofeedback is currently used by many therapists who perform imaginal exposure or systematic desensitization. The patient is progressed through the fear hierarchy only as physiologic stabilization occurs. Studies have reported that when the phobic's fear structure is activated, autonomic arousal (such as increased heart rate or sweat gland activity) occurs. Physiologic monitoring helps determine if the patient's fear structure is activated and, therefore, open to change. It also indicates if the patient is experiencing hyperarousal, which is not desirable. And finally it shows if the patient has become desensitized to a certain aspect of the phobic scenario and should actually be encouraged to move on to the next level of the fear hierarchy so that treatment may progress (26).

The use of VR in the area of mental health is still in its infancy. To further proceed and become a recognized part of therapy, more controlled studies are needed to determine if VR does provide for more rapid, less expensive, more efficient treatment. Systems must also be developed that are easy to use for the nontechnical person and that are inexpensive and allow purchase by practitioners. Virtual environments that allow the patient and therapist to interact so that a wider variety of disorders can be pursued with VR treatment are necessary. As the patient becomes more confident or less phobic, the therapist can slowly withdraw from the virtual world. Improved and variable scenarios are also needed to increase real-life applicability and generalizability for the patient. Advanced features would allow virtual worlds to be easily adapted for particular disorders or to suit particular patient characteristics. Advanced data analysis would allow underlying trends in patients' physiology to be seen as they move through the virtual world. An integrated system incorporating a virtual world and physiologic monitoring may allow real-time data analysis to occur. And finally, the ultimate goal might be to have VR systems that are driven by the patient's own physiology. Perhaps this could even include intelligent software that would automatically control the level of difficulty the patient experiences after he or she achieved specific parameters in training.

## REFERENCES

1. P. M. DiBartolo, S. G. Hofmann, and D. H. Barlow. Psychosocial approaches to panic disorder and agoraphobia: assessment and treatment issues for the primary care physician. Mind/Body Med 1995;1:133–146.

2. C. Kent. NIMH spearheads new anxiety education campaign. Am Med News, Dec 2, 1996:5–6.

3. D. Sobel and R. Ornstein. The cost of anxiety. Mind/Body Health Newslett 1997;6:7.

4. C. Sherman. Multiple somatic symptoms may signal anxiety, depression. Intern Med News, May 15, 1997:21.

5. D. A. Regier, W. E. Narrow, and D. S. Rae. The epidemiology of anxiety disorders: the epidemiological catchment area (ECA) experience. J Psychiatr Res 1990;24:3–14.

6. I. Kowachi, D. Sparrow, P. S. Vokonas, and S. T. Weiss. Symptoms of anxiety and risk of coronary heart disease: the Normative Aging Study. Circulation 1994;90:2225–2229.

7. B. S. Jonas, P. Franks, and D. D. Ingram. Are symptoms of anxiety and depression risk factors for hypertension? Longitudinal evidence from the National Health and

Nutritional Examination Survey I Epidemiologic Follow-up Study. Arch Fami Med 1997;6:43–49.

8. L. D. Kubzansky, I. Kawachi, and A. Spiro III. Is worrying bad for your heart? A prospective study of worry and coronary heart disease in the Normative Aging Study. Circulation 1997;95:818–824.

9. American Psychiatric Association. Diagnostic and statistical manual of mental disorders. 4th ed. Washington, DC: APA 1994.

10. N. Seppa. Psychologists boost anxiety screening. APA Monitor, Dec 1996:31.

11. R. M. Goisman, M. P. Rogers, G. S. Steketee, et al. Utilization of behavioral methods in a multicenter anxiety disorders study. J Clin Psychiatry 1993;54:213–218.

12. J. Reich. The epidemiology of anxiety. J Nervous Mental Dis 1986;174:129–136.

13. J. K. Myers, M. M. Weissman, C. E. Tischler, et al. Six-month prevalence of psychiatric disorders in three communities. Arch Gen Psychiatry 1983;41:959–967.

14. D. H. Barlow. Anxiety and its disorders: the nature and treatment of anxiety and panic. New York: Guilford, 1988.

15. J. C. Masters, T. G. Burish, S. D. Hollon, and D. C. Rimm. Behavior therapy: techniques and empiricals findings. 3rd ed. New York: Harcourt Brace Jovanovich, 1987.

16. P. M. G. Emmelkamp and P. P. Mersch. Cognition and exposure in vivo in the treatment of agoraphobia: short term and delayed effects. Cognitive Ther Res 1982;6:77–88.

17. S. L. Williams and J. A. Rappoport. Cognitive treatment in the natural environment for agoraphobics. Behavior Ther 1983;14:299–313.

18. L. Michelso, M. Mavissakalian, and K. Marchione. Cognitive and behavioral treatments of agoraphobia: clinical, behavioral and psychophysiological outcomes. J Consulting Clin Psychol 1985;53:913–925.

19. L. G. Ost. Age at onset in different phobias. J Abnormal Psychol 1987;96:223–239.

20. M. S. Schwartz, et al. Biofeedback: a practitioner's guide. New York: Guilford, 1995.

21. W. J. Magee, W. Eaton, H. U. Wittchen, et al. Agoraphobia, simple phobia, and social phobia in the national comorbidity survey. Arch Gen Psychiatry 1996;53:159–168.

22. M. M. North, S. M. North, and J. R. Coble. Virtual reality therapy. Colorado Springs: IPI Press, 1996.

23. B. K. Wiederhold and M. D. Wiederhold. A review of virtual reality as a psychotherapeutic tool. CyberPsychol Behav 1998;1:45–52.

24. B. K. Wiederhold, R. Gevirtz, and M. D. Wiederhold. Fear of flying: a case report using virtual reality therapy with physiological monitoring. CyberPsychol Behav in press.

25. J. H. Boyd, D. S. Rae, J. W. Thompson, et al. Phobia: prevalence and risk factors. Soc Psychiatry Psychiatr Epidemiol 1990;25:314–323.

26. E. B. Foa and M. J. Kozak. Emotional processing of fear: exposure to corrective information. Psychol Bull 1986;99:20–35.

27. L. F. Hodges, R. Kooper, B. O. Rothbaum, et al. Virtual environments for treating the fear of heights. Comput Innovat Technol Comput Prof, 1995;28:27–34.

28. B. O. Rothbaum, L. Hodges, and R. Kooper. Virtual reality exposure therapy. J Psychother Pract Res 1997;6:291–296.

29. B. O. Rothbaum, L. F. Hodges, R. Kooper, et al. Effectiveness of computer-generated (virtual reality) graded exposure in the treatment of acrophobia. Am J Psychiatry 1995;152:626–628.

30. B. O. Rothbaum, L. F. Hodges, R. Kooper, et al. Virtual reality graded exposure in the treatment of acrophobia: a case report. Behav Ther 1995;26:547–554.

31. R. Lamson. Virtual therapy of anxiety disorders. CyberEdge J 1994;4:1,6–8.

32. M. P. Huang, J. Himle, K. Beier, and N. E. Alessi. Challenges of recreating reality in virtual environments. CyberPsychol Behav in press.

33. S. Agras, D. Sylvester, and D. Oliveau. The epidemiology of common fears and phobias. Comprehensive Psychiatry 1969;10:151–156.

34. L. F. Hodges, B. O. Rothbaum, B. A. Watson, et al. Virtually conquering fear of flying. IEEE Comput Graph Appl 1996;16:42–49.

35. B. O. Rothbaum, L. Hodges, B. A. Watson, et al. Virtual reality exposure therapy in the treatment of fear of flying: a case report. Behav Res Ther 1996;34:477–481.

36. North MM, North SM, Coble JR. Virtual environments psychotherapy: A case study of fear of flying disorder. Presence 1996;5:1–5.

37. R. M. Rapee. Current controversies in the anxiety disorders. Guilford, New York: 1996.

38. A. S. Carlin, H. G. Hoffman, and S. Weghorst. Virtual reality and tactile augmentation in the treatment of spider phobia: a case report. Behav Res Ther 1997;35:153–158.

39. A. Bullinger, A. Roessler, and F. Mueller-Spahn. 3D-virtual reality as a tool in cognitive-behavioral therapy of claustrophobic patients. CyberPsychol Behav 1998.

40. A. Berger. personal communication, Mar 1997.

41. I. M. Marks. Advances in behavioral-cognitive therapy of social phobia. J Clin Psychiatry 1995;56(suppl 5):25–31.

42. Book of lists.

43. J. H. Greist. The diagnosis of social phobia. J Clin Psychiatry 1995;56(suppl 5):5–12.

44. J. W. Jefferson. Social phobia: a pharmacologic treatment overview. 1995;56(suppl 5):18–24.

45. E. Tanouye. Easing stage fright could be as simple as swallowing a pill. The Wall Street Journal, June 30, 1997:B1.

46. D. H. Barlow, P. A. DiNardo, B. B. Vermilyea, et al. Co-morbidity and depression among the anxiety disorders: issues in diagnosis and classification. J Nervous Mental Dis 1986;174:63–72.

47. E. B. Foa, G. S. Steketee, and B. J. Ozarow. Behavior therapy with obsessive-compulsives: From theory to treatment. In M. Mavissakalian, S. M. Turner, and L. Michelson, eds. Obsessive-compulsive disorders: psychological and pharmacological treatment. New York: Plenum Press, 1985.

48. M. Mavissakalian, S. M. Turner, and L. Michelson. Future directions in the assessment and treatment of obsessive-compulsive disorder. In M. Mavissakalian, S. M. Turner, and L. Michelson, eds. Psychological and pharmacological treatment of obsessive-compulsive disorder. New York: Plenum Press, 1985.

49. J. H. Greist. A telephone interface for simulated behavior therapy of an anxiety disorder. Paper presented at Medicine Meets Virtual Reality IV. San Diego, CA, 1996.

50. K. W. Kizer. Progress on posttraumatic stress disorder. JAMA 1996;275:1149.

51. R. C. Kessler, A. Sonnega, E. Bromet, et al. Posttraumatic stress disorder in the National Comorbidity Survey. Arch Gen Psychiatry 1995.

52. S. Salyer. The dawn of virtual therapy. USA Weekend, July 18–20, 1997:10.

53. A. Canter, C. Y. Kondo, and J. R. Knott. A comparison of EMG feedback and progressive muscle relaxation training in anxiety neurosis. Br J Psychiatry 1975; 127:470–477.

54. I. Beiman, E. Israel, and S. A. Johnson. During training and post-training effects of live and taped extended progressive relaxation, self-relaxation, and electromyogram biofeedback. J Consult Clin Psychology 1978;46:314–321.

**■■■■■ CHAPTER 3**

# Virtual Reality for Health Care

L. BEOLCHI and G. RIVA

Istituto Auxologico Italiano
Verbania, Italy

## 3.1   VR AND TELEPRESENCE

The basis for the virtual reality (VR) idea is that a computer can synthesise a three-dimensional (3-D) graphical environment from numerical data. Using visual and auditory output devices, the human operator can experience the environment as if it were a part of the world. This computer-generated world may

*Information Technologies in Medicine, Volume II: Rehabilitation and Treatment,* Edited by
Metin Akay and Andy Marsh.
ISBN 0-471-41492-1   © 2001 John Wiley & Sons, Inc.

be either a model of a real-world object, such as a house; or an abstract world that does not exist in a real sense but is understood by humans, such as a chemical molecule or a representation of a set of data; or it might be in a completely imaginary science fiction world (1). Furthermore, because input devices sense the operator's reactions and motions, the operator can modify the synthetic environment, creating the illusion of interacting with and thus being immersed within the environment.

However, there are many interpretations of what constitutes VR, some writers even make reference to cave painings of prehistory. The term *virtual reality* was first coined and used extensively in its current context by Jaron Lanier when he set up the first commercial VR company, VPL Inc., in 1987 to sell complete solutions for VR. A key technology making this possible at the time was the development of an affordable head-mounted display (HMD) system.

In today's marketplace VR refers to any computer-based model that uses 3-D graphics to represent an environment, real or abstract, in which the user is able to interact in real time with this environment. Optionally, the environment may be immersive throught the use of HMDs and position-tracking devices; but on the whole immersive VR accounts for only 5% of the market.

Virtual reality has come a long way in since 1990. The technologies making up VR have evolved fast; and as a result of this maturation, the field has adopted the professionally more sober title of virtual environment (VE). The term VR is still in common use in the games and entertainment markets.

The most recent developement of VR has been in the area of networking and the Internet. Networked virtual environments and 3-D interfaces to the Internet are among the latest applications of VR in a growing telecommunications market. Telepresence and teleconferencing, which have so far been dominated by expensive video conferencing technologies, will soon see their role undercut by simple PC-based conferencing facilities based on VE technologies. Developement work in this area is being funded primarily by the games and entertainment industry. A small but increasing proportion of effort, however, is funded by commercial applications developers with industrial, engineering and training needs.

An important role in stimulating this research and development (R&D) activity in Europe is played by the European Commission, with its R&D funding under the Fourth Framework Programme and, more important, its plans for the Fifth Framework Programme (1998–2002).

## 3.2   DEFINITIONS

Virtual reality is an emerging technology that alters the way individuals interact with computers. "Virtual reality is a fully three-dimensional computer-generated 'world' in which a person can move about and interact as if he actually were in an imaginary place. This is accomplished by totally immersing the person's senses ... using a head-mounted display (HMD)"(2), or some other immersive display device, and an interaction device such as a DataGlove or a joystick. "User immersion in a synthetic environment distinctively characterizes virtual reality (VR) as different from interactive computer graphics or multimedia. In fact, the *sense of presence* in a virtual world elicited by immersive VR technology indicates that VR applications may differ fundamentally from those commonly associated with graphics and multimedia systems" (3).

Virtual environments present a unified workspace allowing more or less complete functionality without requiring that all the functions be located in the same physical space. "Virtual environments [can be defined] as interactive, virtual image displays enhanced by special processing and by nonvisual display modalities, such as auditory and haptic, to convince users that they are immersed in a synthetic space" (4). Less technically, "a virtual world is an application that lets users navigate and interact with a three-dimensional, computer-generated (and computer-maintained) environment in real time. This type of system has three major elements: interaction, 3-D graphics, and immersion" (5).

Satava (6, 7) identified five elements that affect the realism of a virtual environment:

- *Fidelity*. High-resolution graphics.
- *Display of organ properties*. Deformation from morphing or kinematics of joints.
- *Display of organ reactions*. Bleeding from an artery or bile from the gallbladder
- *Interactivity*. Between objects such as surgical instruments and organs.
- *Sensory feedback*. Tactile and force feedback

However, realism of the virtual objects is not enough. In addition, the human–computer interaction must provide a realistic environment in which the user can interact (8).

## 3.3 TECHNOLOGY OVERVIEW

### 3.3.1 Head-Mounted Displays

As you move through the world, images of the objects that surround you fall onto your retinas. As you move past a fixed object, seeing it from various angles, the size and shape of the images on your retinas change, yet you effortlessly and unconsciously perceive the object to have a stable position, shape, and size. This innate perceptual ability, honed by your daily experience ever since infancy, is so fundamental and habitual that it seems almost absurd to talk about objects that could change their position or shape or size, depending on how you moved your head. Yet VR gives us simulated objects that change their position, size, and shape as the head moves. The location of these objects appears to change as the head moves around, and their size and shape appear to change, depending on whether they are being viewed directly in front of the user's head or off to the side. In immersive virtual reality, an HMD, rather like a motorcycle helmet, and a head tracker are used to rapidly measure head position and create an image for each eye appropriate to its instantaneous viewpoint.

There are two primary technologies used in HMDs to deliver images to the eye: cathode ray tubes (CRTs), essentially the same component as you find in your living room TV, although much smaller, and LCDs, the type of display used in watches, portable computers, and game systems. Each has certain advantages.

*CRTs*, or cathode ray tubes, create an image by scanning a high-energy beam of electrons across a phosphor-coated glass screen. CRTs can be made small and with high resolution and brightness, and they offer a high contrast ratio. CRTs are proven technology. They have some disadvantages, though. Compared to LCDs, they are heavier, more expensive, and require more power. It is difficult to make a color CRT small enough for HMD use, which typically requires no more than a 1-in. diameter. Finally, there are as yet untested suspicions that the magnetic fields generated by the high power required for the scanning beam (tens of thousand of volts) may pose a health hazard when placed very close to the head.

*LCDs* are not perfect either, although they present certain advantages. They are lightweight and have low power requirements. Color and monochrome systems are available and can be made quite small. The downside of LCD displays is that they are a relatively new technology and not easily available in high resolution. As few as 25% are usable in some manufacturing processes, resulting in a relatively high price. Finally, update, or refresh, rates are considerably slower for LCDs than for CRTs.

A problem with the current generation of headsets is that communication with the VR computer is achieved through direct cable links between the headset and the computer. This limits how far the human can walk. In the near future, cabling will be replaced by remote control scanners to overcome this problem. Later on, the computer will not need to be nearby. Data from users as to where they are, and data from the computer as to what they should be seeing will be delivered using broadband communications networks.

The latest generation HMD is less bulky than the old motorcycle helmets and looks more like a set of heavy-duty industrial goggles, such as someone might use when handling dangerous chemicals. In the future, we can expect VR spectacles, and later on contact lenses; both technologies are already in the post-research phase of development. These systems can provide all the visual clues without the cumbersome weight and represent a major advance. Two other display systems, although not in common use, bear some examination.

One system has been getting a lot of attention but is a long way from delivery. It is the VR laser scanner, developed at the University of Washington. This experimental system uses a modulated laser beam (low power, of course) to paint an image directly on the retina of the eye. The primary advantage of this technology at this point is high resolution and update rate. However, this system is years away from HMD use. Currently, it exists only as a prototype that provides high resolution with low power requirements, but researchers face severe obstacles in reducing its size and providing color output.

Another technology that is in use in a couple of HMD systems is the light pipe. This system uses a collimated fiberoptic bundle to carry an image to a set of mirrors, which then reflect the image into the eye. The image source can be anything that will connect to the feed end of the fiberoptic bundle: a CRT, a slide projector, a microscope, or whatever image generator is appropriate. The system is desirable because of its versatility and the light weight of the HMD itself. It can provide color and high resolution. However, the collimated bundles are expensive and somewhat fragile, limiting the application of light pipe systems to the high end of the application spectrum.

The latest newcomer in the HMD market is Sony with its low-end and high-end helmets, ranging from $599 (NTSC or PAL HMD) to $8999 (SVGA 3D Resolution).

### 3.3.2 Position Tracking

The four technologies used predominantly in tracking are mechanically based; optically based, which uses cameras to examine a point of the body from a distance; magnetically based, such as the Polhemus; or acoustically based, using triangulation of ultrasonic "pings" to locate the position.

Mechanical tracking makes use of a mechanical armature with one side connected to the top of a helmet and the other end connected to an encoding device on the ceiling. As the user changes head pos of the arm are relayed to the computer and the computer can update the screen display. While mechanical position/orientation tracking is the most precise method of tracking, it has the disadvantage of being the most limiting.

Optical tracking makes use of small markers on the body, either flashing infrared LEDs or small infrared-reflecting dots. A series of two or more cameras surround the subject and pick out the markers in their visual field. Software correlates the marker positions in the multiple viewpoints and uses the different lens perspectives to calculate a 3-D coordinate for each marker. One limitation of these systems is the processing time needed to analyze the several camera images and determine each marker's 3-D position. Most of the systems operate in a batch mode, where the trajectories of the markers are captured live, followed by a period of analysis to calculate three-space positions from the 2-D images.

Magnetic tracking uses a source element radiating a magnetic field and a small sensor that reports its position and orientation with respect to the source. Competing systems from Polhemus and from Ascension Technologies provide various multisource, multisensor systems that will track a number of points at up to 100 Hz in ranges from 3 to 20 ft. They are generally accurate to better than 0.1 in. in position and 0.1° in rotation. Magnetic systems do not rely on line-of-sight observation, as do optical and acoustic systems, but metallic objects in the environment will distort the magnetic field, giving erroneous readings. They also require cable attachment to a central device (as do LED and acoustic systems). However, the current technology is quite robust and widely used for single- or double-hand tracking.

Acoustic trackers use high-frequency sound to triangulate a source within the work area. Most systems, such as those from Logitech and the one used in the Mattel, Pow ping from the source (mounted on the hand, for instance) received by microphones in the environment. Precise placement of the microphones allows the system to locate the source in space to within a few millimeters. These systems rely on line of sight between the source and the microphones and can suffer from acoustic reflections if surrounded by hard walls or other acoustically reflective surfaces. If multiple acoustic trackers are used together, they must operate at nonconflicting frequencies, a strategy also used in magnetic tracking.

### 3.3.3 Glove and Body Suit Technologies

The DataGlove is put on the hand, and can then be seen as a floating hand in the VE. It can be used to initiate commands. For example, in virtual spaces where gravity does not exist, pointing the glove upward makes the person appear to fly. Pointing downward takes the user safely back to the ground. In this regard, the virtual hand is like a cursor a standard PC, able to execute commands by pointing at a particular icon and clicking.

Glove devices measure the shape of the hand as the fingers and palm flex. In the 1990s, many researchers built hand and gesture measuring devices for computer input. We describe the more significant ones that have appeared in the literature or in the marketplace.

- *Sayre glove.* Consists of flexible tubes not fce at one end and a photocell at the other. Tubes are mounted along each of the fingers of the glove. As each tube is bent, the amount of light passing between its source and photocell decreases evenly. Voltage from each photocell can then be correlated with finger bending.
- *MIT LED glove.* Uses LEDs and a camera to capture finger motion.
- *Digital Data Entry Glove.* Consists of a cloth glove onto which is sewn numerous touch, bend, and inertial sensors specifically positioned to recognize the Single Hand Manual Alphabet for the American Deaf.
- *DataGlove* Monitors 10 finger joints and the 6 degrees of freedom (dof) of the hand's position and orientation. Physically consists of a lightweight Lycra glove fitted with specially treated optical fibers. Finger flexion bends the fibers, attenuating the light they transmit. The signal strength for each

of the fingers is sent to a processor that determines joint angles based on precalibrations for each user. A 3-D magnetic tracker attached to the back of the hand determines position and orientation of the palm.

- *Dexterous HandMaster (DHM)*. An exoskeleton-like device worn on the fingers and hand. Using Hall effect sensors as potentiometers at the joints, it accurately measures the bending of the three joints of each finger as well as abduction of the fingers and complex motion of the thumb. The DHM measures 20 dof of the hand (4 for each finger and 4 for the thumb). Although originally developed for robotics, the DHM has been successfully marketed as a tool for clinical analysis of hand function and impairment.
- *Power Glove*. Inspired by the success of the VPL DataGlove, the Mattel toy company manufactured a low-cost glove as a controller for Nintendo home video games. The Power-Glove is a flexible molded plastic glove; the plastic on the backs of the fingers are resistive-ink flex sensors that register overall bending of the thumb and index, middle, and ring fingers with two bits of precision per finger. Mounted on the back of the hand are acoustic trackers that locate the glove accurately in space (to 0.25 in.) with respect to a companion unit mounted on the television monitor. The trackers also provide four bits of roll orientation for the hand (rotation of the wrist).
- *CyberGlove*. Consists of a custom-made cloth glove with up to 22 thin foil strain gauges sewn into the fabric to sense finger and wrist bending. A small electronics box converts the analog signals into a digital stream that can be read by a computer's standard serial port. As with the DataGlove and DHM, a 3-space tracker can be mounted on the glove to get hand position in space.
- *Space Glove*. Made of soft molded plastic that fits over the back of the hand. Rings around the fingers and a strap around the wrist hold the glove in place. One flex angle for each finger and two flex angles for the thumb are measured using sensors with 12-bit A/D converters. A 3-space magnetic tracker is incorporated into the back of the glove.

One problem with the glove is the need to provide a sense of touch to increase the haptic experience of the wearer. Consider what happens when a human reaches out to grip a virtual object. Although the virtual image shows he or she is gripping an object, the human cannot feel any resistance to the hand tightening movement. Work is under way to achieve this illusion by making the glove resist further closure. The gloves are not without their difficulties. They can be tiring and feel artificial. Indeed, some commentators question the future of the glove as an input device, though there seems little alternative when it comes to sensual output to the hand, or Frequd in an entire lightweight body suit. This suit has fiber-optic cables or motion sensors at the major joints allowing the VR computers to track the user's movements precisely. The more advanced suits, even those used in arcade style VR games, can cost up to $20,000 (KECU 16.9).

### 3.3.4   Sound Generation

VEs are not necessarily silent, so the person can be surrounded by 3-D sounds, making the experience of the VE all the more convincing. At present, sound systems are relatively crude, but much research is under way to create convincing and realistic 3-D sounds at exactly the right moment, for instance when the DataGlove hits a VR wall.

An auditory interface for VEs should be capable of providing any specified pair of acoustic waveforms to the two ears. More specifically it should have high fidelity, be capable of altering those waveforms in a prescribed manner as a function of various behaviors or outputs to the listener (including changes in the position and orientation in the listener's head), and exclude all sounds not specifically generated by the VE system (i.e., real background sounds). Generally speaking, such results can be most easily achieved with the use of earphones; when loudspeakers located away from the head are employed, each ear receives sound from each loudspeaker and the control problem becomes substantial. Although commercial high-fidelity firms often claim substantial imaging ability with loudspeakers, the user is restricted to a single listening position within the room, only azimuthal imaging is achieved (with no compensation for head rotcteristics of the listening room cannot be easily manipulated. In addition, since the ears are completely open, extraneous (undesired) sounds within the environment cannot be excluded.

Finally, although the tactual cues associated with the use of earphones may initially limit the degree of auditory telepresence, because the user will be required to transit back and forth between the virtual and the real environments, such tactual cuing may actually prove useful. In any case, such cuing is likely to be present because of the visual interface. One set of situations for which loudspeakers might be needed are those in which high-energy, low-frequency acoustic bursts (e.g., associated with explosions) occur. In such cases, loudspeakers, but not earphones, can be used to vibrate portions of the body other than the eardrums.

### 3.3.5   PC-Based VR

It has been a few years since PC-based desktop VR began to be possible. While the cost of a basic desktop VR system has gone down by only a few thousand dollars since that time, the functionality has improved dramatically, both in terms of graphics processing power and VR gear such as HMDs. For now, these improvements mean that a growing number of practical applications of VR are beginning to be deployed. In the near future, desktop VR could become as commonplace as PCs are today, revolutionizing the publishing world. When coupled with innovations occurring in telecommunications, distributed multi-user virtual worlds will soon be a reality.

Several PC-based software packages are available for building and running virtual worlds. Ranging in price from free (www.alice.org) to $8000. Some of them rely exclusively on C or C$^{++}$ programming to build a virtual world, whereas others offer simpler point-and-click operations to develop a simulation. Most of these make it easy to hook up VR gear such as HMDs, trackers, and DataGloves. Sense8 (Mill Valley, CA.), for example, offers WorldToolKit (WTK). This package, one of the leaders in the market, has been around long enough to be pretty well shaken out. WTK and its counterparts, such as Super-scape's (United Kingdom) VRT, are fairly mature in terms of functionality. Indeed, Superscape recently raised the VR development platform a level with a new offering, VRT 5.61 that provides a point-and-click method for non-C programmers to create prototype worlds. The VRT is Superscape's complete graphical environment for the creation of virtual worlds. Through the VRT's editors, users can create and manipulate the virtual world in real time to give it whatever appearance and interactions they want. Over 600 specific commands are available for assigning behaviors within VEs. These can be applied on an object by object basis so that the results can be evaluated immediately. Release 5.61 also includes VRML 2.0 and Direct-X support, VRML authoring, support for all leading VR devices, and real-time resolution switching up to 1280 × 1024, DXF transfer including layering support and virtual humans.

On the hardware side, 1999 has shown significant progress, and industry observers expect even more advances over the next year or so. Much of the graphics display quality of the Silicon Graphics (SGI) RealityEngine, which has been the Rolls Royce of the VR world with a six-digit price tag, can now be achieved with a new Intergraph (Huntsville, AL.) graphics accelerator board (Wildcat 4105) plugged into a Pentium III PC.

The Intergraph board has a $3000 price tag and two boards can be plugged in to render stereo images. The complete system (TDZ2000 GL2) based on dual 600 MHz PIII, 256 MB/9 GB10 K, CD40x, 100 BT sells for $6999 (Nov. 1999). Using the TDZ2000, it is possible to get the same image quality as an high-end Onyx on the PC. The same demonstration running on the at 15 to 20 Hz runs on an SGI Onyx at 30 Hz. But the Onyx is pricey. If you need the frame rate, then you still need a SGI workstation. But if you put the same nonmoving image on a side by-side SGI and TDZ2000, you cannot tell which is which.

Intergraph's accelerator is the first in a series that will hit the market soon. According to many sources, some of the biggest computer companies (IBM, HP, Compaq, etc.) are getting ready to launch mid-range ($1000 to $5000) graphics accelerators for PCs that will compete aggressively with the performance of SGI machines. Several hardware vendors will announce new products in 2000 to 2001 that will bring the price down by 80%. For instance Nvidia and 3dfx are preparing new versions of their low-cost TNT2 and Voodoo 3 graphic cards (now selling for $250) with features and power matching the ones of actual mid-range graphic accelerators. The notion of a special-purpose board is also likely to go away. What will result is a single board and then a chip that will do 24 bit/pixel display graphics, MPEG 2 video, NTSC/PAL TV-out, and VR and 3-D graphics rendering.

The Gartner Group predicts that 3-D desktop visualization will be the first

VR technology to become widespread as soon as 2000. They further predict that by 2001, high-end desktop PCs will be able to generate virtual worlds as well as those generated by 1999's graphics workstations. "'We'll have to get RealityEngine performance for $5,000 for the technology to become ubiquitous,' says Gartner Group's Pimental. 'By the year 2000 it will be possible to get SGI RealityEngine2 graphics for less than $5,000 on a PC. It may come sooner. I wouldn't be surprised if it were here in two to three years'" (9).

Immersion, too, is getting more affordable. For example, Virtual I-O (USA) now has an HMD equipped with built-in head tracking that costs less than $800. Sony distributes its L-55 Glasstron headset for about $600 without head tracking. In 1998, HMDs of the same quality were about 10 times more expensive. But HMDs are still used primarily for entertainment. "'Most people doing practical applications are using monitors or projection systems,' according to Pimental—Gartner Group—'because HMDs have a way to go to get good quality at affordable price. SVGA quality is now about $2,000. It was $70,000, so it's a big breakthrough.'" But that price will probably lose a digit during the next five years.

Input devices for desktop VR today are largely mouse and joystick based. As developers focus on how to make desktop VR practical, this is sound advice. Not only does it keep costs down, but it minimizes the foreignness of VR applications and avoids the ergonomic issues of some of the fancier I/O devices like 3-D mice and gloves that do not provide good hand support. The day will come, however, when DataGloves and other innovative devices move out of the realm of high-end entertainment and research VR systems.

### 3.3.6  Networked VR

The Virtual Reality Modeling Language (VRML) is a file format and run-time description for 3-D graphics elements for use on the World Wide Web (WWW). It includes interaction and animation elements as well as interfaces to scripting languages to provide more general simulation behaviors and interfaces to network services. Currently VRML worlds can be scripted with Java and JavaScript, both of which are familiar to most Web programmers.

VRML 2.0 was designed and implemented in 1995 and has been an ISO standard since 1997 (referred to as VRML97). VRML97 is the only existing open standard for describing 3-D graphics on the Web, though several proprietary packages with similar capabilities exist. The development and maintenance of VRML97 is overseen by the Web3-D Consortium, which counts Sun, Microsoft, SGI, Apple, and Intervista among its members. Along with the variety of open standard VRML authoring tools now freely available on the Web, hardware changes in PCs have accelerated deployment of VRML on the desktop. Currently, available PCs are well able to cope with the requirements of moderately complex VRML97 worlds. In particular, almost all desktop PCs sold since mid-1998 have been shipped with a 3-D graphics accelerator. In addition, VRML97 browsers are now standard in the complete installation of

*Internet Explorer* 5.0 (Intervista WorldView) and *Netscape* 4.7 (CosmoPlayer). Plugin browsers are available for earlier versions of both of these software packages.

Much of the power of VRML over other 3-D technologies is that 3-D worlds can be integrated into and interact with standard 2-D Web page descriptions. Given that the Web page is a familiar front-end to the Internet, and that VRML scripts can access the capabilities of Java scripting, games developers and online shopping providers have been quick to see the potential of hosting thousands of users within a controlled 3-D environment. The overall experience of VRML worlds on the Internet will be vastly improved over the next couple of years as basic technologies (such as second-generation graphics accelerators) and network technologies (such as ADSL) become available.

Java is a platform-independent language that is an integral part of Web browsers including *Netscape Navigator* and *Microsoft Internet Explorer* and allows video, audio and graphics applets, or small sections of a program such as a video clip, to be played directly from the host server, removing the need for the PC to store and process the code. As Java is integrated into VRML environments, less processing and bandwidth requirements are made on the host PC, providing users with high-quality performance.

## 3.4 MARKET ANALYSIS

The VR market is at present immature, without any clear market leaders or clear segmentation of activities. In a paper (10) prepared for the European Commission's IT Policy Analysis Unit (DG III/A.5) on VR, PVN (Belgium) estimates a market of $570 million (MECU 483) by 1998. This figure includes both hardware and software. The bad news for Europe is that it is forecast to have only $115 million (MECU 97) of that market, a poor third behind the United States and Japan (Fig. 3.1). A study into telematics applications of vir-

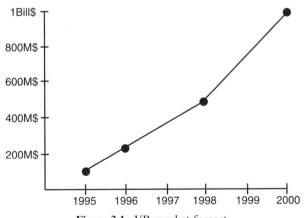

**Figure 3.1.** VR market forcast.

tual environments, carried out by Sema Group (F), Fraunhofer IAO (D) and MIT's Research Laboratory for Electronics (Boston, MA) for the Commission's DG XIII/C in 1994, predicted a market evaluation of "roughly MECU 400–MECU 500 by 1998" with a growth rate "very high, approaching 70-80% per year" (11). What is perhaps less disputed is that the major market activity is in entertainment equipment.

According to a Business Communications Company report (12), by 1996, more than 300 companies will settle sales for about $255 million worth of VR products and services, and behind this figure are multinational brands of military and medical products. By 2000, the VR industry will be posting annual sales of over $1 billion and reaching an annual average growth rate (MGR) of 33%.

In July 1996 Ovum, the UK market research company published another survey on VR markets. They expects the killer application of VR to be in 3-D interfaces to the Internet, used for promoting products and services on the WWW. They predict that in the next 5 years, VR will be widely used as a graphical user interface (GUI) for standard business software, thus replacing icon-based GUIs for such applications as databases, business systems, and networked management software. According to the survey, a large proportion of companies polled indicated that they would use PC-based VR training applications for their employees. Regarding the present uptake of VR in business, the report concludes that "companies are finding virtual reality an important source of competitive advantage" and that "although some companies are taking their time to evaluate VR, which is slowing down the speed of market lift-off, many are reporting significant benefits and are increasing their use of VR technology." It explains this expected increase in uptake by saying that "In many cases, companies have made cost savings of over US$1 million. They have experienced faster time to market, fewer mistakes than when using CAD technologies, greater efficiency in working methods and improved quality in final products."

The report also predicts that the VR market will grow from US$134.9 million in 1995 to just over US$1 billion by the year 2001 and that the largest growth sector will be in the software sector with a 58% annual growth in this period. Another significant finding of the report is that the business market for VR in 1995 represented 65% of the total, with entertainment applications accounting for only 35% (Table 3.1). VR is normally seen to be of major significance to the games market; it is not known whether, and how, the authors distinguish between entertainment and the entertainment business.

The Ovum survey foresees a radical shift in how companies will be using VR between now and the year 2001. Today the majority of VR applications are in design automation: virtual prototyping, interior design and ergonomics, and architectural and engineering design. Expensive, workstation-based systems currently dominate, accounting for 43% of the market. By 2001, however, PC-based VR technology will account for 46% of the business market, where most

**TABLE 3.1. Virtual Reality Market by Application ($ millions, constant 1995$)**[a]

| Application | 1994 | 1995 | 2000[b] | AAGR% 1995–2000 |
|---|---|---|---|---|
| Instructional and developmental | 70 | 95 | 355 | 31 |
| Design and development | 25 | 30 | 150 | 40 |
| entertainment | 60 | 110 | 500 | 35 |
| Medical treatment | 10 | 20 | 50 | 20 |
| Total | 165 | 255 | 1055 | 33 |

[a] Reprinted with permission from Ref. 12.
[b] Forecast.

of the applications will be nonimmersive, using computer screens instead of headsets.

At the current state of the situation all marketing experts converge on the fact that the major market activity is entertainment equipment; leisure technology uses account for the largest VR market value and is foreseen to continue growing at a 35% MGR to the year 2000. The critical mass in marketing terms will be reached with high-scale produced single-user entertainment VR system, this will be the propelling force pushing the market growth from a current 1995 value of $110 million to $500 million by year 2000.

The great market expansion is expect for site-based entertainment. This expectation is based on the evaluation two factors: the low saturation, and dramatic decrease of prices. These phenomena will allow VR technology to be used by all facets of society, including commercial/industrial, the government, military, and university and secondary schools at a stage not comparable with any previous existing situation. A great role will also be covered with in the support to education in general, for instance the instructional and developmental market is expected to widen its share from a $95 million 1995 market figure to $355 million by 2000, resulting in an MGR of 31%. The dimension of this increase will affect technical/engineering colleges and universities, and the developmental VR includes spending on advanced, but as yet noncommercial, applications along with pure science and research systems not included in the other categories.

Applications of the design and development VR market are in engineering, architecture, and chemical design and development a constant shift will bring performance of CAD/ CAMM application to the standards of virtual reality applications . This market will grow from a 1995 market value of $30 million, to $150 million by 2000, reaching an MGR of 40%. The medical treatment VR market will also sustain growth. The 1995 market value of $20 million is projected to reach $50 million by 2000, reaching a 20% MGR.

Current VR products employ proprietary hardware and software. There is little doubt that incompatibility among different systems is restricting market growth at present. It is probable that as the market matures, certain de facto standards will emerge, perhaps when major players become involved. It is probable that the VR market will follow the route of the real-time financial information markets, which found that adopting an open systems approach did not damage sales, as had been feared, but helped encourage the growth of the marketplace. According to the IMO—Information Group at the Policy Studies Institute in London (14) "in the future an open systems approach will emerge for VR as well." At that point, the market is likely to expand considerably.

However, the cost of VR equipment is falling rapidly. For example, head-gear prices have already fallen from hundreds of thousands of dollars to $600 and basic VR software packages are available commercially for $200 or can be freely downloaded from the Internet. Simple VR games software is available in the United States for $70. The Gartner Group (15) predicts that 3-D desktop visualization will be the first VR technology to become widespread as soon as 2000. They further predict that by 2001, high-end desktop PCs will be able to generate virtual worlds as well as those generated by today's graphics workstations.

## 3.5 VIRTUAL REALITY IN HEALTH CARE*

### 3.5.1 Introduction

Virtual environments and related technologies are allowing medical practitioners to help their patients in a number of innovative ways. In particular, three important aspects of virtual reality systems offer new possibilities to medical treatment (1, 18).

***3.5.1.1 How They Are Controlled?*** Present alternate computer access systems accept only one or at most two modes of input at a time. The computer can be controlled by single modes such as pressing keys on a keyboard, pointing to an on-screen keyboard with a head pointer, or hitting a switch when the computer presents the desired choice; but present computers do not recognize facial expressions, idiosyncratic gestures, or monitor actions from several body parts at a time. Most computer interfaces accept only precise, discrete input. Thus many communicative acts are ignored and the subtleness and richness of the human communicative gesture are lost. This results in slow, energy-intensive computer interfaces. Virtual reality systems open the input channel: The potential is there to monitor movements or actions from any body part or many body parts at the same time. All properties of the movement can be captured, not just contact of a body part with an effector.

---

*This section is an adapted version Ref. 16.

Given that these actions are monitored, why can the user control more in the virtual world than in the real world? In the VE these actions or signals can be processed in a number of ways. They can be translated into other actions that have more effect on the world being controlled, for example, virtual objects could be pushed by blowing, pulled by sipping, and grasped by jaw closure. Proportional properties such as force, direction, and speed could become interchangeable allowing the person with arthritic joints to push something harder, without the associated pain, by simply moving faster. They could be filtered to achieve a cleaner signal. Actions can be amplified thus movement of the index finger could guide a tennis racket. Alternately movements could be attenuated giving the individual with large, poorly controlled movement more precise control of finer actions.

**3.5.1.2  *Feedback.*** Because VR systems display feedback in multiple modes, feedback and prompts can be translated into alternate senses for users with sensory impairments. The environment could be reduced in size to get the larger or overall perspective (without the looking-through-a-straw-effect usually experienced when using screen readers or tactile displays). Objects and people could show speech bubbles for the person who is deaf. Sounds could be translated into vibrations or into a register that is easier to pick up. Environmental noises can be selectively filtered out. The user with a spinal cord injury with no sensation in the hands could receive force and density feedback at the shoulder, neck, or head.

For the individual multimodal feedback ensures that the visual channel is not overloaded. Vision is the primary feedback channel of present-day computers; frequently the message is further distorted and alienated by representation through text. It is very difficult to represent force, resistance, density, temperature, pitch, etc., through vision alone. VR presents information in alternate ways and in more than one way. Sensory redundancy promotes learning and integration of concepts.

**3.5.1.3  *What is Controlled?*** The final advantage is what is controlled. Until the last decade computers were used to control numbers and text by entering numbers and text using a keyboard. Recent direct manipulation interfaces have allowed the manipulation of iconic representations of text files or two dimensional (2-D) graphic representations of objects through pointing devices such as the mouse. The objective of direct manipulation environments was to provide an interface that more directly mimics the manipulation of objects in the real world. The latest step in that trend, VR systems, allows the manipulation of multisensory representations of entire environments by natural actions and gestures. This last step may make accessible valuable experiences missed owing to physical or sensory impairments. These experiences may include early object-centered play, and early independent mobility.

In VEs we can simulate inaccessible or risky experiences, allowing the user to extract the lessons to be learned without the inherent risk. Virtual reality systems can allow users to extend their world knowledge.

The following are some examples in which these advantages are used in a clinical setting:

- As the technology develops, a surgeon will be able to operate on a patient in a remote location. Today's remote telesurgery is being developed for the military to enable a surgeon to assist medics in the battle arena. The Advanced Research Projects Agency's (ARPA) Advanced Biomedical Program has demonstrated its robotics surgery system using wireless transmission, with the surgical site located 1 km away from the "robotics arms."
- VEs are useful for local as well as for remote surgery. An example of the local use of VEs is in endoscopic surgery. Surgeons manipulate instruments by viewing a television monitor and manipulating a tool inserted through a tube into the patient.
- VEs are being used to create surgical simulators or trainers. These systems reduce the cost of training surgeons and the risk to patients. For example, a heart-catheterization simulation allows the trainee to guide a balloon catheter through a hollow guide wire to the obstruction, and inflate the balloon to expand the artery and restore regular blood flow.
- Therapeutic uses of VEs include creating interactive systems that help reduce anxiety or stress. For example, dentists are using 3-D eyeglasses to divert patients' attention while in the chair.
- VEs are also used to reduce phobias, to develop skills, and to train those with disabilities. One example of the use of virtual environments for training is a program that substitutes virtual bus rides for the real thing so that disabled individuals can learn to use a public transportation system.

### 3.5.2 Health-Care Applications

The terminology and categories used in this section are an amplification of Satava's (7) schema for health-care applications of VEs and related technologies.

#### 3.5.2.1 Surgical Procedures

*3.5.2.1.1 Remote Surgery or Telepresence.* Telepresence applications link research in robotics and VEs. Telepresence systems are used in medicine to manipulate equipment at remote sites. The surgeon or other medical practitioner has the sense of actually being at the site performing the procedure (1995).

SRI International's Green Telepresence Surgery System was designed to allow surgeons to participate in battlefield operations from sites removed from the front line. The system consists of the "remote operative site and a surgical workstation [that includes] 3-D vision, dexterous precision surgical instrument manipulation, and input of force feedback sensory information." The surgeon operates on a virtual image, and a robot on the battlefield reproduces the surgeon's movements. This one-to-one coupling between the surgeon and the machine has been demonstrated to work from 150 yd away with a fiberoptic connection. The next goal for the military is to replace the fiberoptic connection with a wireless signal (7). As promising as this system is, it will take about 3 years for it to be approved for investigational trials on humans.

Recently, supervisory staff at medical schools such as Johns Hopkins have been using telepresence. The supervising staff member remains in his or her office and holds a laparoscope remotely for the surgeon. The remote interaction is facilitated by two monitors and a hard-wired connection.

The use of VEs and remote surgery opens up new possibilities. Besides the military and the academic examples discussed above, other civilian uses are possible. A specialist could assist a local surgeon by remote connection or surgery could be performed, via a medical center, in a rural setting, a ship at sea, an airplane in flight, or even a space station. Besides solving the distance problem, telepresence offers other benefits, such as minimizing the exposure of surgeons to diseases and reducing potential costs as a result of reduced trauma (7).

The military surgery system and academic application described above fit the narrow definition of telepresence or remote surgery as the manipulation of equipment at a remote site. However, many of the procedures described in the following sections will lend themselves to robotics telepresence in the future.

*3.5.2.1.2 Augmented, or Enhanced, Reality Surgery.* Augmented, or enhanced, reality surgery is being used for minimally invasive surgery. Augmented surgery includes fusing computer images with real-time images or superimposing them on the body using video technology or robots directed by surgeons physically present in the operating room. Table 3.2 shows some applications of these techniques.

Traditionally, surgery is performed by making incisions and directly interacting with the organs and tissues. Recent innovations in video technology allow direct viewing of internal body cavities through natural orifices or small incisions. As with remote surgery, the surgeon operates on a virtual image. The manipulation of instruments by the surgeon or assistants can be direct or via virtual environments. In the latter case, a robot reproduces the movements of

**TABLE 3.2. Applications for Augmented Reality Surgery**

| Technique | Examples |
|---|---|
| Endoscopic surgery | Cholecystectomies (gallbladder) removal |
| Robots used locally | Orthopedics, joint replacement |
| Fusing scanned images and real-time video image | Brain surgery: MRI overlaid on a video image of the patient's head |

humans using virtual instruments. The precision of the operation may be augmented by data or images superimposed on the virtual patient. In this manner the surgeon's abilities are enhanced.

> Surgical practice, particularly in orthopaedics, presents excellent opportunities for robotic and computer-based technologies to improve clinical techniques. Procedures such as total joint replacements are performed in large volumes and at significant cost. The clinical success of these procedures is very dependent on the proper placement and fit of the implants within bony structures. Important contributions to surgical planning and execution can be made by surgical robots and pre-operative planners that utilize computer simulations. Use of robotic assistants significantly augments the skill of the surgeon (20).

In 1989, video technology was employed by a team of surgeons to perform a laparoscopic cholecystectomy (removal of a gallbladder). The use of this minimally invasive therapeutic technique has become standard: "about 90% of all cholecystectomies performed in the last two years have been done using laparoscopic techniques" (21) Use of endoscopes (instruments that use video techniques for visualizing) are now commonly used for surgery.

In 1993, surgeons at Brigham Women's Hospital in Boston, "with help from engineers from General Electric Co.'s imaging and visualization laboratory in Schenectady, N.Y., ... began modeling work to assist operations in real time. As of early November [1993], 17 operations had been performed" with the surgeons using a monitor. In one example, a MRI scan taken earlier was overlaid on a real-time video image of the patient's head (22). This technique can provide an x-ray view of a tumor that might otherwise not be visible if it is deeply embedded in the brain tissue. Similarly, "UNC, Chapel Hill, is overlaying ultrasound images on live video that is then viewed in an HMD [head-mounted display]. [Again], this system essentially gives the viewer the feeling of having X-ray vision" (19). Aligning images in real time is an area for major research.

A low-cost interactive image-directed neurosurgical system is being used in epilepsy surgery. The system has been successfully used in 20 epilepsy surgery cases. The epilepsy surgery is directed by the physiologic and functional data obtained during the preoperative evaluation. Computer-assisted image-directed techniques are particularly well suited for this surgery. An image-directed system melds the preoperative data to the surgical anatomy by defining all the relevant data topographically in 3-D space and coregistering these data to the anatomic image and the patient space.

Fuchs created a VR model that allows the physician to visualize the tumor (from reconstructed 3-D CT scans) inside the individual patient and plan various radiation trajectories to allow lethal doses of radiation to the tumor while avoiding damage to normal organs.

In addition, MRI allows the visualization of temperature changes for thermal surgery procedures, a capability never previously available noninvasively. For the first time, real-time 3-D images of temperature changes can be obtained.

Furthermore, MRI scans show a phase change upon heating, and it is postulated that this occurs when the tissue protein is denatured (i.e., when coagulation takes place). These two capabilities provide MRI with the ability to monitor and control thermal therapies. Tissue ablation can be monitored during the deposition of energy via interstitial laser or focused ultrasound therapy, RF ablation or cryosurgery (21).

### 3.5.2.1.3 Planning and Simulation of Procedures before Surgery.

Virtual environment technology can also be used to improve the way surgeons plan procedures before surgery. When used to simulate a procedure on a particular patient, the technology can be used to integrate the information provided by diagnostic sensors into a realistic model of the actual environment in which the surgeon will perform the proposed procedure. The realistic model or surgical simulator must have accurate detail and must be highly interactive. Specifically, the image must be anatomically precise and the organs must have natural properties such as the ability to change shape with pressure and to behave appropriately in gravity. All the body parts represented must be able to be manipulated by grasping, clamping, or cutting, and they must be able to bleed or leak fluids (7).

Virtual environments can make a critical contribution to the planning of a surgical procedure (Table 3.3). For example, Netra has been used for various precision, computer-assisted surgical procedures. Neurosurgeons use Netra to plan precision biopsies, laser-guided tumor resections, surgery for Parkinson disease and other motor disorders, and surgical implantation of electrode arrays for epilepsy (23). What is unique with this system is its user interface. Users manipulate objects, such as a doll's head, to cause movement of the virtual image on the monitor.

**TABLE 3.3. Applications for Surgical Planning and Simulation**

| Technique | Examples | Who/Where |
|---|---|---|
| VR face model with deformable skin | Plastic surgical procedure and demonstration of final outcome | Rosen, Dartmouth University Medical Center |
| Virtual leg model | Tendon transplant surgery and walking the repaired leg to predict consequences | Delp |
| Creating 3-D images from CT scans | Craniofacial dysostosis repair | Altobelli, Brigham Women's Hospital |
| Netra system, used for various precision computer-assisted surgical procedures | Biopsies, laser-guided tumor resections, surgery for Parkinson disease and other motor disorders, surgical implants of electrode arrays for epilepsy | Department of Neurosurgery, University of Virginia |

Simulators are being developed for all types of surgery. Many of them are used for planning particular procedures. Altobelli's system creates 3-D images from the CT scan of a child with bony deformities of the face (craniofacial dysostosis); using the model created from the CT scan, the bones can be correctly rearranged to symmetrically match the normal side of the face. The procedure can be practiced repeatedly.

Some of the simulations designed for planning a procedure also include a predictive component. Data that could be used to correct a condition are introduced into the model and the results of the proposed actions are calculated and visualized. For example, Rosen's VR model of a face with deformable skin allows the practicing of a plastic surgical procedure and demonstrates the final outcome. Another example is Delp's virtual model of a lower leg on which he can practice a tendon transplant operation and then "walk" the leg to predict the short- and long-term consequences of the surgery (7).

The Fraunhofer-Institute for Industrial Engineering and the Orthopaedic University Clinic Heidelberg. Developed an application for the planning of osteotomy operations. The surgeon, with the aid of tracked shutter-glasses and a 6-D input device, is able to view and rotate the femur and the hip joint. Using a simulated x-ray of the bones, the medical practitioner can determine the angle, allow the computer to perform the surgery, and view the simulated results on the screen. Planning for surgery is always important. With computer-assisted surgical planning, an exact picture can be drafted of the relative positions of the cartilages, the abrasion of the cartilage, and the position of the femur in the hip joint, to help determine the alteration parameters. The planning of an osteotomy can be optimized by using a 3-D image because the operator is more able to evaluate the result. An increase in the rate of successful operations is conceivable. In the future, the application should serve in the planning of patient-specific osteotomies requiring tomographic data from the relevant bones and cartilage (24).

Simulation techniques for improved preoperative planning are of value for orthopedic surgery with or without a robot. It is useful for a surgeon to realistically simulate surgery beforehand to help determine what implant size to use, and what would be its optimal position. Existing planners permit the surgeon make a template of the implant based on 3-D geometry but give no indication of the consequences of the proposed surgery on the initial stability of the system, the presence of implant-bone interface gaps, and the changes in the mechanical environment that are induced in the bone. The inclusion of biomechanical simulations would permit the surgeon to make appropriate changes in the initial surgical a plan, changing such parameters as the implant placement, specifics of the bone preparation, and type and size of implant. Without a robotic tool, however, there is no method for a surgeon to accurately implement a preoperative plan. For example, the simulation may help indicate an optimal bone cavity shape and implant location, but the surgeon will be unable to accurately perform this plan without a robotic device. In this manner, surgical robots actually improve the clinical usefulness of realistic surgical simulations (20).

**TABLE 3.4. Applications for Medical Therapy**

| Technique | Examples | Who/Where |
|---|---|---|
| Controlled virtual environments | To modify eating disorders | Riva, Istituto Auxologico Italiano, VREPAR Project |
| | To provide interventions for the rehabilitation of neglect for the treatment of stroke disorders | Wann and Rushton, University of Reading, VREPAR Project |
| | To treat autistic children to recognize a common object and then to find the object in the environment, walk to it, and stop | University of North Carolina at Chapel Hill School of Medicine |
| | To treat acrophobia | Georgia Institute of Technology and Kaiser-Permanente, San Rafael, CA |
| VR/3-D eyeglasses and headphones for movies or educational programs | To distract dental patients from work being done; to diminish psycho-oncological symptoms in cancer patients | |
| Controlled virtual environment as part of a relax/refresh system | To relax users while monitoring their pulse rate | Matsushita, Japan |
| Building a virtual reality experience from within an altered state | To provide understanding and analysis of hemianopia, proprioceptive disorientation, or muscular damage | Addison, New Media Arts, Palo Alto, CA |

The predictive element is important not only for the medical team but also for the patient's family. It can serve as a model on which to base informed consent of the patient and his or her family. Furthermore, these simulation applications could be used for medical education and training.

***3.5.2.2 Medical Therapy.*** Virtual environments are being used for a variety of purposes, categorized here as medical therapy (Table 3.4). These include treating eating disorders, phobias, and other psychological conditions; diverting patients' attention during medical intervention sessions; providing an appropriate environment for physical exercise and/or relaxation; and providing a means for patients to describe their experiences from within altered states.

Research by Riva (1) has shown the efficacy of the VE for body image modification (VEBIM) theoretical approach. This approach focuses on the treatment of a disturbed body image to resolve eating disorders. Preliminary results show that after the VR experience, the subjects were more satisfied with their actual body image (i.e., less intent on achieving an ideal body image).

After suffering a stroke, patients provided with stimulation interventions attain some degree of recovery of function. One system being developed translates biofeedback to action feedback through a virtual environment. By providing patients with visual information about specific muscular activity, it is expected that they will make significant, if limited, gains (25). Similarly, a VR experimental system is being developed to study motion in some diseases of the basal ganglia, e.g., Parkinson disease. The aim of this research is to develop and use immersive VEs to study the relationship between visual sensory information and control of movement being performed by those suffering from these diseases.

Since the spring of 1993, researchers at Georgia Institute of Technology's Graphics, Visualization, and Usability Center have been exploring the possibility of using virtual environments for therapy of individuals with psychological disorders. One of their research areas has concerned acrophobia (fear of heights). The researchers' goal is to lessen a person's anxieties through practice in well-controlled situations. One of the main advantages of a virtual environment is that it can be used in a medical facility, thus avoiding the need to venture into public situations (3). Lamson is using a similar system for virtual therapy (19). Another application of VR to psychology helped in training autistic children. The study was designed to replicate skill training done by therapists. The goal was to train a subject to find an object in the environment, walk to it, and stop. The two autistic children used as subjects accepted the technology and responded to the learning situation (1)

Another trend is the use of VEs in medical "edutainment". Dentists are using virtual environments to divert patients' attention while in the chair. Using 3-D glasses with headphones hooked up to a tuner and VCR, patients can watch 2-D and 3-D videos or educational programs, listen to music, and play video games. Another example is its use in a medical support program for cancer patients. Cancer patients may experience insomnia and unrest, especially when undergoing chemotherapy. The purpose of the Psycho-oncological VR Therapy (POVRT) application is to diminish these problems through virtual environments. In the virtual space, the patients can feel as if they were outside the hospital. Furthermore, some patients internalize the experience of having had nausea and vomiting when they were first treated with chemotherapy, and they complain in the second chemotherapy session even before the treatment starts. Such anticipatory emesis may be reduced with VE applications (1, 17).

A stationary bike that allows the user to race against the computer or other people, changing gears, braking, and tilting the seat to steer has been developed. A variety of on-screen terrains offers different degrees of pedaling difficulty; going faster causes the feeling of simulated wind resistance. Another product is a massage chair that uses VR images and sound to help relax users; it monitors pulse rate and automatically controls images and sound to match the user's body condition and state of consciousness (17). Still to be developed is the concept of using VR as a medical and patient education and evaluation tool. The idea is to allow a VR experience to be built from within altered states, including hemianopia, proprioceptive disorientation, or muscular damage.

### 3.5.2.3 *Preventive Medicine and Patient Education.*

The areas of preventive medicine and patient education lend themselves to VE applications. Video games are not necessarily VEs, although some use VEs. VEs could become an important educational tool and provide edutainment. For example, a video game series (Health Hero) is being developed for pediatric patient education. The video games are expected to enhance young people's self-esteem, self-efficacy, communication about health, health knowledge and skills, and motivation to learn about health and how these factors can influence self-care behavior and health outcome. This is an area that will benefit from work done in other areas of virtual environments; although to be effective, products must be tailored to the particular applications and users.

### 3.5.2.4 *Medical Education and Training*

*3.5.2.4.1 Education.* Virtual reality allows information visualization (the display of massive volumes of information and databases). Through 3-D visualization, students can understand important physiologic principles or basic anatomy (7). Table 3.5 lists some applications of VEs and related technologies for medical education. In this chapter, the term *education* is used for applications that do not allow the learner to practice a procedure and the term *training* is used when practice is the objective of the application.

One application for the study of anatomy allows the abdomen to "be explored by 'flying' around the organs (a bird's-eye view from the diaphragm) or behind them (watching the bile duct pass through the pancreas under the duodenum) or even inside them. (A trip might start from inside the esophagus,

**TABLE 3.5.** Applications for Medical Education

| Technique | Examples | Who/Where |
|---|---|---|
| Exploring anatomy by flying through the body | Providing an understanding of the organs by flying around them, behind them, or even inside them | |
| Touring a topic of study and then exploring it | Seeing a visual representation, e.g., of shock and navigating through the arterial tree | |
| MMVR | Flying into an organ and grabbing something (e.g., going into the stomach, seeing an ulcer, and grabbing it for biopsy) | Hoffman, University of California, San Diego |

down the stomach, through the duodenum, up the bile duct, and out the gall bladder is a popular route)." The extraordinary perspectives provided by such a learning tool "impart a deeper understanding and appreciation of the inter-relationship of anatomical structure that cannot be achieved by any other means, including cadaveric dissection" (7).

Virtual environments provide both a didactic and an experiential educational tool. A demonstration mode could give a tour of the intended subject, and then an exploration mode would allow the student to actually experience the environment.

Hoffman, is working to create 4-D, the three dimensions of a virtual world and the fourth dimension of time (archived information in multimedia format), in essence, multimedia virtual reality (MMVR). For example in a MMVR simulator of the gastrointestinal tract, a student could fly down into the stomach, see an ulcer, and grab it as if for a biopsy, this would bring up the histologic micrograph of an ulcer, or play a videotape of a Bilroth 2 operation for ulcer disease, or perhaps demonstrate (predict) the healing in response to medication. In this fashion the multiple layers of understanding could be rolled into one, and the change of the processes over time can be graphically represented and personally experienced (7).

The following are additional examples of systems being used in education or training:

- A German system for orthopedic surgery is being used for educational purposes with data records procured from the company Viewpoint Data-Labs. The data records are models from people with average body structure and are therefore suitable for general educational purposes.
- A computing system for visualizing and monitoring human labor and birth, from the Health Sciences Center at Brooklyn, New York, offers an opportunity for the study of large numbers of collected cases, and for modeling scenarios for the purpose of education and research. Particularly instructive labors can be preserved in a computerized teaching file and become objects of instruction for future students in labor.
- The Center for Human Modeling and Simulation at the University of Pennsylvania is developing models of functional anatomy. The center is first modeling the respiratory mechanism because it involves physiologic change, such as pressures and flows, that depends on gross anatomic deformations. Ultimately, using models for other physiologic systems, the center will demonstrate the interactions between systems owing to the physical space they share.

The opportunity for international participation in medical conferences is another potential application currently being explored. Interaction and participation using virtual environments might alleviate some of the stiltedness of current videoconferencing capabilities. This use of a shared VE instead of real-time transmission suggests an application of VEs to telemedicine.

TABLE 3.6. **Applications for Medical Training**

| Technique | Examples | Who/Where |
|---|---|---|
| Virtual reality laparoscopic surgery simulator, consisting of a torso into which the handles of laparoscopic instruments are mounted and provide force feedback | The virtual abdomen (liver and gallbladder) are graphically displayed on the video monitor, and the apprentice surgeon practices specific laparoscopic procedures | Woods and Hon |
| Heart catheterization simulation including feedback | Allows the trainee to guide a balloon catheter through a hollow guiding wire to the obstruction, inflate the balloon to expand the artery, and restore regular blood flow | High Techsplantations Inc., Rockville, MD |
| Virtual abdomen | Created for the immersive, traditional HMD and DataGlove | Satava, Advanced Research Project Agency, Arlington, VA |
| Limb trauma simulator | Will lead to a VR environment | MusculoGraphics, Inc., Evanston, IL |
| Simulating surgery complete with feedback on the force being exerted | Simulates surgery on the human eye | Georgia Institute of Technology, Atlanta |

*3.5.2.4.1 Medical Training.* The use of computers in medical schools is increasing. Table 3.6 lists some examples of applications of virtual environments and related technologies for medical training. In medical research, there is a shortage of cadavers. For students, being able to summon a detailed, lifelike computer image of a human body is a workable replacement. To improve training, companies are developing 3-D computer simulations of medical and surgical procedures.

A system built at Talisman Dynamics, Inc. simulates the rather rare open cholecystectomy procedure. Because the laparoscopic procedure is being addressed by a variety of applications for medical training, Talisman felt that a simulation of the open procedure would lend itself to an overview of the abdominal anatomy in 3-D context that could be useful in anatomic education. Simulating the open procedure allowed the developers "to simulate a large number of different tools and interactions, and to provide a comprehensive spatial context" (26).

High Techsplantations' initial work involved the development of a virtual abdomen. The virtual abdomen or "uro man" can be rotated using a 3-D mouse. After a year of research and development efforts, a laparoscopic lymph node dissection simulation was completed. In parallel, High Transplantations simulated other procedures, including an angioplasty procedure (sponsored by Marion Merrell Dow). This simulation allows the user to use a simulated balloon catheter to practice angioplasty. The software allows for various complications including transection of the coronary vessels, rupture of the balloon, as well as resistive feedback to the end-user. A specially designed catheter, equipped with position sensors and feedback devices was constructed to afford a high-fidelity tactile simulation (27).

Woods and Hon (28) developed virtual reality laparoscopic surgery simulators. These consist of a simple plastic torso into which the handles of laparoscopic instruments are mounted (to provide force feedback); the virtual abdomen (liver and gallbladder) are graphically demonstrated on the video monitor, and the apprentice surgeon can practice the specific laparoscopic procedures. Satava (7) took a different approach: "A virtual abdomen has been created for the immersive, traditional helmet mounted display (HMD) and Dataglove. Using virtual scalpel and clamps, the abdominal organs can be operated upon. This same abdomen can be 'explored' by a student."

The following are examples of additional issues being addressed by simulators recently or currently under development:

- A limb trauma simulator is being developed and is expected to lead to a VR environment.
- Georgia Institute of Technology in Atlanta is trying to simulate surgery on the human eye, complete with feedback on the force being exerted.
- The National Institute for Cancer Research in Genoa, Italy, has developed a VR microsurgical simulator for surgeon training. They want to create a microsurgical training simulator that simulates the suturing of two parts of a vessel under a stereo microscope.
- The National Cancer Center of Tokyo has developed a Surgical Simulation Support System. The surgical procedure simulated is a neurosurgical operation in which a neoplasm of the brain is resected without photomicroscopy.
- Researchers at the Ohio State University Hospital, Immersion Corporation, and the Ohio Supercomputer Center are collaborating

    to create and test a virtual simulator for training residents in the use of regional anesthesiology. Specific issues and difficulties of the epidural technique were used to develop a pilot system.... Limitations of physical models such as mannequins include lack of patient variance, inaccurate representation of biological tissue, and physical wear from repeated use

- Triage is a protocol to assess patient conditions and to decide on medical treatment in mass casualty situations. Education and training on triage protocols can be facilitated with computer-based training facilities, like interactive video. VE training and simulation systems can give the human an experience that is near to reality. In a VE training system, mass-casualty triage in combat situations can be simulated. There is, however, some more research required toward deformation modeling and real-time database management. Present display devices have a resolution in terms of image size that is critical to medical applications.

In addition to building simulators for specific procedures, generic problems are being addressed, such as the introduction of olfactory stimuli in virtual environments. Surgical simulations need to provide the proper olfactory stimuli at the appropriate moments during the procedure. Similarly, the training of emergency medical personnel operating in the field should bring them into contact with the odors that would make the simulated environment seem more real and that might provide diagnostic information about the injuries that simulated casualty is supposed to have incurred.

Another generic issue is the development of low-cost systems for mass distribution. Virtual reality surgical simulators will someday be valuable in medical education, both to reduce training costs and to provide enhanced physician training. However, many surgical simulators rely on real-time volume rendering techniques, and run on hardware costing several hundred thousand dollars. The Departments of Surgery and Computer Science at Stanford University have created a low-cost, interactive VR application for the IBM PC that provides a much clearer perception of surgical anatomy than a surgical atlas while remaining comparable in price. This program could be used to teach hundreds of other surgical procedures.

### 3.5.2.5 *Visualization of Massive Medical Databases.* Virtual reality is a way to visualize, manipulate, and interact with computers and extremely complex data. Interactive image-directed neurosurgery may be considered a primitive form of VR, because it essentially does this in the context of performing surgery. With interactive computer image-directed techniques, the neurosurgeon navigates through anatomic, functional, and physiologic 3-D space defined by digital images obtained from and representing the patient. The image space is a VR dataset representing functional as well as anatomic digital data. The intent of this category is to use virtual environments to symbolically represent data as visual objects in a virtual environment. Table 3.7 lists some applications of virtual environments and related technologies for visualization of massive databases.

Under funding from the Department of Defense, the Ohio State University Hospital's Department of Anesthesiology is creating a system for teaching a specific method of regional anesthesia, the epidural technique. The system will enable the resident to investigate various 3-D reconstructed datasets in a nonthreatening environment. The system can be cued through voice activation to provide additional information in text, audio, or graphical form. Furthermore, the system incorporates the necessary components to allow the resident to feel the technique as performed by the expert.

Henderson created a cyberspace representation of the war injuries from the

TABLE 3.7. Applications for Visualization of Massive Medical Databases

| System | Examples | Who/Where |
|---|---|---|
| Epidural technique | Allowing residents to investigate various 3-D datasets | Ohio State University Hospital |
| War injury statistics | Providing a cyberspace representation of war injuries from the Vietnam Database; allowing complex combinations of war wounds, organ systems injured, mortality, etc. to be visualized as clusters of data points | Henderson |

Vietnam Database. Using a 3-D cube to plot three axes of information, complex combinations of war wounds, organ systems injured, mortality, etc. can be visualized as clusters of data points. These clusters can illustrate and reveal important relationships that otherwise cannot be discovered. Navigating in three dimensions allows different perspectives of the data, permitting different interpretations. This application for visualization has not been exploited sufficiently and holds promise for the field of medical informatics (7).

### 3.5.2.6 *Skill Enhancement and Rehabilitation.* Applications of virtual environments and related technologies for skill enhancement and rehabilitation include those that provide training in the use of equipment, those that allow the exploration of virtual space, those that augment physical abilities, and those that teach skills. Table 3.8 lists some examples.

Imman is using a VE to train disabled children to control motorized wheelchairs. For a child who is learning to use a motorized wheelchair but who has limited control over his or her body, for instance, a virtual environment overcomes several potential safety problems. This VE training might also be motivational, because children accustomed to constant care by others can feel threatened by a wheelchair's mobility.

The use of VEs for rehabilitation in medicine has grown dramatically, resulting in an annual conference devoted to the subject. Greenleaf Medical Systems has created virtual environments for exploration in a wheelchair. For example, an individual with cerebral palsy who is confined to a wheelchair can operate a telephone switchboard, play handball, and dance within a virtual environment. Warner used an eyetracker device from BioControl, Inc. for a quadriplegic child in an effort to provide her the opportunity to develop interactions with the outside world before her disability causes her to become too introverted to communicate. In these circumstances, VR is being used to empower individuals with disabilities.

The visually impaired have difficulty using conventional computer display products. Current products for the visually impaired limit the amount of enlarged imagery to as little as 1% of a document page. Furthermore, it is difficult

**TABLE 3.8. Applications for Skills Enhancement and Rehabilitation**

| Application | Examples | Who/Where |
|---|---|---|
| Training in use of equipment | Training disabled children to control motorized wheelchairs | Imman, University of Oregon |
| Exploration of physical space | Providing VEs for exploration in a wheelchair | Greenleaf Medical Systems, Palo Alto, CA |
| Empowerment of the disabled using an eyetracker device | Providing a quadriplegic child the opportunity to develop interactions with the outside world before the disability causes the child to become too introverted to communicate | Warner, Human Performance Institute of Loma Linda University Medical Center, CA |
| Use of VR to enhance vision of the visually impaired | Providing a virtual computer monitor that moves the user's line of sight across an enlarged virtual monitor | |
| | Providing vision enhancement | John Hopkins University, Baltimore, MD |
| | Using glasses that display a television image to help Parkinson's disease patients overcome their halting, hesitant gait | Weghorst, University of Washington |
| Train to Travel Project | Substituting VR bus rides for the real thing to train individuals to use the public transportation system independently | University of Dayton (OH) Research Institute and Miami (FL) Valley Regional Transit Authority |

to determine the cursor position on the page. A prototype system was designed using a virtual computer monitor (VCM) that moves the user's line of sight across an enlarged virtual document, instead of vice-versa, using a HMD. The wearer's head position is sensed using a head-tracking device, and translated into mouse output in software. The simulated mouse data are used to scan the enlarged computer output across the HMD field-of-view in the opposite direction from the wearer's physical head movement, causing the impression of moving one's view about a fixed, enlarged document.

The University Applied Physics Laboratory at John Hopkins University, is working on an Interdivisional Sensory Engineering Program in cooperation with the Schools of Medicine, Engineering, and Arts and Sciences for the use of virtual reality to enhance vision of the visually impaired.

A primary symptom of Parkinson disease progressively restricts the ability to walk. VR technology provides a way to enable walking, by presenting virtual objects overlaid on the natural world. Normal stride length, and even running, can be enabled, provided the virtual clues are spaced properly and simulate the appearance of staying stable on the ground as the person moves (1). Glasses displaying a television image help Parkinson disease patients overcome the halting, hesitant gait that characterizes the disease. The glasses project a track of objects, currently yellow blocks, at stride-spaced intervals. Wearers step across the track, facilitating nearly normal walking patterns.

The Train to Travel project, sponsored by the University of Dayton (OH) Research Institute in cooperation with the Miami (FL) Valley Regional Transit Authority (RTA), substitutes virtual reality bus rides for the real thing. Students learn independently in the classroom, eliminating the need for a teacher to accompany or follow them on real trips. In the project, students use interactive multimedia to recognize landmarks and learn what to do in case of an emergency. When they master basic skills, they progress to the VR environment, where they use a HMD system with head tracking to look around a computer-generated landscape.

### 3.5.2.7   *Architectural Design for Health-Care Facilities.* Virtual environment testing of architectural designs for health-care facilities could save both time and money. However, considerable research on interaction methods and software system design will be needed before those savings can be realized. To illustrate what is being done, Kaplan of the Harvard Graduate School of Design is beginning to apply virtual reality to architectural design in a project for the operating room of the future.

In one example of using a VE for design purposes, a person in a wheelchair puts on a virtual research helmet equipped with electromagnetic motion trackers. Objects are manipulated via a DataGlove. The architect can point to a representation of a windowsill, for example, and make it higher or lower, or widen a door if it is too narrow. Companies are also using VR to sell their health-care products. For example, one has adopted a relatively low-cost, custom-built system to present interactive layouts of its health-care equipment to potential clients in realtime. Table 3.9 lists examples of applications of VEs and related technologies for architectural design for health-care facilities.

**TABLE 3.9.  Application of VE and Related Technologies in Architectural Design for Health-Care Facilities**

| Application | Examples | Who/Where |
| --- | --- | --- |
| Architectural design testing | Applying VR to architectural design of the operating room of the future<br>Allowing designers to perform work within a VE | Kaplan, Harvard Graduate School of Design |
| Sale of health-care products | Presenting interactive layouts of health-care equipment to potential clients in real time | |

TABLE 3.10. Value Added to Health Care by Virtual Environment Systems

| Value Added | Examples |
|---|---|
| Cost savings | Trauma units in emergency rooms could improve operating efficiency and reduce costs by using telepresence; doing so would conserve resources by limiting the need for part-time specialists to be physically present in trauma units |
| Improved services | Simulations allow surgeons to develop new techniques, to practice unfamiliar techniques, and to predict results of particular surgical procedures |
|  | The success of joint replacement depends on the proper placement and fit of implants within bony structures; surgical robots and preoperative planners using computer simulations can improve surgical techniques and accuracy |
|  | Advantages offered by telepresence systems include enhancing task performance in remote manipulation, allowing controlled application of extremely large or small forces, improving operator perception of the task, and facilitating manipulation in hazardous environments |
| Savings in material resources | The use of simulators saves precious resources such as cadavers and animals. |

## 3.5.3  Discussion

This section presents a discussion of the current applications of the virtual environments and related technologies discussed above. It summarizes the value added of these applications for health care, notes some problems and limitations, and describes some tools currently under development.

### 3.5.3.1  *Value Added.*  Virtual environments and related technologies add value to health care in the areas of cost savings, improved services, and savings in material resources. Table 3.10 summarizes examples of value added in these three areas.

*3.5.3.1.1  Cost Savings.*  Trauma units in emergency rooms could improve operating efficiency and reduce costs by using specialists who are not physically present. With telepresence, experts could be linked to remote patients. This is effective whether distances are great or not. Because the need for specialists in emergency situations cannot be predicted, making use of remote specialists in time of need limits the staffing needs of the trauma units without limiting their effectiveness. Doing this would conserve resources by limiting the need for part-time specialists to be physically present in trauma units.

*3.5.3.1.2  Improved Services.*  Virtual reality is affecting and improving surgical results. Examples include the use of laparoscopic simulators for training, the development of applications that simulate human response to medication (e.g., simulator systems helping train anesthesiologists), and the development of imaging tools that guide surgical tools through brain tissue to the site of a tumor.

Advantages offered by telepresence systems include enhancing task performance in remote manipulation through increased positioning resolution or range, allowing controlled application of extremely large or small forces, improving operator perception of the task, and facilitating manipulation in hazardous environments by isolating the environment from the operator or manipulation in clean environments by isolating the operator from the environment. Common to all telepresence systems is a human operator in a manual or supervisory control loop overseeing task performance. Application areas include operations in radioactive, underwater, space, surgical, rehabilitation, and clean-room environments, as well as the manufacturing and construction industries.

*3.5.3.1.3 Nonrenewable Resource Savings.* Finally, the use of simulators saves precious resources such as cadavers and animals. By allowing medical personnel to train using simulators, the demand for nonrenewable resources can be drastically reduced. The trainee can practice over and over using a realistic, virtual environment without reducing the supply of nonrenewable resources.

### 3.5.3.2 Problems and Limitations of Current Applications.
Many of the current virtual environment applications in health care have problems that limit their effectiveness. Some of these limitations are the result of the state of the art of the supporting technologies.

As noted earlier, the sense of smell in virtual environment systems has been largely ignored. Both Krueger and Keller are developing odor-sensing systems. Smells are extremely important. Not only do they help distinguish specific substances but they give a sense of reality to a situation. The absence of odor is a serious limitation of current telepresence and training systems.

Another major research problem relates to overlaying ultrasound images on live video that is then viewed in a HMD application. The research issue to be addressed is the alignment of images in real time.

The senses of vision and touch are the two main feedback mechanisms used by surgeons when performing a surgical procedure. Improved cameras, high-definition TV, HMDs, and stereoscopes have advanced the sensing and displaying of vision; however, there have been few developments in the area of tactile feedback. The ability to feel tissue is a valuable tool. Procedures that require palpitation, such as artery localization and tumor detection, are extremely difficult when the only form of haptic exploration is in the form of forces transmitted through long, clumsy instruments. The ability to remotely sense small scale shape information and feel forces that mesh with natural hand motions would greatly improve the performance of minimally invasive surgery and bring a greater sense of realism to virtual trainers.

According to experiments conducted by the British Defence Research Agency VR can make you sick (30). This confirms what some users of VR headsets have long suspected. Researchers found that 89 of 146 otherwise healthy adults suffered temporary nausea, dizziness, or impaired vision after using a HMD for just 20 min. Eight became so nauseated they could not finish the 20-min period. Researchers attribute the apparent effects to a couple possible causes. First, VR systems usually have a lag time between when the user moves and when the display is updated; users, accustomed to this lag, may become confused when they take the helmet off. Moreover, virtual reality creates an illusion of three dimensions, even though the screen actually remains at a fixed distance from a wearer's eye. This may disrupt depth perception later (30)

Today simulations trade off less realism for more real-time interactivity because of limited computing power, but the future holds promise of a virtual cadaver nearly indistinguishable from a real person. Initial research in the 1990s in video technology, graphics, computer-aided design (CAD) and virtual reality has given us an insight into some of the requirements for a VR surgical simulator. If graphic images are used, it is estimated a rate of 5,000,000 polygons/s would be required for a realistic reconstruction of the abdomen; current high-level computer-graphics workstations generate 60,000 to 100,000 polygons/s. Using CT or MRI scans would require substantially more computer power. The algorithms for object deformation and gravity are available and continue to evolve. For motion, at least 30 frames/s are necessary to eliminate flicker and response delays; this level of interactivity is available on standard virtual reality systems. The computational power for sensory input and for object reactivity has not been determined (7).

Fujita Research has created a situation in which a construction robot in America can be controlled from Japan. If it can be done with a construction robot, it will not be long before this is applied to telepresence surgery. The biggest problem now is the time delay involved in long-distance communications. Currently, there is a delay of a second or more from the time the command is given until the robot actually moves. The same is true when sending a camera image from the robot. Fujita hopes to cope with the delay problem by employing computer simulations of the robot movements and displaying predicted motions on the operator screen.

VR systems used for interfacing to training equipment require the user to be isolated from the real world and surrounded by the virtual world generated by the computer. This is normally achieved using a HMD enclosed in a rugged casing. One of the challenges for virtual environments is to allow the user to move freely between the virtual and the real worlds.

### 3.5.3.3 *Tools under Development.* There are many types of tools under development that will facilitate the use of virtual environments in health care. These tools provide computer input, computer output, or both. Examples of these are listed in Table 3.11.

Warner is employing virtual environment technologies to provide greater interactivity to people with severe disabilities. He has developed computer interfaces that use eye movements and muscle potentials. Severely disabled peo-

**TABLE 3.11. Examples of Tools for Use in Virtual Environments in Health Care**

| Tool | Use | Who/Where |
|---|---|---|
| Computer input Facial | Using eye movements and muscle to provide greater control to people with severe disabilities | Warner, Human Performance Institute of Loma Linda University Medical Center, CA |
| | Using image processing to recognize gestures and facial expressions as input | Systems Research Laboratory, Advanced Telecommunications Research Institute, Kyoto |
| Props | User manipulating props such as a doll's head to cause the screen image to move | Department of Neurosurgery, University of Virginia |
| Virtual perambulator– bodily movement coordinated with visual images | Coordinating bodily movement with visual images, creating a lifelike model | Iwata, Institute of Engineering Mechanics, University of Tsukuba |
| Visualization of data | VRASP; allows surgeons to interactively visualize 3-D renderings of CT and MRI data | Mayo Foundation |
| | Provides real time MRI and CT scans for the operating room | General Electric Co., Imaging and Visualization Laboratory, Schenectady, NY |
| | Space Interface Device for Artificial Reality; provides haptic display (device for presenting tactile and force sensation) | Sato, Precision and Intelligence Laboratory, Tokyo Institute of Technology |
| Computer output Ability to feel objects in virtual environments | PHANToM; actively exerting an external force on the user's finger(s) creates the illusion of interaction with solid virtual objects | SensAble Devices, Inc., Cambridge, MA |
| | Argonne Remote Manipulator; provides force feedback for molecular modeling applications | University of North Carolina, Chapel Hill |
| | Reflects force with a pen-shaped, 6 dof device | Iwata, Institute of Engineering Mechanics, University of Tsukuba |
| | Reflects force with a 4 dof manipulandum | Northwestern University |
| | Teletactile hand allows doctors to reach out and touch patients electronically at a physical distance | Burrow, Georgia Institute of Technology, and colleagues at the Medical College of Georgia |

| | | |
|---|---|---|
| Ability to feel the visual image of column data on the screen | Volume haptization techniques representing higher-dimensional scientific data by force sensation | Iwata, Institute of Engineering Mechanics, University of Tsukuba |
| computer input and output User characteristics are input and determine output | VRAMS; allows psycho-neuro- physiologic assessment and rehabilitation | VREPAR Project, Commission of the European Communities (CEC) |
| Ability to smell objects in virtual reality | Allows transmission of olfactory data | Keller, Pacific Northwest Laborating, Richland, WA, and Krueger, Artificial Reality Corp. |

ple have been able to navigate through virtual environments using biologic signals from muscles over which they retain control.

Researchers at the Systems Research Laboratory of the Advanced Tele-communications Research (ATR) Institute in Kyoto are working on a system that uses image processing to recognize gestures and facial expressions as input. Such a system would provide a more natural interface without requiring the operator to wear any kind of special gear.

Iwata has a virtual perambulator under development. In this project, he wants to build an apparatus that will take the previously separated bodily sensations and handle them together. The perambulator uses a HMD. The walker's upper body is fixed in place, and a goniometer detects the position of the head. Ultrasonic wave generators are attached to the walker's toes. The time required for the ultrasonic waves to reach receiver units determines the positions of the walker's feet. These motion data are sent to a computer that generates a virtual space, and the view through the HMD changes in real time in response to the walker's movements.The perambulator is made so that the tension on wires attached to the feet produces the sense of reaction or resistance associated with climbing or descending stairs. When the walker ascends a step, the wire length is regulated so that the take-off foot feels the force of resistance. To represent the reaction force involved in opening a virtual door, the virtual perambulator includes a manipulator having 6 dof.

The ability to feel objects in VEs can markedly enhance the effectiveness of many applications, particularly for training, scientific visualization, and telepresence. Haptic displays, devices for presenting tactile and force sensations, are being developed in several laboratories, but are not yet widely used elsewhere. Most of the haptic displays being developed are electromechanical devices that deliver force feedback to the hand or arm within limited ranges of movement.

For example, Sato developed a force-reflecting system called the Space Interface Device for Artificial Reality (Spidar). With this system, the user inserts his or her thumb tips and index finger into a pair of rings, each of which have four strings attached to rotary encoders. The encoders are located at the corners of a cube. String movements can be restricted with brakes, providing touch sensations. Spidar is being applied in a virtual environment for collaborative design.

The PHANToM actively exerts an external force on the user's finger(s) creating the illusion of interactions with solid virtual objects. Users can actually feel the tip of the stylus touch virtual surfaces. Surgeons can practice procedures on virtual patients.

The Phantom consists of a finger thimble mounted on the end of a small robot arm. When the thimble hits a position corresponding to the surface of a virtual object in the computer, three motors generate forces on the thimble that imitate the feel of the object. The Phantom can duplicate all sorts of textures, including coarse, slippery, spongy, or even sticky surfaces. It also reproduces friction. And if two Phantoms are put together a user can "grab" a virtual object with thumb and forefinger. Researchers are using the PHANToM™ for surgical training, proto-typing, and drug design (31).

Other force feedback tools include a system under development at the University of North Carolina, Chapel Hill, which uses an Argonne Remote Manipulator (ARM) to provide force feedback to the arm for molecular modeling applications. Iwata of the developed a pen-shaped, 6 dof, force-reflecting device. A 4 dof, force-reflecting manipulandum was developed by Northwestern University.

Iwata developed volume haptization techniques that represent higher-dimensional scientific data by force sensation. The system maps voxel data to the three dimensions of force and three dimensions of torque in the force display. The operator thus feels the visual image of column data on the screen.

Addressing the issue of incorporating the sense of smell in virtual environments, Keller's group developed a chemical vapor sensing system for the automated identification of smells. An electronic nose will potentially be a key component in olfactory input to a telepresent VR system. The identified odor would be electronically transmitted from the electronic nose at one site to an odor generation system at another site. This combination would function as a mechanism for transmitting olfactory information for telepresence. This would have direct applicability in the area of telemedicine because the sense of smell is an important sense to the physician and surgeon.

Burrow and colleagues at the are developing a teletactile hand that will someday enable doctors to electronically touch a patient in a remote area with few medical specialists. A related project at Georgia Tech uses tactile feedback to help students practice surgery.

Practicing Mayo Clinic surgeons are committed to assisting with the development, evaluation, and deployment of the VRASP system discussed earlier. VRASP will bring to the operating room all of the presurgical planning data and rehearsal information in synchrony with the actual patient and operation to optimize the effectiveness of the procedure, minimize patient morbidity, and reduce health-care costs.

Modules of the Virtual Reality All-purpose Modular System (VRAMS) being developed as part of the Commission of the European Communities (CEC) VREPAR Projects are being used to study and treat eating, stroke, and movement disorders. The goal of this system is to provide psycho-neuro-physiologic assessment and rehabilitation (1, 17).

### 3.5.4  Areas for Further Research

Virtual environment applications for health care are currently available and are being used to achieve the benefits discussed earlier. The demands of surgery, training for surgery, and telepresence surgery require a high degree of realism in terms of transmitted images. Additional large-scale research is necessary in the

TABLE 3.12. **Research Areas for Virtual Environments in Health Care**

| Research Area | Examples | Who/Where |
|---|---|---|
| User studies | Research among physicians to find out what their problems are and how VEs can help them perform their jobs better | |
| | Evaluation of the physiologic effects of VE itself, and investigation of the physiologic meaning of VR simulations to humans | VREPAR Project, Commission of the European Communities (CEC) |
| Telepresence surgical procedures | Development of a telepresence microsurgical robot for eye surgery | Hunter, MIT |
| | Development of a simulated beating heart that would allow surgery on a beating heart | Hunter, MIT |
| Enhanced system reality | Development of olfactory information transmission | Keller, Pacific Northwest Laborating, Richland, WA; Krueger, Artificial Reality Corp. |
| | The addition of spoken language for virtual environment commands | SRI International, Menlo Park, CA |
| Improved system architecture | Use of fast parallel hardware to solve the CT and MR image time bottleneck and the segmentation and classification problems | |
| Improved functionality | Hardware that runs faster; a display that is brighter, sharper, and higher resolution; system software that supports the faster hardware; networking that supports real time multiuser environments; interaction device that provides force feedback and supports 3-D navigation, object interaction, and flawless speech generation and recognition | |

following areas: user studies, use of robots for telepresence surgical procedures, enhanced system reality, improved system architecture, and improved functionality. Table 3.12 summarizes research needs in each of these areas.

**3.5.4.1 *User Studies.*** There is need to do research among physicians to find out what their problems are and in what ways telepresence and other forms of

VEs can help them perform their jobs better (32) Because VE enhances the interaction between users and systems, investigation into how people interact with the systems and how they systems can best be employed for instruction, training, assessment, rehabilitation and other people oriented applications are being undertaken as part of the VREPAR Project (1, 17).

In terms of future research, it is necessary to upgrade the system by improving not only VR-related parts (such as developing a high-resolution HMD and the enriching the VR experience) but also other parts such as the vibration pattern and massage contents. Also, it is necessary to evaluate physiologic effects of virtual reality itself and to investigate more about the physiologic meaning of virtual reality stimulations to the human (1, 17).

**3.5.4.2 Telepresence Surgical Procedures.** Hunter is developing VE technologies for teleoperated surgical procedures. The initial application uses a teleoperated microsurgical robot for eye surgery. A virtual model of the eye has been developed to practice teleoperated surgery under simulated conditions. Hunter is also developing a simulated beating heart that would allow surgery on a beating heart.

**3.5.4.3 Enhanced System Reality.** Although inclusion of the visual, aural, and tactile senses into VR systems is widespread, the sense of smell has been largely ignored. A mechanism for transmitting olfactory information for telepresence is needed. This would have direct applicability in the area of telemedicine, because the sense of smell is an important sense to the physician and surgeon.

The Virtual Perception Program at SRI International has been exploring the use of spoken language for virtual environment commands with SRI's Decipher, a speaker-independent, continuous-speech recognition system. Spoken language proved useful for discrete commands, such as selecting virtual objects and changing their attributes less useful for continuous commands such as navigating through a virtual environment. Spoken commands for movement to specific locations, such as a chair, also were useful.

**3.5.4.4 Improved System Architecture.** Demand for enhanced-reality services is being helped by minimally invasive surgery, such as endoscopy, in which the cunican guides an optical-fiber light probe and tiny camera through the patient while looking at a video screen. Instruments are inserted through puncture holes and manipulated from outside the body. A 3-D environment to use human depth perception might aid this work, as might tactile feedback, because often cancerous tissue is detected by touch

There have been attempts of 3-D visualization in medicine; most of them follow the vector-based approaches of the VR world. The main sources of medical 3-D data are CT and MR images. Fast parallel hardware can and will solve the time bottleneck; and within the next few years, VEs in medicine will be realized if the segmentation and classification problems can be overcome.

***3.5.4.5  Improved Functionality.*** To achieve improved functionality in virtual environments for health care, the hardware should run faster. The display should be brighter, sharper, and have higher resolution; when coupled with a HMD, it should also be more lightweight and contain faster and more accurate head tracking. The system software should support the faster hardware. Networking should support real-time multiuser environments, eventually allowing an infinite number of users to network with real-time results (including speech) over, say, a telephone line. The interaction device should provide force feedback and support 3-D navigation, object interaction, and flawless speech generation and recognition.

## 3.6  TELEMEDICINE*

There is a growing trend toward the development of telemedicine applications: "In 1994, 37 telemedicine projects were launched, joining some 20-odd telemedicine pilots already in progress" (33). The potential for involvement ranges from what has become traditional telemedicine functions (diagnosis and monitoring) to remote surgery. Table 3.13 list some specific applications of virtual environments and related technologies for telemedicine being explored in current projects. Clearly the potential for expanded and enhanced telemedicine is great.

One key area of telemedicine applications is for the delivery of trauma care in the field. For example, the health-care system in a battlefield situation demands timely and efficient evaluation, development and implementation of a treatment plan for severely traumatized patients. A delivery system should increase the efficiency of centrally located experienced trauma specialists by assisting medics at the remote site.

Also challenging is the delivery of expert medical care in remote areas of the United States as well as in developing countries. A map etitled "1995 Telemedicine across the U.S." (34) shows telemedicine hubs in all but two states. Other reports indicate that the missing states have at least remote referral sites.

The use of digital compression to send high-quality video images from rural areas to big-city hospitals for diagnosis has been instrumental in bringing specialized care to rural America.

Packets of information, such as patient records, X-rays, or pathology slides, can be sent over the telecommunications link to be stored digitally for review by a specialist. These data can be simple text, the primary care physician's notes on an initial examination, for example, or contain high-resolution images from CT or MRI scans.

---

*Adapted from Ref. 16.

**TABLE 3.13. Applications for Medical Diagnosis and Monitoring**

| Technique | Examples | Who/Where |
| --- | --- | --- |
| Virtual clinic | Providing diagnoses and treatment for Parkinson disease patients in rural areas | University of Kansas, Kansas City |
| Mobile units consisting of wireless data communications and laptop computers | Allowing nurses to receive doctors' orders, chart patients' progress, review medical reference books, and show educational videos to patients at home | Carnegie Mellon University, Pittsburgh, PA |
| Videoconferencing pilot | Enabling rural nurses and doctors to treat 95% of patients who would have been referred to a specialist hundreds of miles away | Eastern Montana Telemedicine Project, Deconess Medical Center, Billings |
| Home computer and modem | Allowing patients to test themselves daily, record the results, and transmit them weekly to a database | Finkelstein, University of Minnesota |
| Interactive video and medical diagnostic equipment in the home | Allowing "revolving-door" hospital patients suffering from chronic conditions to avoid hospitalization | Medical College of Georgia, Augusta |
| Telemetry/fetal monitoring equipment provided to patients | Applying telemedicine to private obstetrics, monitoring baby's heart rate and mother's contractions for babies with cord entanglement problems | Collins, Pregnancy Institute, Slidell, LA |
| Communications network | Linking three main medical institutions | Iowa Communications Network |
| | Linking the largest prison in North Carolina and two rural hospitals to diagnose and prescribe medications, and have access to a digital stethoscope, a graphics camera, and a miniature, handheld dermatology camera | East Carolina University School of Medicine at Greenville |
| | Linking a prison project to a hospital | University of Texas at Galveston |
| | Linking the Watauga Medical Center in Boone, to the carolinal medical center for a monthly tumor board meeting | The Carolina Medical Center, Charlotte, NC |
| | Linking an emergency room/ trauma center to a major hospital | Letson, Cleveland Memorial Hospital in Shelby, NC |

**TABLE 3.13** *(Continued)*

| Technique | Examples | Who/Where |
|---|---|---|
| | Allowing limited transmission of the reports and slides for which the Health Care Financing Administration will reimburse | Oklahoma Telemedicine Network, Oklahoma University Health Sciences Center, Stillwater |
| | Providing communications and telemedicine to frontier areas | High Plains Rural Health Network, Colorado |

In addition to interactive videoconferencing, which allows patient and doctor to see and hear each other, new devices let physicians listen to a patient's heart, take blood pressure readings, and otherwise thoroughly examine a patient without actual physical contact. Once the capability exists to display registered images at the remote site, an expert can guide a remote medic by manipulating the graphics that appear on the screen.

The needs of developing countries are not being ignored. For example, the Cleveland Clinic Foundation is exploring opportunities for providing expertise abroad. Clearly telemedicine is a developed technology. However, telemedicine applications vary from limited electronic exchange of records for review to sophisticated interactive systems with extensive diagnostic equipment.

A cost-cutting trend is to treat more patients at home using telemedicine technologies rather than in the hospital. A project by Carnegie Mellon University has combined wireless data communication and laptop computers to help nurses provide care at patients' homes. The system allows nurses to receive doctors' orders, chart patients' progress, review medical reference books, and even show educational videos to patients. Such systems allow trained medical personnel to provide home monitoring and also allow self-monitoring.

A recent study by Finkelstein illustrates the potential of such a system. In his experimental setup, lung transplant patients, who benefit from monthly check-ups after surgery, test themselves, record the results, and transmit the results reliably from their homes. Not only may costs be cut but daily tests (of blood pressure and best blows into a spirometer) could help detect trends before symptoms indicate a problem. All the measurements were performed daily, stored automatically, and transmitted weekly to a relational database. The Medical College of Georgia is putting interactive video and medical diagnostic equipment in the homes of "revolving-door" hospital patients suffering from chronic conditions. Sanders, who founded a telemedicine network that has grown to include 59 Georgia hospitals and clinics, claims the network has allowed 86% of the patients who would have been transferred out of a rural hospital for specialized care to stay put.

Another example of home care began with Collins's (35) search for a way to better monitor babies with cord entanglement problems. "He performed a clinical study ... in which the patients were given telemetry/fetal monitoring equipment so that they could perform the monitoring themselves, without a nurse." The doctor linked into the woman's computer and studied the baby's heart rate and the mother's contractions.

Other specialized telemedicine units are also being developed. For example, a virtual clinic at the University of Kansas in Kansas City provides diagnoses and treatment for Parkinson disease patients in rural areas, many of whom might otherwise go untreated. Another example is the monthly tumor board meeting of the Carolina Medical Center in Charlotte and the Watauga Medical Center in Boone (NC). The team of expert oncologists, pathologists, and radiologists reviews the particularly complex cases at Watauga's cancer center from its specially equipped telemedicine room at the Carolina Medical Center. The facility has a videocamera, communications capability for real-time video transmission, and a 60-in. color monitor. The experts are thus able to interact with the audience of 30 surgeons, chemotherapy specialists, and health-support workers in Boone.

Physicians see and talk to the patients via the telemedicine link and then diagnose and prescribe medications, when necessary. Practitioners have access to a digital stethoscope, a graphics camera, and a miniature hand-held dermatology camera to aid in patient examination.

Another innovative use of telemedicine is in prisons. East Carolina University is performing telemedicine consultations to the largest prison in North Carolina Originally established to provide only emergency consultations for trauma cases, this network's usage has expanded to include 31 School of Medicine physicians from 15 medical disciplines. The network is being expanded to six rural hospitals and a large naval hospital. A similar telemedicine prison project at the University of Texas, Medical Branch at Galveston, handles 45 to 65 telemedicine cases per week.

There are a number of pilot projects involving regional telemedicine. The following are some examples:

- In Iowa, the three main medical institutions are linked over the statewide fiberoptic backbone called the Iowa Communications Network. The network has hosted 10 telepathology consultations (using the Roche Image Analysis System), 10 telecardiology sessions, 100 echocardiography cases, and 250 noninvasive vascular imaging transmissions.
- The Eastern Montana Telemedicine Network's videoconferencing pilot, had a 95% success rate in its first year of operation; rural nurses and doctors successfully treated patients who would have been referred to a specialist.
- Cleveland Memorial Hospital in Shelby, North Carolina, operates one of the busiest emergency rooms in the state. Telemedicine is used to improve the operating efficiency of this busy trauma center. Because of the costs

involved, the Oklahoma Telemedicine Network, which will ultimately connect 45 rural hospitals in the state, has decided not to include any videoconferencing in its initial phase. Instead, the prime focus is on the limited transmission of reports and slides that the Health Care Financing Administration will reimburse.

- The High Plains Rural Health Network is a growing network of providers. It covers the frontier areas ($<6$ inhabitant $mi^2$) of northeastern Colorado, northwest Kansas, and southwest Nebraska.

## REFERENCES

1. G. Riva. Virtual reality in neuro-psycho-physiology: cognitive, clinical and methodological issues in assessment and rehabilitation. Amsterdam: IOS Press, 1997.
2. R. M. Satava. Surgery 2001: a technologic framework for the future. Surg Endosc 1993;7:111–113.
3. L. F. Hodges, R. Kooper, T. C. Meyer, et al. Virtual environments for treating the fear of heights. IEEE Comput 1995;28:27–34.
4. S. R. Ellis. What are virtual environments? IEEE Comput Graph Appl 1994;14:17–22.
5. D. R. Pratt, M. Zyda, and K. Kelleher. Virtual reality: in the mind of the beholder. IEEE Comput 1995;28:17–19.
6. R. M. Satava. Virtual reality surgical simulator: the first Steps. Surg Endosc 1993;7:203–205.
7. R. M. Satava. Medicine 2001: the King is dead. Interactive technology and the new paradigm for healthcare. Washington, DC: IOS Press, 1995:334–339.
8. W. Barfield and C. Hendrix. Factors affecting presence and performance in virtual environments. Interactive technology and the new paradigm for healthcare. Washington, DC: IOS Press, 1995:21–28.
9. Virtual Reality Report. May. 1996.
10. European Commission paper.
11. Telematics study.
12. RGB 175/the virtual reality business.
13. Orvum.
14. IMO.
15. Gortner Group.
16. J. Moline. Virtual reality in health care: a survey. In G. Riva, ed. Virtual reality in neuro-psycho-physiology. Amsterdam: IOS Press, 1997:3–34.
17. G. Riva, B. Wiederhold, and E. Molinari. Virtual environments in clinical psychology and neuroscience: methods and techniques in advanced patient-therapist interaction. Amsterdam: IOS Press, 1998.
19. D. K. Bowman. International survey: virtual-environment research. IEEE Comput 1995.

20. A. M. DiGioia III, B. Jaramaz, R. O'Toole III, et al. Medical robotics and computer assisted surgery in orthopaedics: an integrated approach. Interactive technology and the new paradigm for healthcare. Washington, DC: IOS Press, 1995:88–90.

21. Blumenfeld. 1995.

22. J. A. Adam. Technology 1994: medical electronics. IEEE Spectrum 1994;31:70–73.

23. J. C. Goble, K. Hinckley, R. Pausch, et al. Two-handed spatial interface tools for neurosurgical planning, IEEE Comput 1995;28:20–26.

24. (p. 315)

25. J. P. Wann, and J. D. Turnbull. Motor skill learning in cerebral palsy: movement action, and computer-enhanced therapy. Bailliere's Clini Neurol 1993;2:15–28.

26. A. Lasko-Harvill, C. Blanchard, J. Lanier, and D. McGrew. A fully immersive cholecystectomy simulation. Interactive technology and the new paradigm for healthcare. Washington, DC: IOS Press, 1995:182–186.

27. J. R. Merril, G. L. Merril, R. Raju, et al. Photorealistic interactive three-dimensional graphics in surgical simulation. Interactive technology and the new paradigm for healthcare. Washington DC: IOS Press, 1995:244–252.

28. Woods and Ham.

29. J. S. McDonald, L. B. Rosenberg, and D. Stredney. Virtual reality technology applied to anesthesiology. Interactive technology and the new paradigm for healthcare. Washington DC: IOS Press, 1995:237–243.

30. A. C. M. Dumay. Triage simulation in a virtual environment. Interactive technology and the new paradigm for healthcare. Washington DC: IOS Press, 1995:101–111.

30. R. Langreth. Virtual reality: head mounted distress. Pop Sci 1994;245:49.

31. R. Langreth. Virtual reality: breakthrough hand controller. Pop Sci 1995;246:45.

32. G. Wagner. As grant comes to a close, Iowa ponders future of DS-3 telemedicine network. Healthcare Telecom Rep 1995;3:1–4.

33. A. Laplant. A virtual ER. Forbes ASAP 1995;6:48–58.

34. Global Telemedicine Report map.

35. J. Collins. Louisiana physician gears up for expanded tele-obstetrics. Healthcare Telecom Rep: 1995;3:1–2.

# CHAPTER 4

# Robot-Assisted Microsurgery Development at JPL

HARI DAS, TIM OHM, CURTIS BOSWELL, ROB STEELE, and
GUILLERMO RODRIGUEZ

Jet Propulsion Laboratory
California Institute of Technology
Pasadena, California

Microsurgeons use a microscope with 20 to 30 times magnification to help them visualize the microscopic field they work with. However, they still use their hands to hold instruments that manipulate tissue with feature sizes from fifty to a few hundred microns. A microsurgical manipulator that can scale down the surgeon's hand motions to the microscopic field would allow the average surgeon to perform at the level of the best surgeons and allow the most skillful surgeons to perform at unprecedented levels of dexterity (1). Development of practical systems for assisting microsurgeons in this way is a growing field of

*Information Technologies in Medicine, Volume II: Rehabilitation and Treatment,* Edited by
Metin Akay and Andy Marsh.
ISBN 0-471-41492-1   © 2001 John Wiley & Sons, Inc.

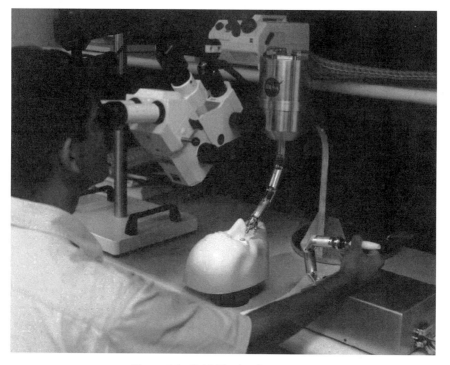

**Figure 4.1.** RAMS telerobot system.

research. Microtelerobotic workstations systems that have been developed for biomedical applications include those reported by Hunter et al. (2), Dario et al. (3, 4), and Hannaford et al. (5).

The work reported here is the result of collaboration between researchers at the Jet Propulsion Laboratory (JPL) and Steve Charles, a vitreo-retinal surgeon. The Robot-Assisted Microsurgery (RAMS) telerobotic workstation developed at JPL is a prototype of a system that will be completely under the manual control of a surgeon (6–8). It is unique in its combination of compact size, light weight, and high precision. The system, has a slave robot that holds surgical instruments (Fig. 4.1). The slave robot motions replicate in 6 degrees of free-dom (dof) those of the surgeon's hand measured using a master input device with a surgical instrument–shaped handle. The surgeon commands motions for the instrument by moving the handle on a master device in the desired tra-jectories. The trajectories are measured, filtered, and scaled down then used to drive the slave robot.

We present the details of this telerobotic system by first giving an overview of the subsystems and their interactions and then presenting details. The chapter concludes with a description of a recent demonstration of a simulated micro-surgery procedure performed at JPL.

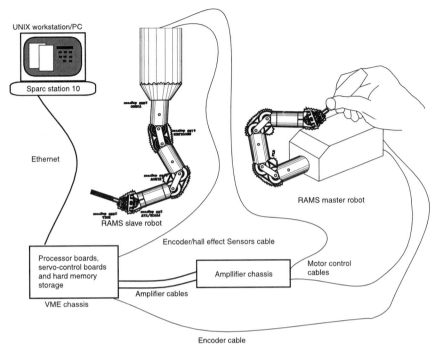

**Figure 4.2.** RAMS telerobot system.

## 4.1 SYSTEM DESCRIPTION

Figure 4.2 shows an overview of the hardware components of the RAMS tele-robotic system. Components of the RAMS system have been categorized into four subsystems (Fig. 4.3): mechanical, electronics, servo-control, and high-level software. The mechanical subsystem consists of a master input device and a slave robot arm with associated motors, encoders, gears, cables, pulleys, and linkages that cause the tip of the robot to move under computer control and to measure the surgeon's hand motions precisely. The electronics subsystem consists of the motor amplifiers, a safety electronics circuit, and relays within the amplifier box (Fig. 4.2). These elements of the subsystem ensure that a number of error conditions are handled gracefully.

The servo-control subsystem is implemented in hardware and software. The relevant hardware parts of the subsystem are the servo-control boards and the computational processor boards. Servo-control software functions include setting up the control parameters and running the servo loop on the servo-control board to control the six motors, implementing the communication between the computation and servo-control boards, initializing the servo-control system, communicating with the electronics subsystem, and communicating with the high-level software subsystem. The high-level software subsystem interfaces

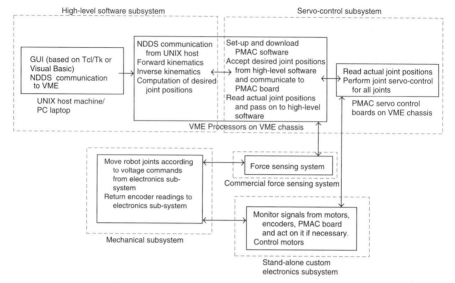

**Figure 4.3.** Subsystems of the RAMS telerobot.

with a user, controls initialization of the system software and hardware, implements a number of demonstration modes of robot control, and computes both the forward and inverse kinematics (Fig. 4.3).

## 4.2 MECHANICAL SUBSYSTEM

The RAMS slave manipulator is a 6 dof tendon-driven robotic arm designed to be compact yet exhibit precise 10-μ relative positioning capability and maintain a high work volume. Physically, the arm measures 2.5 cm in diameter and is 25.0 cm long from its base to tip. It is mounted to a cylindrical base housing (12 cm in diameter by 18 cm long) that contains all of the drives that actuate the arm (Fig. 4.4). The joints of the arm are as follows:

- A torso joint rotating about an axis aligned with the base axis and positioned at the point the arm emerges from its base.
- A shoulder joint rotating about two axes that are in the same plane and perpendicular to the preceding links.
- An elbow joint that also rotates about two axes that are in the same plane and perpendicular to the preceding links.
- A wrist joint consisting of pitch, yaw, and roll rotations.

The master device, kinematically similar to the slave robot, also has six tendon driven joints. It is 2.5 cm in diameter and 25 cm long. Its base houses high-resolution optical encoders requiring a larger volume (a 10.8-cm by 18.4-cm

**Figure 4.4.** RAMS slave robot.

by 23.5-cm box). Gear transformation ratios in the master arm are reduced to allow backdrivability (Fig. 4.5).

The slave wrist design, based on the kinematics of the Rosheim (9) Omni-Wrist uses a dual universal joint to give a 3 dof, singularity free, mechanically decoupled joint that operates in a full hemisphere of motion (up to 90° in any direction). The master wrist design uses a universal joint to transmit rotation motion through the joint while allowing pitch and yaw motions about the joint, resulting in singularity free motion over a smaller range of motion in 3 dof. The fourth and fifth axes of the master and slave robots are unique joints that rotate about two axes and allow passage of cables to pass through the joint for actuating the succeeding joints without affecting their cable lengths. The sixth axis is a torso joint, which simply rotates the manipulators relative to their base housing. For the slave robot, the torso range of motion is 330° and the master it is 30°.

Features resulting from the unique mechanical design of the arms are listed below.

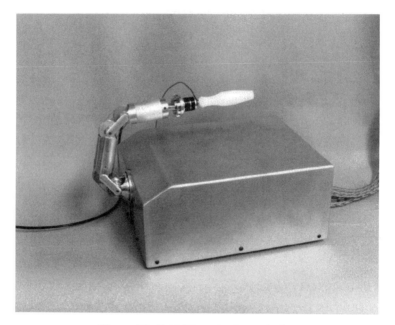

**Figure 4.5.** RAMS master input device.

- *Drive unit separability.* Drive motors and optical encoders on the slave robot cannot survive an autoclave environment and are designed to be removable for sterilization.
- *Zero/low backlash.* Low backlash (free play) is essential for doing fine manipulation, especially because the position sensors are on the motor shafts.
- *Low stiction.* Stiction (stick/slip characteristic) must be minimized to achieve small incremental movements without overshooting or causing instability.
- *Decoupled joints.* Having all joints mechanically decoupled simplifies kinematic computations and provides for partial functionality should any joint fail.
- *Large work envelope.* A large work volume is desirable so that the slave arm's base will not have to be repositioned frequently during tasks.
- *High stiffness.* A stiff manipulator is necessary for accurate positioning under gravitational or environmental loads, especially when position sensing is at the motor drives.
- *Backdrivability.* The master arm has been designed to be easily backdrivable.
- *Compact/lightweight.* In some applications, a restricted workspace warrants a small manipulator to minimize interference (e.g., visual interference).

- *Fine incremental motions.* Human dexterity limitations constrain surgical procedures to feature sizes of 20 to 50 μ, whereas the slave arm is designed to achieve better than 10 μ relative positioning accuracy.

- *Precise position measurement.* The master arm has been designed to be able to measure commanded hand motions down to a relative position resolution of 25 μ, whereas the slave robot can read its tip position to a resolution of 1 μ.

- *Tool wiring provisions.* Tools requiring electrical or pneumatic power can have cabling routed through a passageway through both the master and slave arms.

The end effector of the slave robot is a force sensor–instrumented micro-forceps actuated by a miniature dc motor. Simultaneous sensing of force interactions at the robot tip and manipulation with the forceps is possible with the end effector. Force interactions measured with the force sensor are processed and used to drive the master arm to amplify the sense of touch at the master handle (Fig. 4.6).

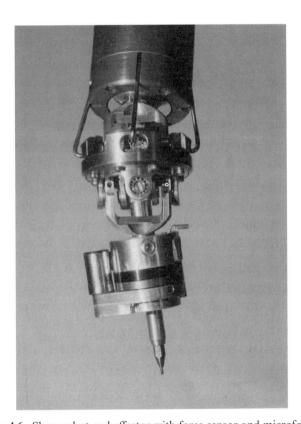

**Figure 4.6.** Slave robot end effector with force sensor and microforceps.

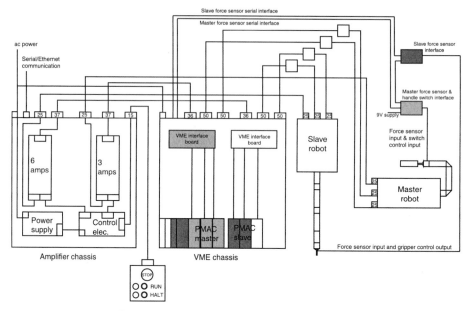

**Figure 4.7.** Electronics components and cabling.

## 4.3   ELECTRONICS SUBSYSTEM

The RAMS electronics subsystem design includes off-the-shelf and custom designed electronics (Fig. 4.7). Components of the electronics subsystem are a VME chassis, an amplifier chassis, and safety electronics. The VME chassis houses the VME backplane and three Motorola processor boards—one MVME-167 and two MVME-177 computer boards used for high-level system control. The VME chassis also contains two sets of PMAC servo-control cards, power supplies ($\pm 15$ V) and two cable interface boards. The VME chassis front panel contains main power control (ac) for the system. The rear panel provides access to the control computer's serial communications port (RS-232). All components above are off-the-shelf items except the cable interface board.

The VME computer boards are the hardware portions of the high-level control system. The RS-232 interface provides communication for control and observation of the robot system functions. The PMAC servo-boards generate two phase drive signals for sinusoidal commutation of the system's brushless dc motors. The PMAC receives optical encoder feedback from the motor shafts and provides low-level control of the motors. The six input/output (I/O) blocks and cable interface board handle signal and power distribution to the connectors on the rear panel.

The amplifier chassis contains the six slave robot motor and three master robot motor drive amplifiers, system-control electronics board, amplifier power supply and amplifier subsystem power. The amplifier chassis has interfaces to

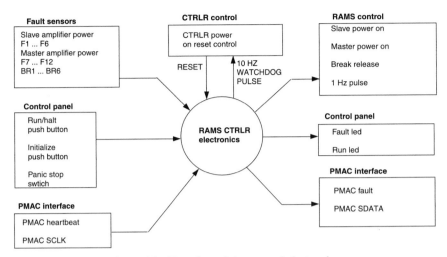

**Figure 4.8.** Function of the control electronics.

the VME chassis (analog inputs and control signals), the master and slave robot motor drive signals, and the CTRL panel subsystem (panic stop, run, and initialize). The VME chassis provides the amplifier chassis with its ac power. The amplifier subchassis secures the individual amplifiers to the amplifier chassis. This is designed to provide a thermal path to the chassis and to provide a favorable orientation with respect to the chassis air-flow pattern. The frame of the amplifier subchassis contains all necessary amplifier interface wiring. This makes the design highly modular to facilitate rapid check out and troubleshooting.

The safety control electronics consists of the control electronics board and the brake relay board (Figs. 4.8 and 4.9). The purpose of the braking function is to hold the motors in place when they are not under amplifier control. Programmable logic devices (PLDs) in the safety control electronics module monitors amplifier power, operator control buttons, and Panic-halt button, and a watchdog signal from the high-level software and control processors (indicating that they are healthy). Any anomaly triggers brakes to be set on the slave robot joint and a fault LED to be lighted. The operator must reset the safety control electronics to re-activate the system.

## 4.4 SERVOCONTROL SUBSYSTEM

The RAMS servo-control system is implemented on processor boards and servo-control boards installed in a VME chassis. One Motorola MVME-167 and two MVME-177 boards, named Proc0, Proc1, and Proc2, are installed on the VME chassis and run under the V*x*Works operating system. Proc0 performs

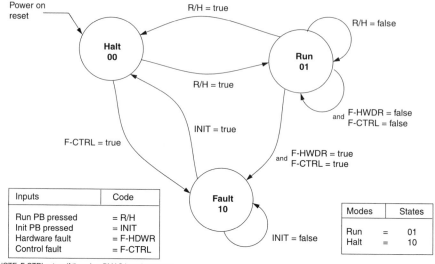

**Figure 4.9.** Control electronics state transitions.

kinematic, communication and high-level control functions for the master robot. Proc1 performs the same functions for the slave robot (described later). Calls to subroutines that read and set joint angle positions of the robot are made from the high-level real-time software on Proc0 and Proc1. These routines, through shared memory implemented between Proc0 and Proc2, provide set points and read current joint angles of the robot. Proc2, in turn, passes the set points for controlling the robot to the servo-control board and retrieves the joint angles measured by the servo-control board. The servo level control system uses the PMAC-VME board by Delta Tau. The interface for reading the force sensor is also implemented on Proc2.

Low-level, high-speed communication between Proc0, Proc1, Proc2, and the PMAC-VME boards is through shared memory. The PMAC board has a large variety of features for motor control, with a customer base largely from industrial installations. The key features used for control of the RAMS robot include digital sine-wave commutation, automatic trajectory generation, shared memory interface, built-in amplifier/encoder interface, and robust closed loop control.

## 4.5   HIGH-LEVEL SOFTWARE SUBSYSTEM

There are a number of components to the high-level software for the RAMS slave robot (Fig. 4.10). Embedded in the computational blocks of the real-time control software are the kinematic control algorithms. They are based on algorithms developed at JPL (10, 11) for the unique geometry of the robot. Wrist

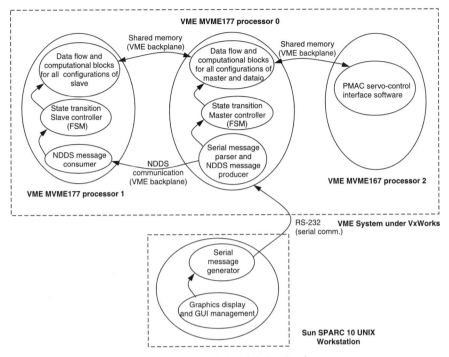

**Figure 4.10.** Parts of the high-level software.

kinematics for the slave robot are based on the work of Williams (12). The demonstration of different control modes of the robot was implemented using a software development tool for real-time systems called Control Shell (13, 14). Handling of operator commands in the real-time software, transitions between states of control, changes in data flow owing to transitions of states in the software, and the algorithms executed within computation blocks. The user specifies the control modes of the system through a graphic user interface (GUI) implemented with Tcl/Tk (15). Commands entered into the GUI are transmitted over an ethernet connection or by a serial interface and are received on the real-time software side of the system. The message passing between the two parts of the software system uses NDDS (16). A producer part creates the messages and broadcasts them from the GUI part of the system and a consumer part receives the messages and processes them.

## 4.6  SIMULATED SURGERY

In September 1996, a demonstration of a simulated eye microsurgery procedure was successfully conducted using the RAMS telerobotic system. The procedure demonstrated was the removal of a 0.015-in.-diameter particle from a simulated

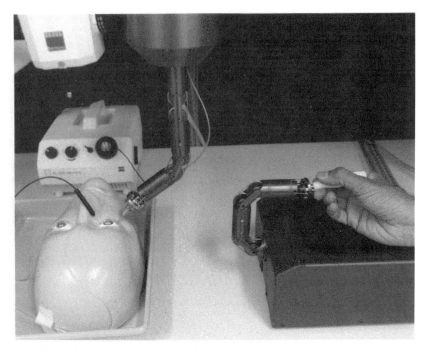

**Figure 4.11.** Eye microsurgery demonstration with the RAMS system.

eyeball. Features added to the RAMS system to enable successful performance of the eye surgery demonstration were switch-operated indexed motion, a surgical instrument mounted on the slave robot tip, and a pivoting shared control algorithm to automatically compensate for pitch and yaw orientation of the surgical instrument while the operator controled the $x$-, $y$-, $z$-, and roll motions of the instrument (Fig. 4.11).

A dual-arm suturing procedure was also demonstrated. Two prototypes of the RAMS system (Fig. 4.12) were configured as left and right arms for performing the procedure. To successfully close a 1.5-mm-long puncture in a thin sheet of Latex rubber, 9-O nylon suture was used.

## 4.7 VR APPLICATIONS

While the RAMS system was not developed as a virtual reality (VR) system, components of it are applicable in VR. The master arm is a unique haptic device that can present virtual or real force interaction to the user. Its ability to measure hand motions to 25 $\mu$ in translation and to 0.07° in orientation and its pencil grasp make it ideal as an interface for positioning and feeling a probe in a virtual environment. Simulated spring-damper and constrained-motion-with-

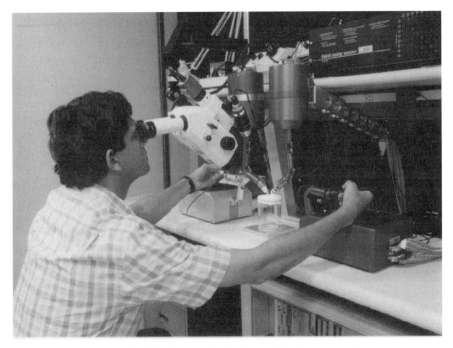

**Figure 4.12.** Dual-arm telerobotic suturing demonstration.

in-a-shpere environments have been implemented in tests conducted on the master device.

Synthetic fixtures or virtual augmentation to the real environment was also implemented on the RAMS system to assist the user in performing complex tasks. In the eye microsurgery simulation procedure, constraints on the motion of the slave robot were implemented to allow the surgical instrument mounted on the slave robot to pivot freely about the entry point in the eyeball. Activation of this mode caused loss of user control in 2 dof of the slave robot; the automated control system prevented motion that would move the instrument against the eyeball wall. An alternative to this strategy would be to simulate forces on the master handle that would guide the user into making safe motions.

Although we have not implemented this, the user interface part of the RAMS system can also be used as a simulator to train for microsurgical procedures. Expert guidance to a novice can also be implemented by having the motions made by an expert on a master device be replicated on a similar device held by the novice.

The RAMS system can also serve as a data collection system for measuring the hand motions made by an operator of the system. These data are useful for characterizing the performance of the user. Much may be learned from analysis of the data, including characterizing the potential microsurgical abilities of surgical residents, predicting the skill level of a surgeon at any time, and providing some insight into the nature of highly skilled manual dexterity.

## 4.8   CONCLUSION

The RAMS project at JPL was recently concluded as planned at the end of its 4-year development. A number of accomplishments resulted from this work. We demonstrated dramatic improvement over manual surgical instrument positioning. Microsurgeons who have evaluated or seen the prototype built have been enthusiastic about its potential. There is a growing commercial interest in this technology and its application partly as a result of the success of this development. We demonstrated practical utility of the technology in microsurgical settings. The products from this work have been transferred to our industry partner, MicroDexterity Systems, Inc., for further development and commercialization. Further augmentation to this system with advanced control and sensors would enable the performance of new procedures not possible with current techniques. The technology developed in this project has the potential to revolutionize the practice of microsurgery by extending the manual dexterity of microsurgeons, allowing more surgeons to perform the difficult procedures currently performed only by the most skilled surgeons.

## ACKNOWLEDGMENTS

This work was carried out at the Jet Propulsion Laboratory (JPL), California Institute of Technology, under contract with the National Aeronautics and Space Administration. The engineering development at JPL was done in collaboration with Dr. Steve Charles and MicroDexterity Systems, Inc.

## REFERENCES

1. S. Charles. Dexterity enhancement for surgery. In R. H. Taylor, S. Lavalle, G. Burdea, and R. Mosges, eds. Computer integrated surgery: technology and clinical applications. Cambridge, MA: MIT Press, 1996.
2. I. W. Hunter, T. D. Doukoglou, S. R. Lafontaine, et al. A teleoperated microsurgical robot and associated virtual environment for eye surgery. Presence 1993; 2:265–280.
3. P. Dario, M. C. Carroza, L. Leniconi, et al. A micro robotic system for colonoscopy. Paper presented at the International Conference on Robotics and Automation. Albuquerque, NM, Apr 1997.
4. P. Dario, C. Pagetti, N. Troisfontaine, et al. A miniature steerable end-effector for application in an integrated system for computer-assisted arthroscopy. Paper pre-

sented at the International Conference on Robotics and Automation. Albuquerque, NM, Apr 1997.

5. B. Hannaford, J. Hewitt, T. Maneewarn, et al. Telerobotic remote handling of protein crystals. Paper presented at the International Conference on Robotics and Automation. Albuquerque, NM, Apr 1997.

6. S. Charles, H. Das, T. Ohm, et al. Dexterity-enhanced telerobotic microsurgery. Paper presented at the 8th International Conference on Advanced Robotics. Monterey, CA, July 1997.

7. P. Schenker, H. Das, and T. Ohm. A new robot for high dexterity microsurgery. Paper presented at the 1st International Conference, CVRMed. Nice, France, Apr 1995.

8. P. Schenker, S. Charles, H. Das, and T. Ohm. Development of a telemanipular for dexterity enhanced microsurgery. Paper presented at the 2nd Annual International Symposium on Medical Robotics and Computer Assisted Microsurgery. Baltimore, MD, Nov 1995.

9. M. E. Rosheim. Robot wrist actuators. New York: Wiley, 1989.

10. G. Rodriguez, K. Kreutz, and A. Jain. A spatial operator algebra for multibody system dynamics. Astronaut Sci 1992;40:27–50.

11. G. Rodriguez. Kalman filtering, smoothing, and recursive robot arm forward and inverse dynamics. IEEE Trans Robotics Automation 1987;3:624–639.

12. R. L. Williams III. Forward and inverse kinematics of double universal joint robot wrists. Paper presented at the Space Operations, Applications and Research (SOAR) Symposium. Albuquerque, NM, June 26–28, 1990.

13. Control shell programmer's reference manual. Vol. 1. Sunnyvale, CA, Real-time Innovations, Inc., 1995.

14. Control shell programmer's reference manual. Vol. 2. Sunnyvale, CA, Real-time Innovations, Inc., 1995.

15. J. K. Ousterhout, Tcl and the Tk Toolkit. Reading, MA: Addison-Wesley, 1994.

16. NDDS programmer's reference manual. Sunnyvale, CA, Real-time Innovations, Inc., 1995.

# CHAPTER 5

# Virtual Reality and the Vestibular System: A Brief Review

ERIK VIIRRE, ZSOLT LORANT, MARK DRAPER, and THOMAS A. FURNESS, III

Human Interface Technology Laboratory
University of Washington
Seattle, Washington

Problem 1. A 25-year-old man sits in a flight simulator and plays with the instrument for 2 h. Afterward he feels nauseated and unsteady, experiences imbalance, and vomits. The symptoms quickly disappear, but he must wait several hours before driving home.

Problem 2. A 25-year-old male patient comes to the emergency room complaining of sudden attacks of spinning dizziness, nausea; he vomits several times. The acute symptoms gradually go away; however, for months afterward he feels unsteady and experiences instability in his vision (the world jiggles when he walks or drives a car).

What is the connection between these two situations? In both cases, the description of the individuals are the same and the symptoms are similar. The

*Information Technologies in Medicine, Volume II: Rehabilitation and Treatment,* Edited by Metin Akay and Andy Marsh.
ISBN 0-471-41492-1   © 2001 John Wiley & Sons, Inc.

symptoms indicate the involvement of the nervous system, the gastrointestinal tract, and the vestibular (balance) system. In both cases, the origin of the disturbance is the vestibular system. In Problem 1, the extended time spent in the flight simulator caused motion or simulator sickness. The second example describes a case of labyrinthitis, which is an inflammation of the vestibular organ. The connection is the vestibular system, which was affected two different ways. A disturbed balance system causes motion sickness. People without working vestibular apparatus do not experience motion sickness. The virtual reality (VR) simulation can modify the balance system, one consequence of which is motion sickness. This modifying effect of VR may also be beneficial for patients with balance disorders, as discussed below.

## 5.1  THE VESTIBULAR SYSTEM

### 5.1.1  Anatomy

The vestibular system is located in the temporal bone on each side of the human head. This system, which is the nonauditory component of the inner ear, contains the three semicircular canals and the two sack-shaped otolith organs. The apparatus is connected with the hearing organ (cochlea). The input from the vestibular system travels to the brain through the vestibular nerve. Figures 5.1

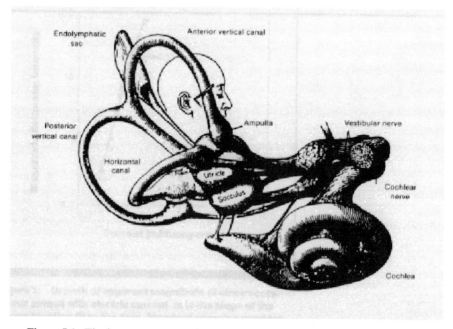

**Figure 5.1.** The inner ear organs. (Courtesy of Engineering Data Compendium.)

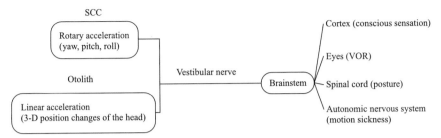

**Figure 5.2.**  The connections between the vestibular apparatus and the nervous system.

and 5.2 show the inner ear organs and the orientation of the semicircular canals and the otoliths.

### 5.1.2  Function

The vestibular system generates signals arising from head movement and head position changs. The input is carried to the brainstem (as coded signals), where this information is distributed to several areas of the central and peripheral nervous system (Fig. 5.2). The information used in the cortex is responsible for the conscious sensation of the head position and movement. Furthermore, the connection with the eye movement system (the vestibulo-ocular reflex; VOR) stabilizes vision during head movements. The connections with the spinal cord play a role in maintaining the posture through controlling signals to the muscles of posture. The vegetative symptoms (nausea and vomiting) of motion sickness demonstrate the junction to the autonomic nervous system.

## 5.2  VIRTUAL REALITY

### 5.2.1  Definition

The strict definition of VR is interactive computer graphic environment. Broader definitions of related terms are as follows (1):

- *Virtual environment.* Representation of a computer model or database that can be interactively experienced and manipulated by the virtual environment participant(s).
- *Virtual image.* Visual, auditory, tactile, and kinesthetic stimuli that are conveyed to the sensory end organs so that they appear to originate from within the three-dimensional (3-D) space surrounding the virtual environment participant.
- *Virtual interfaces.* System of transducers, signal processors, computer hardware and software that create an interactive medium.

VR is motion illusion. We experience a similar illusion when we view a movie or television. A movie is a series of still pictures projected on the screen quickly one after each other. The human eye cannot distinguish between the rapid still pictures because of the processing time required by the visual nervous system. The more pictures projected per second the better the quality of the illusion up to a frequency of approximately 60 frames per second. At this rate, we have the perception of continuous smooth movements on the screen.

## 5.2.2  VR Systems

In a virtual environment, we view images with a head-mounted display (HMD), which shows a virtual image corresponding to the current direction of gaze. The position of the head is sensed by a head-tracker device, which sends the information to a CPU, where the data are processed. The VR computer uses these data to correlate the image to the head position and sends the updated new image to the displays. We have the illusion of being in a real place (called immersion or presence), because as we use natural head movements—the same ones we use in the real world—and we are given a view that meets our expectation of the change in direction of gaze.

There is an interesting similarity between the connections to the nervous system and the vestibular apparatus and connections of a VR system. Both have a motion detector connected to a central processing system that sends signals to stabilize gaze. The vestibular system stabilizes gaze by moving the eyes and a

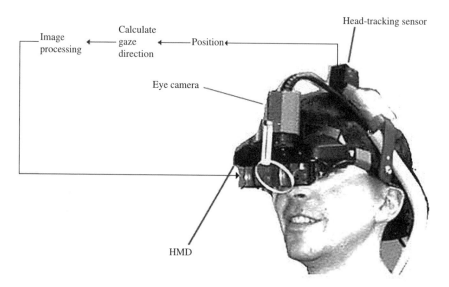

**Figure 5.3.** The HMD-VR system. Note that the eye camera shown is used in the Human Interface Technology Laboratory's VR Effects Laboratory to study influences of VR on the vestibular system's eye stabilization function.

VR stabilizes gaze by changing the image to be viewed to correspond to the user's changing gaze direction. There are useful higher-order analogies between the systems, such as the use of predictive algorithms to improve performance.

## 5.3  MOTION SICKNESS IN VR

### 5.3.1  Definition

Motion sickness is a widely researched area, and there have been numerous theories for it through history. Such theories are not surprising, because the symptoms have been described for centuries; but our forms of transportation, movement, and motion have changed drastically and have given us new means for creating motion sickness. The newest technologies, simulators and VR have given rise to a new terminology: simulator sickness. Simulator sickness was observed when the first simulators appeared, and its distinct symptoms have been studied since.

The most popular theory of motion sickness is the cue conflict, or sensory conflict theory. It states that motion sickness occurs when there is conflict between different sensory signals (visual, vestibular, proprioceptive) in response to motion stimuli. Inside a boat, where there is no access to windows, there is cue conflict because the visual system detects an apparently stable environment, but the vestibular apparatus is sending information to the brain indicating motion. When out on the deck the horizon can be viewed, giving the visual system information of self-motion relative to gravity, the cue conflict is reduced and correspondingly, motion sickness is reduced. As mentioned, people without vestibular function generally do not get motion sickness. It should be noted that cue conflict theory does not explain all phenomena related to motion sickness, nor is it the only theory. The teleologic explanation for cue conflict theory is the idea that land-dwelling mammals experience conflicting signals between the vestibular system and the visual system only if there is a vestibular system malfunction, presumably from poisoning. Thus nausea and vomiting occur to stop ingestion of further poison and eject that which had been taken in.

### 5.3.2  Why It Occurs

#### 5.3.2.1  *The Simulation.*  VR is simulation and certain environments in the real world provoke motion sickness. One can sit in a simulator showing an empty classroom and experience no motion sickness. However, a simulation of violent flight maneuvers in a modern fighter jet in the same system rapidly produces nausea, as the real vehicle would. Our exuberance for VR includes the possibility of creating experiences that we would not normally have. These novel experiences may also include novel ways of generating illness. This is not just of theoretic interest, because the appearance of illness in users may prevent them from using a useful simulation for training, or might even result in nega-

tive training where maneuvers useful in the real world are avoided because of motion sickness.

***5.3.2.2 Characteristics of VR.*** Beyond what is being simulated, motion sickness in VR may occur because of the system itself. Such simple factors such as the weight and temperature and closed-in feeling of the HMD can exacerbate the symptoms. Most important, the potential for cue conflict is inherent in a VR system. Motion of the head has to be detected, calculated, and converted into a new gaze direction by the VR system in real time to give the illusion of presence. There are two possible failures in this transformation: either the transformation can take too long, called transport delay or the transformation can be incorrectly done, called geometric distortion.

Recent research at the Human Interface Technology Laboratory (University of Washington, Seattle) focused on these specific issues of VR. Draper (2) carried out a controlled study to determine the contribution of geometric distortion versus time delay in the appearance of motion sickness in VR users. A 3 degree-of-freedom (dof) (rotations only) VR system was used in which subjects could actively interact with a series of environments. A control condition was compared to geometrically distorted views (a magnification and a minification) and to conditions in which time delays of 125 and 250 ms were introduced. Interestingly, even though the time delay condition was definitely a cue conflict condition (subjects commented on it), it did not provoke any significant motion sickness. In contrast, the distortion conditions, particularly the minification condition, were highly provocative. These results correspond to other studies of motion sickness and delay in simulations.

Based on these findings we present a short guideline on how can the negative effects of VR exposure be reduced.

1. Image size should stay close to $1.0 \times$ magnification. Any other sources of distortion, such as head trackers should be carefully examined.
2. Simulations should be of non-nauseogenic conditions, especially for naive viewers or those prone to motion sickness.
3. Limit the exposure time ($> 5$ min) to dramatic motion environments to minimize sickness and adaptation effects, especially with naive subjects.
4. Allow peripheral vision around the display to stay in closer connection with the real world. Several studies show drastic differences between restricted and clear peripheral vision conditions. The restricted vision had serious sickness stimulating effect.

### 5.3.3 The VOR

The VOR is a basic eye movement reflex that functions to keep images stabilized on the retina during movement of the head. When the head starts to move in any direction the vestibular apparatus senses this movement and sends information to the oculomotor system. The result is a corresponding eye movement in an equal but opposite direction. The latency is low, the compensatory eye movements begin 10 to 20 ms after the head rotation starts. The function of the VOR is to reduce retinal slip, i.e., motion of the image of the real world on the retina when the head is moving.

Gain and phase are two main metrics of the VOR. VOR gain is calculated as the slow-phase eye velocity divided by head velocity. It is a measure of the amplitude of eye movement velocity for a given head movement. Phase indicates the relative timing of eye movements in response to head movements. Phase is considered the angle between head movement and eye movement.

**5.3.3.1 Adaptation of the VOR.** The vestibulo-ocular reflex demonstrates a surprising capacity to adapt to alterations in environment and anatomy. This plasticity is owing the prominent role of the cerebellum, which acts to adjust the gain of the reflex. Modification of the reflex is necessary with aging, certain diseases, and new correction lenses. A common experience of millions of people is a change in glasses prescription. If a 1-diopter change in prescription occurs, there is a corresponding change in magnification of about 10%. The visual world becomes unstable and the glasses wearer may have transient dizziness, imbalance, and unsteadiness. However, the VOR will adapt and compensation for the change in magnification will make the visual world stable and the symptoms will disappear.

If image stabilization in a VR system is not done properly, the user will experience a situation similar to the wearer of a new glasses prescription. The VOR will adapt or attempt to adapt to the destabilized image. Kramer et. al. (3) described the ability of the VOR to adapt to retinal image slip in a HMD VR system. Draper (2) found appropriate changes in VOR after adaptation was allowed to occur.

The importance of these findings are not only that researchers of the vestibular system can manipulate the vision-stabilizing VOR but also that conditions in VR systems in regular use may induce changes in this neurophysiologic reflex. As with the glasses prescription changes, there may be attendant symptoms, and awareness by the designers can avoid or reduce the problems.

**5.3.3.2 Applications of VR for Vestibular Patients.** The ability to modify the VOR may be useful therapeutically for patients with vestibular disorders. These patients present with dizziness, imbalance, and oscillopsia. When tested, they are often found to have a deficient VOR. The VOR deficiency may occur for two reasons: The adapative capability of the VOR is defective or it has been overwhelmed. It has been found that small defects in the VOR are more readily adapted to than large defects. If the VOR has been overwhelmed, the control over visual scene movement in a virtual environment might be useful for these patients.

We tested six subjects with a history of vertigo and VOR gain $< 0.5$ in an adaptation protocol. The purpose of the step protocol is to incrementally increase the VOR gain. Our results showed an average of 16% VOR gain increase in a period of 30 min, with a total increase in image magnification of approximately 20%. These preliminary results are leading us to further research using the VR technology to determine if permanent changes in the neurophysiologic reflex can be created.

Current research is in the process of developing materials and procedures for assessing vestibular contributions to spatial cognition. Because of the difficulty of spatial orientation perception, the goal is to evaluate computer-generated animations as a potential tool for studying self-orientation and self-motion perception (4).

Finally, virtual environments are being used to treat patients with various phobias, such as fear of heights and fear of flying. Repeated exposure to a virtual environment that simulates such patients' phobic stimului appears to reduce the fear they have to the real thing. Vertigo patients often develop a phobia for experiences such as driving on a freeway or riding on a open escalator. Virtual environments have the possibility to be usefully employed to desensitize patients with these problems. This is a subject for future research.

## REFERENCES

1. W. Barfield and T. A. Furness. Virtual Environments and Advanced Interface Design. Oxford University Press, New York, 1995.
2. Draper M: The adaptive effects of virtual interfaces: Vestibulo-ocular reflex and simulator sickness. Seattle, WA University of Washington, 1998.
3. Kramer et al. Context specific short-term adaptation of the phase of the vestibulo-ocular reflex. Exp. Brain Res. 120:184–192, 1998.
4. Don Parker, personal communicating, 1998.

# PART II

# TELEMEDICINE AND TELESURGERY

# CHAPTER 6

# Computer Imagery and Multimedia Techniques for Supporting Telemedicine Diagnoses

QINGLIAN GUO, KATSUNOBU MUROI, and MIEKO OHSUGA

Mitsubishi Electric Corporation
Tsukaguchi-Honmachi, Amagasaki, Hyogo, JAPAN

Telemedicine involves delivering medical diagnoses and health-care advice to distant patients. A nurse providing clinical advice over the telephone is the

*Information Technologies in Medicine, Volume II: Rehabilitation and Treatment,* Edited by Metin Akay and Andy Marsh.
ISBN 0-471-41492-1   © 2001 John Wiley & Sons, Inc.

simplest example. Recent telemedicine systems, however, have typically used advanced image and audio capabilities by exploiting ongoing technical advances in communications, imaging, and multimedia.

The object of our current research is to provide medical doctors with patient images in a wider visual field and higher in resolution during a telemedicine diagnosis. To achieve this, computer image processing and multimedia techniques are used in constructing our telemedicine system. The creative functions of this system provide a medical theater with more information about the patient and enable a more effective and accurate telemedicine diagnosis to be carried out.

We discuss the background of this research and describe the limitations and problems of existing telemedicine systems. Then we present a global view of our system construction and highlight its advanced features. Next we present our special devices for inputting (catching) a patient's image and how to automatically composite wide- and high-resolution images from small pieces of images (digital imagery mosaicking techniques). Finally we present our human interface for supporting medical doctors' operations, and discuss the limitations of the system, and give a description of future work.

## 6.1 BACKGROUND AND PURPOSE

Telemedicine projects in the United States, such as that developed by the Georgia Institute of Technology, have been used to support health-care management of patients in their homes (1–3). The prototype allowed patients in their homes and care providers in their clinics to see and hear each other over a video conferencing link and to monitor a variety of vital signs from a central monitoring station. The teleconferencing system can also enable doctors living in geographically different places to work together to administer medical care to patients in rural areas. In Europe, a project called ATTRACT (4) is being designed to take advantage of emerging cable television network infrastructures to offer cost-effective health care to patients at home. This objective will be achieved through a set of broadband network applications that provide low-cost interactive health-care services at home competitively. In Japan, in contrast, a medical information network between Kyoto and Osaka Universities employs video image communications for educational, research, and experimental purposes.

In many countries, telepathology systems, which transform microscopic images to support remote pathologic diagnoses, are being routinely used. The hospital is connected through a communication network to a pathology specialist located far away, so that tissue images under a microscope are transferred to the specialist's site. Then the specialist examines the images and makes a diagnosis based on the display on the monitor. The results are then transfered back to the hospital.

In these existing telemedicine projects, various advanced techniques are being employed, including touch-sensitive monitors and graphical user interfaces (GUIs) for assisting nontechnical users to easily use the system, signature recognition and coding techniques for maintaining information security, and various data-compressing equipment for high-speed communication. The effectiveness of telemedicine systems, however, varies widely, depending on the quality of the visualization conditions.

In telemedicine, when a doctor may not be able to meet a patient face to face, it is important for the doctor to obtain sufficiently high-quality video images of the patient to make the correct diagnosis. For different clinical examination purposes, different parts of the body are emphasized. However, the primary requirement should be to obtain a wide field of view and high-resolution images for doctors working in pediatrics, dermatology, gynecology, and even surgery. When a doctor meets the patient face to face, he or she can quickly get a global image of the patient's state that corresponds to a wide view and can simultaneously focus on a detailed region that corresponds to a high-resolution view.

Most existing systems use a single high-resolution camera to take images of a patient. Unfortunately, the camera's field of view is always smaller than the eye's field of view, so large objects cannot be captured in a single frame. By shortening the distance between the patient and camera, it is possible to capture images with high accuracy. A problem arises in that visualized area will be limited. If only such image scaled down in resolution and narrow in visual field is possible, information much less than practical, thus causing a problem for medical examination. Using a wide field of view (fish-eye) lens is one solution (5, 6). However, the images may feature substantial distortions, and mapping an entire scene into the limited resolution of a video camera may compromise image quality.

In this chapter, we present an alternative solution that solves the above problems. Our approach is to simultaneously use several high-resolution video cameras to take images of a patient. That is, we divide the entire field of view into several small regions and then compose a wide-angle and high-resolution image by overlapping the small frames, each corresponding to one of the cameras. Here, we apply digital mosaicking techniques in computer graphics to automatically transform a composite of the small frames into a large image, along with original efforts to keep the calculation cost low enough for on-line processing.

Digital mosaicking is a technique for aligning different pieces of a scene (small frames) into a large picture of that scene (mosaic) and then to blend the frames together. Photographic mosaicking was first implemented for aerial and satellite images to provide wide-angle color pictures of the earth's surface for use in geologic studies, analysis of land use, and weather and climate analyses. Recently, various mosaicking software products have become popular, enabling users to compose a wide panoramic view from several individual images obtained by tilting and panning a hand-held video camera (7–11). The completed

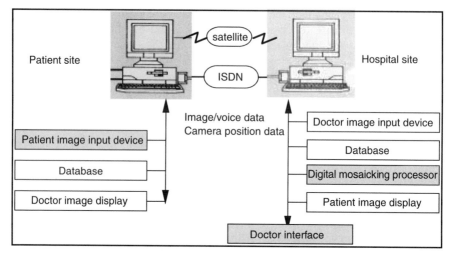

**Figure 6.1.** Construction and processes of our telemedicine diagnosis system.

wide scene is registered quite well, with little or no distortion. More complex systems, using a large collection of video images and supporting camera motion control, can map mosaics onto a modeled three-dimensional (3-D) space to establish virtual environments, making possible a virtual walk through an old palace (12–17).

## 6.2 CONSTRUCTION AND CHARACTERISTICS

Our work represents the first attempt to use digital mosaicking for telemedicine application. Figure 6.1 illustrates the basic construction of our telemedicine system. Through an ISDN network (128 Kbps) or communication satellites, various types of data, such as images, sounds, and parameters, are transferred in two directions between a patient site and a hospital site to allow interactive diagnosis between doctors and their patients. Our system is realized with three key features.

First, our special patient image input equipment consists of several high-resolution digital video cameras in combination with a multimedia device. Although a one-camera system may be adequate for the most basic use, despite being hampered by poor visibility, our multicamera device can cover a larger patient space and take detailed high-quality patient images to support telemedicine diagnosis. It is also possible for a doctor to remotely control the cameras through a doctor interface on at his or her site.

Second, our mosaicing algorithm is sufficiently simple and effective to enable the mosaicking processor to compose mosaics from video frames on-line in real time; therefore, interactive telemedicine diagnosis is made possible based on wider high-resolution patient images. Our input devices have many functions to simplify image registration and image blending, providing a substantial decrease in calculation costs.

Finally, our visual human interface is designed to support to doctors by making it easy for them to use the system. Because they need not concern themselves with computer-related issues, doctors can focus on carrying out their medical tasks. A large-screen monitor for displaying the image synthesized by the digital mosaic processor is provided. The large-screen monitor has a size capable of displaying human body image in a substantially life-size from. At the same time, it displays the menu at the side so that it does not dominate the screen space.

Because of its remarkable capabilities, our system has provided a major advance toward overcoming the drawbacks of existing telemedicine systems. It is now possible for a doctor to view a wide-angle and high-resolution video image of a remote patient during a telemedicine diagnosis. This allows patients to be treated in a more individualized manner and with more accurate visual diagnoses. Progress in the doctor interface has allowed doctors to work at lower stress levels. Applications of our research are possible for health-care, monitoring, emerging treatment, telepathology, and tele-education systems. In the following sections, we give more detailed descriptions of these three features.

## 6.3  PATIENT IMAGE INPUT EQUIPMENT

We constructed special equipment that uses several high resolution video cameras for taking patient images. The shooting range of each video camera is limited, but by using several cameras together at the same time it is possible to cover a wide patient field by arranging each camera to correspond to a square area, thus keeping a high shooting resolution.

### 6.3.1  Type 1

Figure 6.2 illustrates one of the special devices for capturing a patient's image. A patient is instructed to assume a prone position. Four high-resolution video cameras suspended over the patient are mounted on a computer-controlled mechanism. The video cameras are located on the same horizontal or vertical plane orthogonal to the direction of patient's eyes. A lattice frame enables cameras to move on under the action of driver mans. It is assumed that the four cameras are set at the same distance and view in a parallel direction. It is possible to translate the position and change the focal length of each camera individually. However, we assume that changes in focal length are minimal so that each camera covers the same size of viewing field. Thus the four cameras divide the patient space into four row-and-column regions, allowing composition of a global-view image of the patient from four video frames collected at the same time.

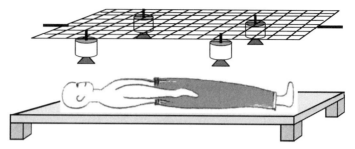

**Figure 6.2.** Patient image input equipment of type 1.

By using this device, we may get 1 to 4 video frames from each of the individual camera for every moment. Each frame is indexed by the two parameters of time and camera position and saved in a two-dimensional (2-D) buffer with a resolution of $m \times n \times k$ bit element, where $n$ and $m$ match the resolution of the screen and $k$ is determined by how many colors and gray scales the system can display. The digital mosaic image resulting from a composite of the four frames will be much wider at the same high resolution as the individual frames. Because objects in the mosaic appear in the same shape and size as in the video frames, it is possible to completely avoid scaling, distortions, and loss of resolution.

On the input device, for the purpose of mechanical control, small artificial retinas that link video cameras with image processing functions are used together with the video cameras (18). The function of the artificial retinas is to overview a patient's space and take low-resolution global images to automatically determine the position (or angle) of each video camera.

Another characteristic of the device is the background board printed with one of several stripe patterns, so that the images can be composite together with further precision. The background pattern may include one obtained by varying the thickness of lines along a predetermined direction, by varying the distances between adjacent lines, or by dividing a background into a plurality of blocks and forming patterns every blocks (Fig. 6.3). The function of the background pattern is to provide referable side information for the mosaicking processing so that the image registration processor proceeds more effectively and is not affected by the particular patient state (a patient may be in a dressed or undressed; the images are more difficult to form into a composite when the patient is undressed, because there are much fewer feature edges that can be extracted for image processing).

### 6.3.2 Type 2

Another type of input device consists of three high-resolution cameras fixed on a camera base that can move up or down (Fig. 6.4). The cameras can freely

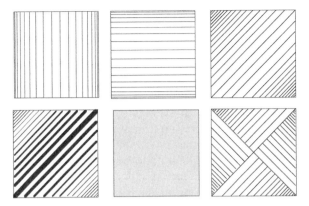

**Figure 6.3.** Examples of background patterns for the patient image input equipment.

adjust to viewing direction, i.e., they may view the patient's space from different angles. The angles can be incrementally changed between 0° and 90° but will be fixed during a diagnosis. The video frames in this case represent the views of the scene at a different orientation, so we need to store each frame together with its parameter of viewing angle.

## 6.4 DATABASE MANAGEMENT

It is an important task to manage the medical database, which may contain various image data, sound data, and parameter data. Users need not care about

**Figure 6.4.** Patient image input equipment of type 2.

what types of data exist in the database or how data management is carried out, but they may want to know what information can be obtained from the database; furthermore, they need to select patient data from the database at anytime it is required.

In our system's database, diagnostic information about a patient involves several items: patient identification number, name, body position during diagnosis (lying down or sitting), diagnosis region, and diagnosis frequency. As for the patient input equipment, there is information about camera location, camera shooting angle, and camera resolution. Patient images taken by the video cameras are transported to the doctor's site for diagnosis, and they do not need to be saved into a database. However, doctors may need the records of patient images at certain moments during a diagnosis for subsequent checking. As medical image data, digital x-ray pictures, CT scans, MRI scans, and pathologic images are commonly saved into databases. To manage such complex databases, a conventional relational database is considered ineffective because many items are closely related to the time parameter.

A recent commonly used software application, Illustra DataBlade, can provide a satisfactory platform for managing our database. The software is capable of understanding time-series data and time data. Users need not care about the details of data management but instead can concentrate on high level processes while using these data. The software also has functions for operating on and managing image data. These functions can be applied to any user-developed system, which decreases the necessary development time usually needed by a complex application for images. It is also possible to extent the relational model, to change data format and to perform various data management operations. Illustra DataBlade also provides functions for analyzing and estimating patient data, for ensuring data security, and for supporting simultaneous access from multiple patients or doctors.

To minimize data transformation time and obtain a response as soon as possible, a special network with high-speed transfer capability may be advantageous. However, we only have the standard communication and data compression method employed by almost all of the telemedicine systems throughout the world. Further research the significance of time constraints (a situation often faced in the real networking process) is desirable in the near future. Here, we focus only on a compromised solution to image composition problems.

## 6.5  TECHNOLOGICAL CHALLENGES

As mentioned, a variety of mosaicking techniques have been used. Each technique has proved to work remarkably well, providing good results under different camera calibration conditions and at different calculation costs. Most mosaics are composted from multiple image streams that are taken by moving or panning a camera. Images are aligned by affine transformation or planar-projective transformation to correct for relative translation shifts, rotational difference, scale differences, and even differences in view perspective. Generally, a mosaicking processor uses the following basic procedures:

• Performing color correction, image intensity normalization, or other similar preprocessing to images to decrease nonuniformity in densities owing to cameras capturing these images under different illumination conditions.

• Determining the initial alignment of images with respect to the cameras' positions and view angles.

• Performing warping and perspective transformation to images to correct image distortions owing to dynamic catching conditions.

• Refining the alignment of each frame by using an image-registration algorithm to obtain perfect and precise joining of frames. Often it is possible to eliminate or minimize alignment error by proper control cameras; however, in many cases a posterior registration and subsequent correction must be performed.

• Blending together the individual contributions of images in their overlapping areas to decrease color discontinuity, which is present even when images are perfectly aligned, and to obtain a smooth mosaicking.

• Cutting and displaying process clips for only the region selected by the doctor from mosaics, and showing the image of this region on a large-size monitor screen.

The more complex the camera's motion, the more complex the mosaicking programs need to be, and usually calculation costs increase. The mosaicking program used in our system is simple but fast enough for on-line processing. This was achieved by choosing the simplest calibrating conditions, i.e., fixed camera location, fixed view angle, and fixed focal length. Therefore, our mosacking algorithms do not include all the above procedures but just the necessary procedures.

### 6.5.1 Program 1

When patient input equipment of type 1 is used, the planer mosaic is composted from four video frames taken at the same time by applying mosaicking program 1, which includes the following procedures (Fig. 6.5)

• Performing color correction and image intensity normalization to images to decrease nonuniformity in their densities.

• Determining the initial alignment of images with respect to the cameras' positions.

• Refining the alignment of each frame by using an image registration algorithm to obtain perfect and precise joining of frames.

• Blending together the individual contributions of images in their overlapping areas to decrease color discontinuity.

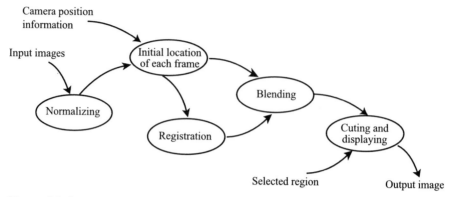

**Figure 6.5.** Image mosaicking program 1, corresponding to image input equipment type 1.

- Cutting and displaying process clips for the doctor-selected regions from mosaics, and showing the image of this region on a large-size monitor screen.

When using the equipment of type 1 with all the cameras shooting with different focus centers, the difference in their densities and colors will occur even under a globally uniform lighting condition. To normalize the intensity of the set of images, we first transform red, green, blue (RGB) images into their hue, saturation, value (HSV) representations (the models most used for representing colors); set one of the frames to be the reference image; and calculate a histogram of the V, S, H items (e.g., HIS1, HIS2, and HIS3). Based on HIS1, HIS2, and HIS3, the V, S, and H items of other images are adjusted. As a result, all of the images will have the similar brightness and color.

The second and third procedures for aligning frames are important, but not always necessary. As shown in Figure 6.5, these procedures are necessary only when a doctor selects a new region to be examined, causing camera displacement to occur. When the alignment procedures are applied to the initial set of video frames, the concurrent coordinate relationship between them will not change until camera displacement occurs again. This is especially important for decreasing calculation cost to make active video image processing possible.

Because camera position is not guaranteed for correct registration among images, it is necessary to adjust the relative positions of the adjacent images vertically or horizontally by pixels. This is because when an object is relatively close to cameras even slight misalignment cannot be tolerated. The following discussion is focused on the image alignment and image blending procedures, which are the most fundamental parts of the mosaicing program.

### 6.5.1.1 *Image Registration.*
To align two frames that have overlapping regions, we first determine their initial locations from the camera position information. Suppose the cameras are located at the position of $(C_{x_i}, C_{y_i})$ for

$I = 1, 2, 3, 4$, and each frame has the same width $J$ and height $K$ (in milli-meters), on a coordinate system corresponding to the doctor's side; the position of each frame can then be represented by its upper left corner $F(x_i, y_i)$ as

$$F_{x_i} = (r/J)(C_{x_i} - J/2)$$
$$F_{y_i} = (r/K)(C_{y_i} - K/2) \tag{6.1}$$

where the unit is pixel, and $r$ indicates the resolution of cameras.

In the next step, to finely adjust the locations of these frames, we need only to translate their locations in the $x$- and $y$-axes, and noncomplex transformations such as rotation or scaling are necessary. For the registration of a pair of images, template matching is used for finding out their most similar area to determine their corresponding positions.

Template matching is one of the most fundamental means of object detection within an image field (19–22). A replica of an object of interest is compared to all unknown objects in the image field, if the template match between an unknown object and the template is sufficiently close, the unknown object is labeled as the template object. In operation, the template is sequentially scanned over the image field and the common region between the template and image field is compared for similarity.

Here, we use the template-matching technique to determine the unknown translation differences that ensure precise joining of frames. Let $F_{1(j,k)}$ and $F_{2(j,k)}$, for $1 \leq j \leq J$ and $1 \leq k \leq K$, represent two discrete images to be registered, where $F_{1(j,k)}$ is considered to be the reference image (Fig. 6.6). Letting $F(m, n)$ denote the overlapping area of the two images, we refer to $F(m, n)$ as a search area. First, we take a small rectangle region $P \times Q$ of interest from the image $F_1$ on the left side within the boundary of the search area, and denote the small region as a template $T_{(x_1, y_1)}$. The central point of the template is $(x_1, y_1)$ at the coordinate of the left side image. Then we raster scan a window with the same size as the template $T_{(x_1, y_1)}$ over the image $F_2$ on the right side, and then compare the template with its replica in the image $F_2$.

The comparison is done to produce a difference measure between the template and all of the replicas on the right side. $T_{(x_1, y_1)}$ is deemed to be matched at a position $(x, y)$, when the difference measure between $T_{(x_1, y_1)}$ and a certain replica $t_{(x, y)}$ gets a minimal value, and $(x, y)$ is the central point of the replica at the coordinate of the right side image.

A common procedure is to produce a difference measure $D_{(x, y)}$ between the template and its replica. The template is deemed to be matched whenever the difference is smaller than some established level $L_{d(m,n)}$. Normally, the threshold level is constant over the image field. The usual difference measure is the mean-square difference or error as defined by

$$D_{(x, y)} = \sum_{i=1}^{P} \sum_{j=1}^{Q} [t(x + i - P/2, y + j - Q/2) - T(x_1 + i - P/2, y_1 + j - Q/2)]^2$$

$$\tag{6.2}$$

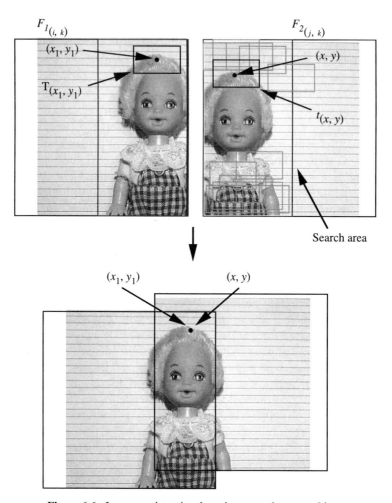

**Figure 6.6.** Image registration based on template matching.

where $F_{(m,n)}$ denotes the image field to be searched. $T_{(x_1, y_1)}$ is the template, $P$ and $Q$ are the width and height of the template window, respectively. The search area must cover their overlapping area and can be larger than the overlapping area. When

$$D_{(x, y)} < L_{d(m,n)} \qquad (6.3)$$

a template match exists at coordinate $(x, y)$. Thus we can determine a 2-D rigid translation

$$V_x = x - x_1$$
$$V_y = y - y_1 \qquad (6.4)$$

where $(V_x, V_y)$ denotes the translation difference between the two images. In detail, if we refine the location of the right image (or the coordinate of its upper-left corner point) by a translation of $(V_x, V_y)$, the two images will be perfectly aligned (joined) to each other.

Obviously, the stripe pattern used as the background for the patient image input device provides unique constant information for carrying out image registration more effectively. Also, the size and localization of the template $P \times Q$ affect the accuracy of image registration a great deal. Basically, a template should not be too small. We used a size of one third the height of the overlapping area, and the same width as the overlapping area. If we are able to use other techniques to find a characteristic area as a template, the size of the template can be made even smaller. Because we used a rectangular window as a template, the searching area should also be a rectangle, covering the overlapping area. It is rather effective to use the template-matching method for our registration, where template matching is limited to a small search area and there is no need formation or magnification of the template window.

***6.5.1.2 Image Blending.*** For the frames that are registered in location to be composted into a mosaic, blending processing is applied to the pixels on their overlapping areas to "combine" the colors and intensities of overlapping pixels. We begin by recording each frame into a lager data buffer to obtain the information on the state of frames overlapping at each pixel. As shown in Figure 6.7, the data buffer is as large as the boundary box containing all the frames, and the frames are copied into the buffer in correspondence to their locations. For a pixel where two or more frames overlap, the buffer will save two or more records on the original color information of each frame at that pixel. Consequently, the pixels of the buffer would be occupied by a non-frame or by one to four frames.

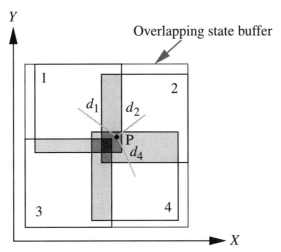

**Figure 6.7.** A buffer used to record the overlapping state of four image frames by pixel.

Based on the occupation state given in the buffer, we move to the next step and calculate the blended color for each pixel. For a pixel occupied by a non-frame, its color remains black; for a pixel occupied by one or more frames, for example the pixel $P_{(x, y)}$ in Figure 6.8, it takes the average of the colors of corresponding pixels of the frames. A color-blending process involves using the following calculation for R, B, and G elements, respectively.

$$r = \frac{1}{3D} \sum_{i=1}^{4} (D^2 - d_i^2) r_i$$

$$g = \frac{1}{3D} \sum_{i=1}^{4} (D^2 - d_i^2) g_i \qquad (6.5)$$

$$b = \frac{1}{3D} \sum_{i=1}^{4} (D^2 - d_i^2) b_i$$

where

$$D^2 = \sum_{i=1}^{4} d_i^2$$

and $r$, $g$, and $b$ are blending results for pixel $P$; $d_i$ depicts the distance from pixel $P$ to the center of the $i$th frame; $r_i$, $g_i$ are $b_i$ are the RGB color of the pixel at $i$th frame.

Figures 6.6 and 6.8 show processing results of our mosaicking program. Figure 6.6 shows the mosaic of two pieces of images taken with two video cameras. Figure 6.8 is a mosaic of a pathologic picture, based on compositing four pieces of small-size tissue images under a microscope.

### 6.5.2  Program 2

To create a wide panoramic scene by forming a composite of the three frames from the type 2 input device, a mosaic program should include the following procedures:

- Performing image intensity normalization to decrease nonuniformity in their densities.
- Determining the initial alignment of images with respect to the cameras' positions and view angles.
- Performing warping and perspective transformation to images to correct image distortions owing to dynamic catching conditions.
- Blending together the individual contributions of images in their overlapping areas to decrease color discontinuity.

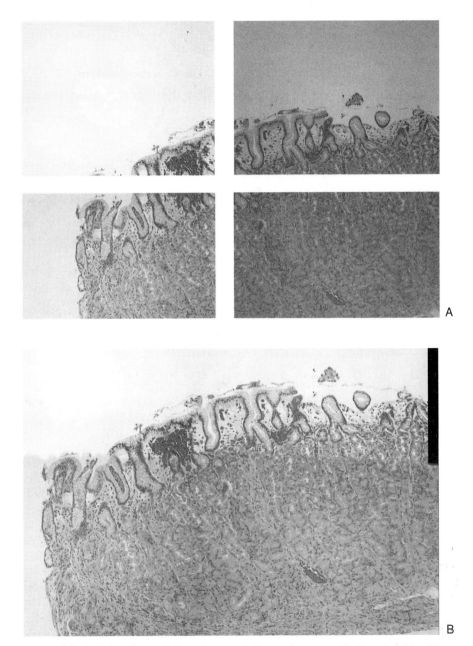

**Figure 6.8.  A**, Four pieces of tissue images under a microscope. **B**, A mosaicking image from the four small pieces.

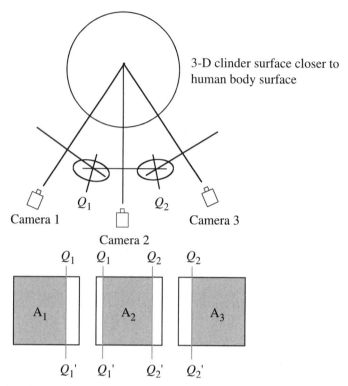

**Figure 6.9.** When composting three frames of images from the equipment of type 2 to create a wide-scene mosaic, a nonlinear connection problem has to be considered.

• Cutting and displaying process clips of the doctor-selected region from mosaics, and showing the image of this region on a large-size monitor screen.

Because the three video cameras shoot from different view directions, if we simply composite the three frames of images to create a wide-scene mosaic, there would be high-frequency (not smoothly varying) distortions occurring on the mosaic. As illustrated in Figure 6.9, the three frames lie on different planes, overlapping in space and intersecting with each other. $Q_1 Q_1'$ and $Q_2 Q_2'$ indicate the intersecting lines between the planes. Note that the three frames are connected at $Q_1$ and $Q_2$, but the connections are nonlinear, or nonsmoothing. Owing the nonlinear connections, high-frequency distortions would occur on a composted mosaic from the three frames.

For handing the nonlinear problem and for creating a panoramic mosaic from the three frames with minimal distortion, the frames are projected onto a smooth curved surface where they are composited. The curved surface is part of a cylinder that is supposedly closest to the human body surface. The cylinder centers at the cross point of the lines on the cameras' view directions and has a specified radius $R$.

Suppose a geometric coordinate system is defined as shown in Figure 6.10A; the coordinates of each point on the curved surface is determined. By using the dotted lines starting at the cylinder center, we can divide the curved surface uniformly into several four-cornered polygons and divide the three frames into the same number of small regions, as well as establish the correspondence between each pair of a small region and a polygon. Then, the problem of mapping the three frames to the curved surface becomes a task of mapping a 2-D texture onto a polygon in 3-D space.

For convenience, we assumed that each of the rectangles as a 2-D texture pattern defined in a texture coordinate system $UV$. We can scale the texture coordinates to vary over the interval $[0, 1]$. To map a four corners texture plane $[u_i, v_i]$ for $i = 1, 2, 3, 4$ to a polygon $[x_i, y_i, z_i]$ for $i = 1, 2, 3, 4$ in 3-D space, a series of procedures is necessary. In the discussion that follows, we use concepts of general transformation matrix and homogeneous coordinates; details are available in the literature (23–25).

First, adding a perspective transformation to each of the four vertices of the polygon

$$[x', y', z', w'] = [x, y, z, 1] \begin{bmatrix} 1 & 0 & 0 & 0 \\ 0 & 1 & 0 & 0 \\ 0 & 0 & 1 & r \\ 0 & 0 & 0 & 1 \end{bmatrix} = [x, y, z, rz + 1] \qquad (6.6)$$

where, $[x', y', z', w']$ or $[x, y, z, rz + 1]$ is the coordinates of a vertex $[x, y, z]$ under a homogeneous coordinate system.

As a second procedure, for displaying the curved surface on the screen, we need to project the curved surface (or the polygons) onto a specified 2-D view plane by using an orthographic projection. If the projection plane is defined as $z = 0$, and a projection center is given on $z$-axis, $z = zc = -1/r$, then we have

$$T = \begin{bmatrix} 1 & 0 & 0 & 0 \\ 0 & 1 & 0 & 0 \\ 0 & 0 & 1 & r \\ 0 & 0 & 0 & 1 \end{bmatrix} \begin{bmatrix} 1 & 0 & 0 & 0 \\ 0 & 1 & 0 & 0 \\ 0 & 0 & 0 & 0 \\ 0 & 0 & 0 & 1 \end{bmatrix} = \begin{bmatrix} 1 & 0 & 0 & 0 \\ 0 & 1 & 0 & 0 \\ 0 & 0 & 0 & r \\ 0 & 0 & 0 & 1 \end{bmatrix} \qquad (6.7)$$

where $T$ defines a perspective projection. Perspective transformations preserve parallel lines only when they are parallel to the projection plane. Otherwise, the lines converge to a vanishing point. This has the property of foreshortening distant lines. The projection of $[x, y, z]$ onto the $z = 0$ plane would be

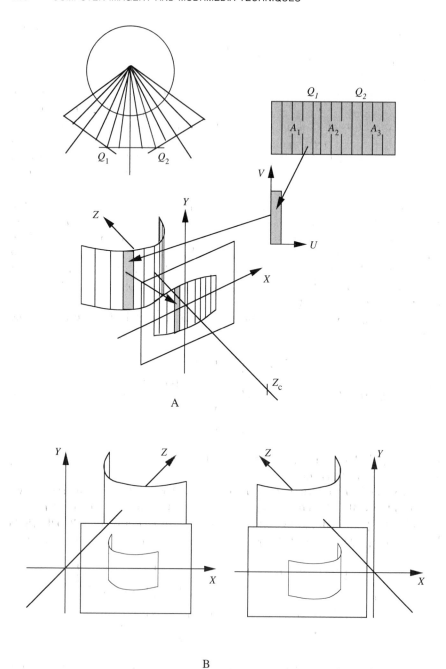

**Figure 6.10.** The process for mapping the three frames onto a smooth curved surface.

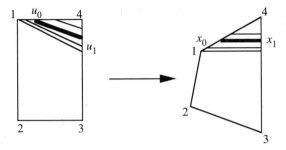

**Figure 6.11.** Four corners polygon mapping using the Gouraud shading method.

$$[x, y, z, 1]T = [x, y, 0, rz + 1]$$

$$= \left[\frac{x}{rz + 1}, \frac{y}{rz + 1}, 0, 1\right] = [x', y', 0, 1] \tag{6.8}$$

So we get a quadrilateral $[x_i', y_i']$ for $i = 1, 2, 3, 4$ on the projection plane. The quadrilateral also related to the rectangle $[u_i, v_i]$ in the texture coordinate system. If the view plane is moved around the cylinder, it is also possible to obtain side view images also (Fig. 6.10B). The purpose of using the equipment of type 2 and the 3-D curved surface model is for getting additional side views to supply more information about patients. Now we need only consider how to map from the texture $[u_i, v_i]$ to the quadrilateral $[x_i', y_i']$ in the screen coordinate system.

For determining the correspondence for all interior quadrilateral points, we used the Gouraud shading method; which is effective purpose (26–29). Ground shading fills a quadrilateral with texture while operating in scanline order. This means that the output screen is rendered in a raster fashion, (e.g., scanning the polygon from top to bottom, with each scan moving left to right). This spatial coherence lends itself to a fast incremental method for computing the interior intensity values (Fig. 6.11).

The following segment of C code is offered as an example of how to process a single scanline.

```
dx=1.0/(x1-x0);      /* normalization factor */
du=(u1-u0) * dx;     /* constant increment for u */
dv=(v1-v0) * dx;     /* constant increment for v */
dz=(z1-z0) * dx;     /* constant increment for z */
dw=(w1-w0) * dx;     /* constant increment for w */
for (x=x0;x<x1;x++){     /* visit all scanline pixels */
        if(z<zbuf[x]){   /* is new point closer ? */
            zbuf[x]=z;   /* update z-buffer */
            scr[x]=tex(u/w,v/w);
            /* write texture value to screen buffer */
    }
```

```
    u=u+du;      /* increment u */
    v=v+dv;      /* increment v */
    z=z+dz;      /* increment z */
    w=w+dw;      /* increment w */
}
```

This procedure assumes that the scanline begins at $(x_0, y_0, z_0)$ and ends at $(x_1, y_0, z_1)$. These two end points correspond to points $(u_0, v_0)$ and $(u_1, v_1)$, respectively, in the input texture. For every unit step in $x$, coordinates $u$ and $v$ are incremented by a constant amount, e.g., $du$ and $dv$, respectively. Because a perspective transformation is a ratio of two linear interpolations, it is possible to achieve theoretically correct results by introducing the divisor, i.e., homogeneous coordinate $w$. We thus interpolate $w$ alongside $u$ and $v$, and then perform two divisions per pixel.

Because the curve surface may contain occluding polygons, the $z$-coordinates of visible pixels are stored in $z$-buffer for the current scanline. When a pixel is visited, this $z$-buffer entry is compared against the depth of the incoming pixel. If the incoming pixel is found to be closer, we update the $z$-buffer with the depth of the closer point, and use the function $tex_{(u,v)}$ to sample the texture at point $(u, v)$ and return RGB values that are stored in $scr$, the screen buffer. Otherwise, the incoming point is occluded, because no further action is taken on that pixel.

## 6.6 VIRTUAL DOCTOR WORK DESK

This section gives a detailed description of the human–computer interface constructed for supporting the work of doctors. The interface is called the virtual doctor work desk, through which doctors can easily and freely interact with the computer and a remote patient, even if the doctors do not have any experience with using a computer. We explain our ideas on medical-purpose human–computer interfaces; describe the functions and features of the virtual doctor work desk; and further explain the visualization and multimedia techniques that are applied to illustrate a patient's diagnostic data, to construct multiresolution icon switches, and to control the remote patient image input device from the hospital side in real time.

### 6.6.1 Requirements from Medical Doctors

In designing an interface for medical work, it is important to give consideration to the entire working environment of a doctor to provide adaptive and supportive functions to help doctors carry out their tasks. First, we need to choose an appropriate input device for doctors. There are many possibilities: keyboard, mouse, trackball, pressure tablet, and so on. It is often possible to use several devices together to achieve a given goal easily and quickly. However, using several devices together can give additional stress to the users. Doctors would be sensitive to the changes in how they work when using computers, so they would not want a complex interface that would bring them more stress and constraints. A well-designed interface for medical use is considered based on the following principles:

- Provide a simple interface with one or two input devices, requiring few functions that might impede the users from carrying out their tasks. The simpler the interface, the less confusion the users will experience. Once a function menu gets longer than, say, 10 items, it would be cumbersome to the users. Moreover, in some cases, many of the items that are placed on the menu are not of interest to the users. Therefore, we decided that our doctor interface should have few functions and occupy only a small portion of the screen space. The other portion of the screen is reserved for displaying the mosaic image.
- Provide a visualized interface that lets doctors easily learn and efficiently use the system. Vocabulary and syntax formats used in command-line interfaces would be disastrous to medical doctors. An interface using conventional icons to show its range of capabilities, database, and user controllable parameters would be preferable for a medical interface, because graphical icons are more quickly recognized than text.
- Provide the users with the ability to interactively control relative parameters. It is especially important for our telemedicine system to enable a doctor to select the part or region of the patient's body to be examined and to control remote camera equipment.

## 6.6.2  Design and Features

Figure 6.12 shows a configuration of the visual interface. We decided to use a keyboard, a mouse, and a microphone as input devices. The keyboard is provided for doctors to write a diagnosis memo, which is saved into the database. The microphone is used for doctors to specify the part to be examined when a sound input function is switched on. All of the other operations can be performed with the mouse, because most users are able to input position information quickly and easily with a mouse device.

The interface menu consists of three parts: function icons, an overview image of the patient's site, and a 2-D graphical human model. The overview image is taken by using a low-resolution CCD camera, together with the patient image input device at the patient site. Within the overview window, camera icons are displayed to show the concurrent camera positions. Therefore, the system gives doctors a global and dynamic map of the patient site, how high a patient is, where the patient is, and where the cameras are positioned.

Based on the overview image, even a static one, the system automatically constructs the human model consisting of 15 pieces filled with color and texture

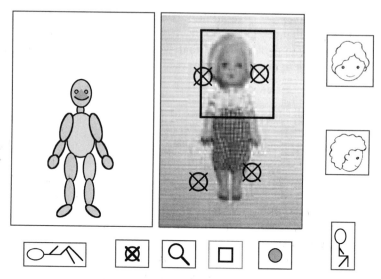

**Figure 6.12.** Virtual doctor work desk.

to represent each individual patient. There are four types of human models—front and side models for patients lying down or sitting up (Fig. 6.13)—and each can change width and height. Furthermore, the color and texture of the pieces can also be changed. The available functions of the interface include the following:

- *Front and side images.* For doctors to specify either a front view or a side view of the patient.
- *Input equipment type.* For doctors to specify which input device to use.
- *Select parts.* For doctors to select body parts (head, hand, and so on) from the 2-D graphical human model and to make a visual clinical record of a diagnosis for an individual patient. For example, a doctor selects the parts of breast and right leg, next the system shows the selected parts in the graphical model with different color or texture, and then it automatically opens a small window where the doctor can write a clinical memo such as "one chest bone and thighbone broken" through a keyboard. The diagnosis record will be stored in the related medical database and can be later reviewed in a similar visualized style.
- *Select range.* For doctors to choose a rectangular region in the window showing the overview of patient site and thus indicate the specific region for examination.
- *Select camera position.* For doctors to control the location of each video camera of the input device. A selected camera icons can be shifted or animated to a new position corresponding to the movement of the mouse

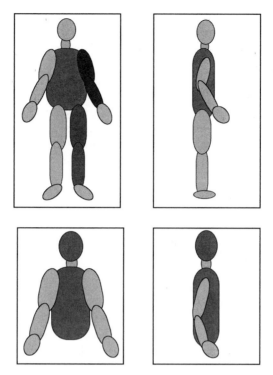

**Figure 6.13.** Four types of 2-D human body models.

cursor. Such position information is transferred to patient-side system to move the video cameras.

- *Sound input.* For doctors to send messages or commands to a computer through a sound recognition device. Here the sound input function is different from the voice conversation between doctor and patient, and it is used for the "communication" between doctors and computer. Because the limitation of the ability of sound recognition techniques, it is still impossible to convert natural language or long sentences. So we require only simple words within an application area, such as numbers or names of parts of human body. It is assumed that a doctor uses number or name to specify a part of human body to be examined through the microphone, then the system catches the characteristics of the sound and recognize its meaning by comparing the sound with what has been saved in the database, so the voice command could be converted to body part information.

- *Zoom in.* For doctors to view a magnification of the patient's image. When magnifying an image, each input pixel becomes many output pixels. Clearly, this one-to-many mapping will result in a degradation of image quality.

### 6.6.3  Multimedia Technique for Remotely Controlling Cameras

When a doctor chooses the "select range" function, he or she can select a region to be examined by dragging a mouse and drawing a rectangle on the overview image of the patient's site. It is possible to obtain this overview with a common panorama video camera. Such images contain a large amount of information that present image processing systems cannot analyze in real time. This is because present systems separate image sensing and image processing: Images are sensed by a camera and processed by a computer. Consequently, performance is limited by slow camera frame rates and low transmission rates between camera and computer.

In our system we choose to employ multimedia techniques. We used a new device produced by Mitsubishi (18): artificial retinas that combine video cameras with image-processing functions. The device is considered particularly useful because it integrates image sensing and image processing to take TV camera-like images at the same time that it performs edge extraction. This means that we can take a global color image of a patient, which is low resolution and take an outline picture of the patient's figure in real time. Of course, it is possible to perform edge extraction on the colored patient image by performing Sobel edge detector or Prewitt edge detector on the computer to obtain the outline, which is the most commonly used method; but by using this camera we can obtain edge information much more quickly, that is, in real time.

In our system, the information on the patient's outline is necessary for two purposes: First, for building a 2-D graphical human model representing an individual patient, we need such data on the patient's height, width, leg length, and so on. From an outline of a human figure, these data can be approximately estimated automatically. Second, for mapping the region a doctor selects for examination to camera position information.

We use this camera to obtain a low-resolution global scene of the patient's site, display the image to the doctor so he or she can understand the particular patient's situation (e.g., where the patient is lying or sitting), and allow the doctor to select a region by dragging the mouse across the overview image. According to the distance of each camera from the doctor's selected region, the system then automatically determines whether one, two, or four cameras should be used to take the patient's image and where each camera should be located.

The basic decision-making rules are (1) covering a larger area than the doctor's selected region, to ensure sufficient shooting ranges in consideration of overlapping between individual frames, (2) using and moving the cameras that are comparatively nearest to the selected region to minimize the amount of movement of each camera; and (3) using as few cameras as possible.

To give more detailed description, for example, when the selected region is smaller than one camera's shooting area, move the nearest camera to the center of the region, and taking patient images with it. When the region is not larger than an area that can be covered by two cameras, the system compares the region with any of the four possible areas covered by two cameras in their default positions. If such an area cannot be found, those two cameras are used for photographing a patient image. If no area is possible, the selected region must be located at the central area, which automatically requires using the four cameras at their default positions.

### 6.6.4  Visualization Techniques

This section presents primitive visualization techniques we used to improve user friendliness of our interface. The techniques are based on visual changes in color icon to help individual users with the interface (30). A change should not break the common rule of consistency, an important aspect of human–computer interface. Here, consistency means that mechanisms should be used in the same way wherever they occur. But this does not mean things do not changing. Accordingly, the changes we adopted are the sort of changes that do not cause the users confusion but rather make the user more confident in using computers.

*6.6.4.1  Visual Changes in Icons.*  Because users have been found to respond more rapidly to icon sings than to text sign, the superior visibility of the icon is frequently used in a GUI. The appearance of an icon depends on its location, size, shape, and the pattern filling it. Figure 6.14 shows the icons designed for the function switches of our interface. Here, we assume that the size and color of an icon may change with the frequency it is selected by users. It suggests the potential for creating personal icon menu using a combination of icon size and selection frequency.

To provide the means of displaying icons according to frequency of use on a user interface screen, we need to prepare icon images with different levels of resolution in our database, e.g. we have three types of images for the icon switch of "showing patient front image": a simple sketch, a filled gray illustra-

**Figure 6.14.** Icon switches that may change in size, color, and resolution with the frequency by which they are selected by users.

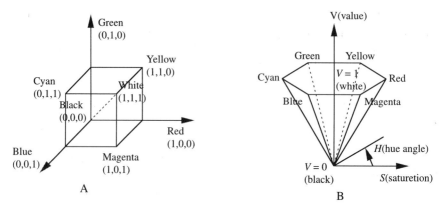

**Figure 6.15.** Color-representing models, A, The RGB model. B, The HSV model.

tion, and a color illustration. When the icon size gets bigger, the features of the icon image are shown in more detail.

### 6.6.4.2 *Visual Change in Intensity.*
Human vision is much more sensitive to intensity than it is to color. For this reason, we applied visible change in intensity to icons and 2-D human model, to express things that could not be as effectively represented by textures. A 2-D human model consists of 15 pieces of body parts, each of which can change intensity according to frequency to be selected. The difference in intensities give a visible highlight of patient's history records. By reviewing the 2-D model, the doctor can roughly estimate which part is diagnosed most.

There are several color models used for representing colored light. The RGB model is used to represent the red, green, and blue intensity settings of a color monitor or television display. The RGB color space may be pictured as rectangular coordinates with black at the origin (Fig. 6.15A).

Another color model is the HSV model, which is a more efficient representation of a color image intended for a human observer. Value is the intensity of the maximum of the red, blue, and green components of the color. Value has the same "feel" as brightness but is easier to calculate. Saturation indicates how much white light is mixed with the color; hue or tone is the pure color of the light. Saturation of 0 means no color; we see white and gray. VHS is often plotted in a cylindrical coordinates with hue the angle, saturation the radius, and value the axis. (Fig. 6.15B) The converts from RGB to HSV, or HSV to RGB can be done easily by using simple converting algorithms.

HSV model employs color descriptions that have are more intuitive to use. We can specify a hue and the amount of white and black to add to the color to obtain different shades, tints, and tones. In our system, a pure color is defined by a pure hue, which specifies the hue angle H and $V = S = 1.0$. If one wants to make change in intensity, tint, or tone, V or S is changed, which means adding either black or white to the pure hue. For example, we start with a pure blue color: H = 240, V = 1.0, and S = 1.0. To get a dark blue, V could be decreased to V = 0.4 with S and H are held constant. Similarly, when parameter S is decreased while keeping V and S constant—e.g., S = 0.3—a light blue could be designated. If one wants some black and some white added, both V and S are decreased. Generally, various intensities are represented with values S = 1 and $0 \leq V \leq 1.0$. When HSV color parameters are used for representing and calculating colors, these parameters have to be transformed to the RGB settings for displaying the color on monitor. Programs for converting between the HSV and RGB models are available (23, 29).

## 6.7 CONCLUSION

We presented a computer system for improving performance in telemedicine efforts by emphasizing high-quality video imaging. The system incorporates strong capabilities to create wide high-resolution mosaics of the scene at the patient site. This permits doctors in hospital sites to carry out telemedicine diagnosis more effectively by viewing the high-resolution images on a large-size video screen. The mosaicking processor is simple but quite effective, providing such extraordinarily fast performance that mosaic images can be created in real time. The system also has an visualization interface that provides a means for doctors to select specific portions for examination, remotely control the camera equipment installed at the patient's site, store clinical data into a database, and visually show diagnosis records with graphical human models representing each individual patient. The system can decide the positions of cameras as soon as the doctor selects a region. This is necessary for enabling an on-line telemedicine diagnosis to be carried out interactively. The interface used in the system has a several significant features, foremost of which is the use of multimedia techniques in place of software for providing an easy and powerful way to carry out the communication interactively. As a result, our system provides a breakthrough approach to solving the existing problems of low-quality video images of patients. Furthermore, this work has explored interesting new directions for telemedicine and research into health care.

One possible disadvantage of our system is that it may require a higher communications cost because of the greater amount of transmitted information. The communication network depends a great deal on computer power and data transformation capability. However, if mode switching is implemented to allow a single video camera to operate depending on the task at hand, it would be possible to carry out more efficient telemedicine diagnoses.

Future research on the doctor interface may include functions to illustrate visual data, enabling patients to review their own data, and displaying guidance to support health care action at home. Help functions should also be provided, but they should never be considered a substitute for a good interface. Help should be context sensitive; it should not take the user away from the task at hand. Helpful interfaces could include displayed dialogs, animation, and many other ideas yet to be explored. However, the general philosophy for designing an interface will remain the same: To establish an easy and simple interface. This will require our continuing efforts and cooperation with medical doctors.

We should add that the perceptions of a computer interface also depend on the current hardware constraints. When more hardware capabilities that become available and their costs decrease, an interface with 3-D icons, constructed on 3-D models and 3-D rendering techniques, may be more widely used. 3-D icons could, for example, look like the various goods on a shop's shelves, with 3-D formations that are more visually appealing and meaningful. A 3-D icon may also be easier to manipulate. With multiple faces, additional space in which the icon can supply additional information to the user, and the relationships between icons can be shown more directly in 3-D virtual spaces. Also, they would be capable of moving through 3-D databases as interfaces become more adaptive and supportive.

## REFERENCES

1. J. Peifer, A. Hopper, and B. Sudduth. A patient-centric approach to telemedicine database development. In J. D. Westwood, H. M. Hoofman, D. Stredney, and S. J. Weghorst, eds. Medicine meets virtual reality. IOS Press 1998:67–73.
2. E. Flavell. The PAECESDT project, Paper presented at the International Teleconference Symposium. 1984.
3. D. A. Perednia and A. Allen. Telemedicine technology and clinical applications. JAMA 1995;273:483–488.
4. G. Anogianakis, S. Maglavera, and A. Pomportsis. ATTRACT—application in telemedicine taking rapid advantage of cable television network evolution. In J. D. Westwood, ed. Medicine meets virtual reality. IOS Press 1998:60–66.
5. G. Furnas. Generalized fisheye views. Paper presented at ACM SIGCHl. Apr 1986.
6. M. Sarkar and M. Brown. Graphical fisheye views of graphs. Paper presented at ACM SIGCHI. Monterey, CA, May 1992.
7. S. E. Chen. QuickTime VR—an image-based approach to virtual environment navigation. Paper presented at the Computer Graphics Annual Conference. 1995.
8. B. Rousso, S. Peleg, and I. Finci. Generalized panoramic mosaics. Paper presented at the DARPA Image Understanding Workshop. New Orleans, LA May 1997.
9. R. Szeliski and H. Shum. Creating full view panoramic image mosaics and environment maps. Paper presented at the Computer Graphics Annual Conference Series. 1997.
10. M. Irani, P. Anandan, and S. Hsu. Mosaic based representations of video sequences and their applications. Paper presented at the Fifth International Conference on Computer Vision. Cambridge, MA, June 1995.
11. M. Hansen, P. Anandan, and K. Dana, et al. Real-time scene stabilization and mosaic construction. Paper presented at ARPA Image Understanding Workshop. Monterey, CA, Nov 1994.

12. L. A. Teodosio and M. Mills. Panoramic overviews for navigating real-world scenes. Paper presented at MULTIMEDIA'93. 1993.

13. P. Jaillon and A. Montanvert. Image mosaicing applied to three-dimensional surfaces. Paper presented at the 12th International Conference on Pattern Recognition. Jerusalem, Israel, Oct 1994.

14. R. Kumar, P. Anandan, and M. Irani, et al. Representation of scenes from collections of images. Paper presented at IEEE CVPR. 1995.

15. L. McMillan and G. Bishop. Plenoptic modeling: an image-based rendering system. Paper presented at the Computer Graphics Annual Conference Series. 1995.

16. S. Peleg and J. Herman. Panoramic mosaics by manifold projection. Paper presented at IEEE CVPR. 1997.

17. R. Szeliski. Video mosaics for virtual environments. IEEE Virtual Reality 1996, 22–30.

18. K. Kyuma, E. Lange, and J. Ohta, et al. Artificial retinas—fast, versatile image processors. Nature 1994;372:197–198.

19. G. J. Vandenburg and A. Rosenfeld. Two-stage template matching. IEEE Trans Comput 1997;C26:384–393.

20. D. J. Hall, R. M. Endlich, D. E. Wolf, and A. E. Brain. Objective methods for registering landmarks and determining cloud motions from satellite data. IEEE Trans 1972;C21:768–776.

21. E. A. Smith and D. R. Phillips. Automated cloud tracking using precisely aligned digital ATS pictures. IEEE Trans 1992;C21:715–729.

22. D. I. Barnea and H. F. Silverman. A class of algorithms for fast digital image registration. IEEE Trans 1972;C21:179–186.

23. J. D. Foley, A. van dam, S. K. Feiner, and J. F. Hughes. Computer Graphics; principles and practice. 2nd ed. Reading, MA: Addison-Wesley, 1990.

24. D. F. Rogers and J. A. Adams. Mathematical elements for computer graphics. New York: McGraw-Hill, 1990.

25. S. Harrington. Computer graphics—a programming approach. 2nd ed. New York: McGraw-Hill, 1987.

26. H. Gouraud. Continuous shading of curved surfaces. IEEE Trans Comput 1971;20:623–628.

27. G. Wolberg and T. E. Boult. Image warping with spatial lookup tables. Comput Graph 1989;23:369–378.

28. G. Wolberg. Digital image warping. Los Alamitos, CA: IEEE Computer Society, 1990.

29. P. Heckbert. Fundamentals of texture mapping and image warping. Masters thesis, University of California at Berkely 1989.

30. E. J. Selker. Method and apparatus for improving visibility and selectability of icons. U.S. Pat. 5,565,888 (Oct. 15, 1996).

# CHAPTER 7

# Implementing a Picture-Achieving and Communication System (PACS) and Teleradiology System: Practical Issues and Considerations

JIHONG WANG, Ph.D.

Department of Radiology
University of Texas Southwestern Medical School
Dallas, Texas

*Information Technologies in Medicine, Volume II: Rehabilitation and Treatment,* Edited by
Metin Akay and Andy Marsh.
ISBN 0-471-41492-1   © 2001 John Wiley & Sons, Inc.

This chapter presents the practical experiences and issues of implementing a clinical PACS. Checklists are included for potential PACS buyers so that they can address some of the common issues involved in the planning, installation, and postinstallation maintenance of a PACS and teleradiology system. The process of implementing a PACS is presented step by step. Specific details and considerations within each step of the implementation process will be discussed, and the University of Texas Southwestern Medical School's (UTSMS) *experiences are presented as examples of each step.* One of the goals of this chapter is to provide the potential PACS buyer with a practical guide throughout the maze of PACS and teleradiology implementation.

## 7.1   PLANNING

Planning is always the most important phase in implementing almost any project. To successfully implement a PACS, detailed planning is required because a PACS is a complex system. Compared to the installation of even highly sophisticated radiology equipment, such as MRI or CT, implementing a PACS requires more planning work of the buyers. First, one has to justify the purchase of the PACS. The hospital administration will want to know why the hospital needs such an expensive system that does not generate revenue. Therefore, the financial justification of implementing a PACS must be done, and it may not be as straightforward as the justification of adding a MRI or CT scanner. Second, implementing a PACS involves multiple departments such as the information service, the facility service, the clinical departments served by the PACS, and so on. Obviously, a well-planned project will have a smooth and cost-effective implementation.

Although the radiology department usually is (and rightly so) the leading force in the implementation of a PACS, the PACS is really an integral part of the hospitalwide patient management system. Radiologic images are part of the patient's electronic medical record (EMR). One needs to convince the hospital administration that it is not just a radiology capital expenditure. It should be treated as part of the information infrastructure similar to the telephone and computer network systems within a hospital. In addition one has to understand that PACS is also a system that enables the radiology department to provide better and faster service to the clinicians. In the end, departments other than radiology may be those who benefit the most from PACS. In fact, it is the primary-care physicians and ultimately the patients who will benefit most from the PACS. Therefore, one must first find the needs and define the problems that PACS intends to solve, such as excessive film loss and improvement of service. These improvements of the efficiency and quality of patient care will consequently reduce cost, especially within the managed-care environment.

### 7.1.1 Organizing the Team

The buyer should first organize a PACS planning and implementation team. The charges of this team are to identify the problems or the areas that need improvement and to study the potential benefits the PACS will provide. At the beginning, the team should include a small number of people so that it can stay focused, thus goals and expectations will be well defined. This small group should also serve as the steering force in the future expanded team as the implementation progresses. The team should clearly define the goals and expectations of the PACS project.

I recommend that the following people should be included in the team:

Radiologist
Physicist
Information service administrator
Radiology administrator
Network engineer
Facility manager
Technologist
Patient scheduling personnel

After the team is organized, the members can meet and discuss the goals and expectations of the PACS.

### 7.1.2 Defining Goals and Expectations

In the 1990s, several PACS projects around the country made the mistake of not defining specific goals before the implementation. Their goals and expectations were not well defined. Consequently, PACS users had unrealistic expectations and ended up with strong disappointment. Like many other technologies, PACS cannot solve all the problems in a radiology department. It provides only the technical means to improve some aspects of patient care, such as instant access to the patient image and elimination of film loss. Still the human factor is most important in the PACS. For example, it is often found that some radiologists initially are not comfortable with reading images on computer monitors. Lack of confidence in the monitor display and other such hesitations in using the PACS can be the biggest obstacles in implementing the PACS. Acceptance of PACS by the primary-care physicians is also critical to its success.

There are various reasons for implementing a PACS. From reduction of film loss to providing teleradiology services, the goals defined by the team will directly determine the scale of and steps toward implementing a PACS. The goals thus defined can serve as guidelines in the contract negotiation. The goals and expectations should be communicated with the users as soon as the implementation of the PACS begins. In this way, there will be no surprises for the users after deployment.

The following are the most common reasons for implementing a PACS:

Excessive film loss.

Long delay in the availability of radiologic images and associated diagnostic reports.

Repeated films owing to poor image quality and film loss.

Required simultaneous access to the same patient's images at different physical locations by several involved physicians.

Need to build a campuswide complete EMR (or electronic patient chart).

Cost of film and chemicals.

Image file room cost.

Need for teleradiology service to remote clinics.

*What the UTSMS Did.* We started with a small group of people, which consisted of radiologist, physicist, vice president in charge of information service (IS), and radiology administrator. This group met and defined the goals and areas for which PACS may have the greatest improvement on the efficiency of radiology service. We found that the emergency room (ER), intensive care unit (ICU), and neurology and Neurosurgery constituted 70% to 80% of CT and MRI services. In addition, CT and MRI are inherently digital and DICOM conformant. These factors have made them the ideal candidates for the first phase of the PACS implementation. We decided that ER, ICU, and neurology and neurosurgery department would be included in the first phase of PACS implementation. Based on each of the department's needs, we decided the number and type of workstations installed at various locations. This small group of people has been the steering force for the later enlarged team that also has included technologist, patient scheduling manager, IS engineer, facility management personnel, etc.

### 7.1.3  Justification Analysis of PACS

There are two major aspects of justification for PACS. One is the financial justification of implementing a PACS and the other is the justification of improving clinical service, which in turn will have indirect financial effect on the institution as a whole. PACS may not be for everybody. In fact, for some hospitals or clinics, it may not pay off financially to implement a PACS at present. For most cases, however, the economical justification analysis is required. It will decide the scope of the PACS. With today's pricing structure of PACS, economical justification by film saving alone is hardly justifiable unless a large amount of examinations is done and one can turn the radiology department film-less overnight. The real savings come from the improvement of radiology service to other departments who benefit from zero film loss, faster, simultaneous access to the radiology images. For example, instantaneous access to the radiologic images by the primary physicians while the patient is still in hospital may save another patient visit for the same medical problem. It will cut down the time that primary physicians wait for the radiologic images. Thus the hospital can provide a faster, better care to patient at lower cost by avoiding the multiple visits.

*What the UTSMS Did.* Our PACS project was not justified based on the possible financial savings within the radiology department. Rather it was justified by the fact that we could improve radiology services to other departments, benefiting the entire the hospital.

### 7.1.4 Workflow Analysis

Workflow analysis is one of the most important steps in the planning phase of a PACS. It determines the layout and archive configuration of the PACS. It also determines the network bandwidth requirement. In the workflow analysis, the team must study the current workflow pattern. Based on the clinical needs, the team must also define when and what locations images will be sent to. It must define the rules of when, where, and what images can be retrieved. In addition, it must define the rules of when, what, and how images should be archived. Based on the number of images and size of images, frequencies of images transferred among the workstations, one can define the network speed and capacity requirements.

Each institution's workflow is different, depending on the services it provides and amount of image data that needs to be sent. There may also be differences in policies as to whether the images should be released to the clinicians without the radiologist's report and, if so, when they can be released. The team should not overlook the effect of PACS on these policies and the politics involved. These customs and traditions tend to be difficult to change and will directly affect the acceptance of PACS among users.

*What the UTSMS Did.* The planning team met numerous times to map out the workflow of CT and MRI services. We carefully studied the current needs of the various departments that use CT and MRI services. Then we decided the configuration of physician's workstations. We analyzed their needs and decided how and when physicians could access the images. We decided to make CT and MRI images immediately available to the physicians as soon as they are acquired. For example, we have decided the flow of CT images is as shown in Figure 7.1.

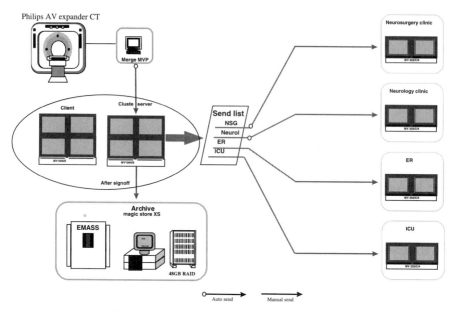

**Figure 7.1.** CT Workflow from 8 A.M. to 5 P.M.

From 8 A.M. to 5 P.M.: The CT sends images to the Merge MVP, on which the images are converted to DICOM format, and sent to the MV1004 cluster server. New CT studies with the patient ward name for the neurosurgery node are stored on the diagnostic reporting workstation MV1004 server for reporting, and after signoff are sent to the Magic Store archive. The images are also sent immediately to the neurosurgery workstation for immediate viewing. Should neurosurgery wish to print images on film, the images are sent to the Easyvision (EV1) print server where they may be printed on the Imation Dry-View laser camera. Selected images from the CT studies are manually sent to the ER department workstation or the ICU workstation. The MRI image routing scheme is similar (Fig. 7.2).

## 7.1.5 Network Requirement Analysis

Depending on the amount of data flow, the existing network infrustructure may or may not be adequate for the successful operation of PACS once installed and in clinical operation. In fact, lack of proper network analysis was another common mistake made in the early days of implementing PACS. It was one of the main reasons several PACS projects failed and created a general resistance to PACS. In one incidence, a third-party dealer sold a PACS to a community hospital without any workflow analysis and network requirement analysis. The existing network was only a 10-Base T ethernet, and the dealer sold a PACS intended to handle CR, MRI, CT images together. Of course, the project was

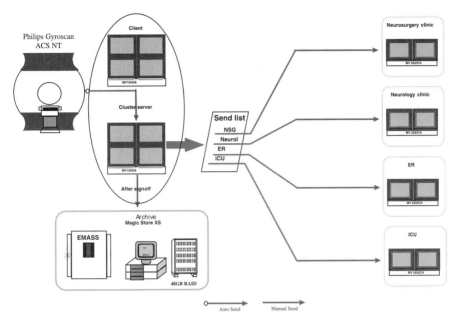

**Figure 7.2.** MRI Workflow from 8 A.M. to 5 P.M.

doomed to fail. It was only after the hospital upgraded the network infru-structure that the PACS project was revived. However, the bad impression of PACS has been established in the minds of many users at that hospital as a result of the lack of planning.

Usually the network analysis requires an experienced network (or IS) engi-neer. Most of time, the PACS network can be segmented from the hospitalwide network so that the heavy traffic within the PACS network will not slow down the functionality of other departments on the same network.

*What the UTSMS Did.* Based on the workflow, we calculated the amount of image data that needed to be transferred from one place to another. Figure 7.3 indicates the scope of the first phase of the PACS implementation. Based on the workflow analysis, we looked at our institution's network infrustructure and found that it was capable of handling the data flow. We decided to use the ex-isting FDDI network as the backbone for the PACS network. We also decided to segregate the PACS network from the main hospitalwide network.

### 7.1.6 Estimation of Achieve Need

The database management piece is the most important component of a PACS. It is the brain and heart of a PACS, and controls the prefetching and autor-outing of previous images to the workstations around the hospital in additional

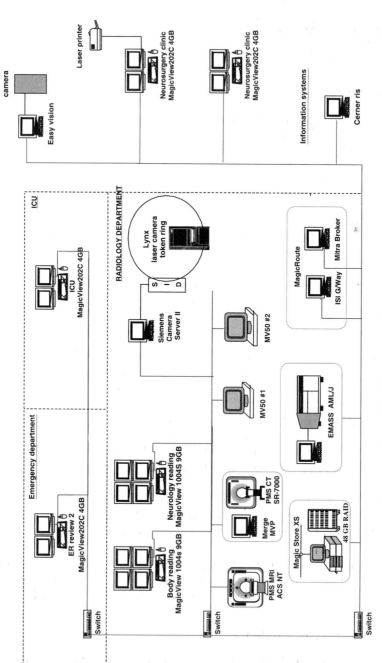

**Figure 7.3.** Network requirement analysis.

to data management in the archive. The archive usually includes both a short-term, fast-access component and a long-term, slow-access component. It is crucial that the users decide correctly how much archive capacity should be purchased and when. Because the price of archive media decreases constantly, it makes little sense to spend a lot of money up front for some storage media that one can purchase in a few months for a lot less. On the other hand, the initial installation of a PACS should have enough capacity to handle the operational requirements. In other words, one should have enough archive to keep newly acquired data stored for a relative short duration and add the required media (such as the tapes or CD) as needed.

The planning team should look at the amount of imaging data generated per month and decide what kind of archive media to purchase. Then it should decide what the initial archive capacity will be. The long-term expandability of the archive media selected should also be addressed. Currently the short archive, which keeps the data online with fast access, is usually a RAID. A RAID often has capacity in tens of gigabytes. The long-term archive can be MOD or tape drive. There is always some new technology on the horizon, such as DVD at present. The buyer should study the options and decide what type of long-term archive media to use.

*What the UTSMS Did.* Based on the study of the amount of data generated for the previous few months, we decided that keeping 2 to 4 weeks of MRI/CT images online would be adequate. Thus a 48-GB RAID was purchased to be the immediate short-term archive device. It provides fast, reliable access for the most recent patients' image files. For the long-term archive, we decided to purchase at least 1.5 to 2 years of image archive initially and purchase more storage capacity when needed. A robotic tape drive with 10-TB capacity was purchased. However, we purchased only 10 tapes initially and will add tapes as we need them.

## 7.2 EQUIPMENT AND VENDOR SELECTION

In the next phase of the planning, the scalability and future expansion of the PACS must be considered. Because PACS involves primarily computer hardware and software, it is critical to keep the system open to future upgrades and to the integration of a piece of equipment not necessarily made by the PACS vendor. One should not have to be locked in to any specific vendor's product. It is only because of DICOM that such an open PACS is possible. Therefore, one must *insist* on DICOM conformance of the system purchased. In fact, one should not waste time looking at a proprietary system if the function can be performed by a DICOM-conformant one.

DICOM is a quite complex standard. The detailed document may be obtained at NEMA (www.nema.org). It includes many functional specifications called service classes. Each service class specifies a particular function. For example, the storage class specifies the function of sending the image data in the standard way so that the receiving party (storage class provider) can receive it properly. The party, which is capable of sending DICOM images, is called the storage class user. A vendor's product may not support all the service classes. In fact, at the present no vendor claims that it supports all the service classes specified by the current DICOM standard.

Further, ACR/NEMA has specific guidance for the vendors to claim DICOM conformance. A sales person from a vendor does not necessarily understand the full meaning of DICOM conformance. The system specification should be studied carefully. An expert's consultation may be helpful.

## 7.2.1 Writing Specifications

Request for purchase (RFP) can serve as the basis of the final purchase contract. It is, therefore, important to specify the system requirements in detail. Unfortunately, accomplishing such a goal is not a trivial task because PACS is a complex system and not yet a mature technology. Therefore, hiring a professional to help with the RFP may be a reasonable option.

Two approaches are common when generating a PACS RFP. The first approach, which is also the most common in radiology equipment purchase, is to specify every technical detail about the system. Government agencies often use this method. This approach works well for a known, mature product such as an x-ray or CT unit. It may not work well for an institution considering a PACS purchase. The second approach is to ask specific technical questions and let the vendors answer them. For example, instead of specifying the type and the speed of network that should be used with the PACS, one can ask how long the PACS takes to prefetch certain images from one point to the other. Once the information is obtained from all vendors, the purchaser can compare the competitive PACS products.

One must also realize that conformance to DICOM standard is an incremental thing. All the commercially available PACS products at the present time are only partially conformant to DICOM standard, which itself is under constant update. Therefore, a vendor should not be excluded solely based on lack of support for a single DICOM service class. However, the buyers may ask that specific DICOM functions be provided at no or minimal cost once the functions become available within a certain period of time from the first purchase.

The principal things to look for when selecting a PACS vendor are as follows:

- Conformance to DICOM standard.
- System openness and network topology.
- Database distribution.
- Workflow management ability.
- User interface design of PACS workstation.

- Interfacing ability to RIS, HIS.
- System function and performance.
- Reliability.
- Service and technical support.
- Existing installation or customer base.

At a minimum the system should support the following DICOM classes: storage, query/retrieve, worklist management service, and print. Later in this chapter is a list of questions that the buyer should ask the PACS vendor is given. One can use it to request for information about competitive PACS products.

*What the UTSMS Did.* We did not write a RFP; instead, we researched all the major PACS vendors' products carefully. Because PACS is a fast-evolving product and there is no perfect PACS product, it probably does not gain the buyer much to specify a product that no vendor can produce. We found a vendor who had a PACS product that met our needs, and then we negotiated directly with that vender. However, not every institution or community hospital can take this approach for various reasons. Therefore, a RFP may be critical for some institutions.

## 7.2.2  RFP Analysis

Once the bids and quotes from the vendors are received, the team should meet to analyze the bids carefully. The main functionality should be compared among the PACS products. There are major differences in PACS products. Some use centralized archives, some distributed. Some have more DICOM service class conformances, some fewer. It is critical to have an expert who has PACS experience to analyze the bids. Sometimes a consultant may provide the necessary help. When analyzing the bids, consider the principal factors listed above plus the system's capability to interact with other vendors' products, the network communication protocols, the design of the database and archive, the image analysis tools, and security measures.

*What the UTSMS Did.* We did not go through the bid analysis because we selected the PACS vendor based on our research of all the existing PACS products. We selected the PACS product that fit our needs.

## 7.2.3  Site Visit

During a site visit, the buyers can see the PACS in clinical operation. The buyers may find clinical operation issues that are different from those at their own institution. Some operational issues may be unique and they may need to be addressed to ensure the success of the PACS. In addition, during a site visit, the buyers may find something not revealed by the marketing people of the vendor (good or bad). In addition, it is always a good idea to talk to people who are currently using the PACS and find out the true story about a vendor's system performance. During site visit, one should concentrate on workflow, archive, and the user interface of the PACS workstation.

*What the UTSMS Did.* We went to several sites to look at various PACS products. During these visits, we not only focused on the PACS product itself but also investigated the workflow and operational issues. We found it beneficial to our decision-making process in selecting the PACS vendor. From the site visits, we found that most of the problems or issues related to the interfacing between HIS/RIS and the PACS and the interfaces between image acquisition modalities and the PACS. Fortunately, more and more image acquisition modalities such as CT/MRI are becoming DICOM conformant so that some of the minimum DICOM functions, such as storage and query/retrieve, are easily available. However, there are still minor problems and glitches in the interfaces. For example, the slice location indicator (or cut lines) on a scout view in MRI and CT are not available on the PACS side simply because the information is not transferred in the image files. Detailed issues such as this need to be addressed with the PACS vendor before a purchase is made, especially because some vendors may charge the customer for any so-called added functions.

### 7.2.4   Contract

As in any negotiation process, the purchaser of PACS should fully use his or her own purchasing power. Oftentimes the purchaser has more power than is thought. For example, the purchaser may be in a geographic location that a PACS vendor wants to use as a show site to compete with other existing vendors in the same area. Or the buyer may belong to a multihospital purchasing group. Or the vendor is approaching the end of a fiscal year. Or the local sale force may desperately need some sales, and they are willing to pull some strings within their organizations to make the sale, and so on.

In the contract, the purchaser should address the clinical flow issues so that there will be no last-minute surprises or even excuses for the vendor's installation team's delay. It is better to specify the criteria by which the PACS is deemed acceptable. In addition, the buyer should specify some of the critical functions that the PACS must perform, such as whether the user shall be able to print from one workstation to an arbitrary printer. The vendor should provide such information in the RFP to the buyer. Because there are so many details to the PACS and there are so many options available with the PACS, putting the technical details in the contract can avoid a lot of misunderstandings and frustrations. For example, the buyer should have the vendor lay out all hardware and software requirements of performing a certain function (such as direct print to a particular laser printer from a specified workstation). This will insulate the buyer against last-minute additional costs when adding so-called optional software needed to perform a certain critical clinical function on the PACS.

Furthermore, the buyer should insist that the price of the PACS components be itemized, although most PACS vendors try to sell it as a whole package. This will give the pricing information for the buyer to consider for future expansion (e.g., adding an another workstation). The vendors were and some still are hesitant to do this for two reasons. First, the major PACS vendors started as imaging acquisition device manufacturers who are used to selling a MRI scanner for such and such price with few options. Their internal pricing schemes differ from the computer industry, which is used to separating the price of hardware from software. The second reason is that by pricing PACS as a whole package, the hidden costs will not be visible to the customer, realizing a higher profit margin for the vendor. It is beneficial to the buyer to have an itemized pricing structure for a PACS product. It has been demanded by many PACS buyers so that many PACS vendors are in the process of changing their pricing practice to meet this need.

In the contract negotiation, the buyer should also address the after-sale service of the PACS. It is often found that in the first few weeks or months after the installation PACS, the users may want to reconfigure the PACS to meet some specific needs. For example, the user may decide to send images to somewhere else or the IP address of certain PACS nodes need to be changed. It is important to put some service clauses in the contract so that such requests be met in a timely fashion. It is mutually beneficial to both the buyer and the PACS vendor to build a good, long-term relationship so that the future expansion of the PACS can be smooth and painless. However, the buyer should also be aware the tactic used by some unethical sale persons. One commonly used phrase is that they are willing to "develop a joint partnership" with the buyer. The buyer should ask what makes his or her institution so special so that the vendor is willing to give them a "huge" discount.

It may be a good ides to get your legal department involved early in the contract negotiation process, depending on the institution's internal policy. It is always a good idea to put some penalty and payment clauses in the contract so that the vendor has some incentives to get the installation done on schedule. One common practice is to pay 80% at shipment of equipment, 20% after completion and acceptance by the user.

*What the UTSMS Did.* Once we selected the vendor for our PACS project, we negotiated with the vendor for a multiphase, multiyear project. We asked for the itemized price of all the PACS components. We agreed that our hospital would become a show site for the vendor in exchange for a price discount. One regret we have is that we did not specify the printing function very clearly, necessitating the purchase of additional software options if we want to print from some workstations to a specific printer.

## 7.3 INSTALLATION AND IMPLEMENTATION

### 7.3.1 Installation Team

When the purchase order is issued, the purchaser should assemble the installation team as soon as possible. This team should include the network engineers from the hospital, project engineers from the vendor, facility managers from the hospital, and anyone who will be involved in the installation. Anyone who may be involved in the installation should be invited at least once to understand the scope and timeline of the installation. The team should meet regularly or as needed during the installation.

Usually the project engineers from the vendor will coordinate most of the configurations and software upload onto the workstations. However, the hospital should also appoint a person to coordinate the work needed to be done within the hospital, such as network cabling and testing, facility modification, and so on. The installation team can still serve as a useful channel of communication among all parties involved. With regular meetings, it is much easier to resolve issues that come up during the installation.

*What the UTSMS Did.* We enlarged our initial PACS planning team to include network engineers from information service and facility management. We also included the HIS/RIS representative to coordinate the interfacing issues. Occasionally, we invited the MRI/CT vendor's representatives to coordinate the DICOM connectivity problems related to MRI and CT.

### 7.3.2 Timelines and Clinical Area Downtime Planning

Careful planning of the PACS installation is important for a busy clinical setting because minimal interruption of the clinical operation is highly desirable. Usually, installation of PACS workstations does not interfere too much with routine clinical operations. Configuration of the PACS workstation can be done at prestaging when the software is loaded into the system. Installation of the archive and storage device can be time-consuming but it has minimal interruption to clinical operation.

However, interfacing the acquisition devices such as MRI and CT scanners with the PACS requires time on the scanners. To minimize the interruption to the clinical operation, it would be better to do the interfacing over a weekend or in late evenings. Usually, the DICOM configuration of the CT and MRI scanners takes less than a couple of hours if the image acquisition devices are already DICOM *conformant*. However, it may take a longer time if an interface box is required to convert the proprietary images to the DICOM files.

The biggest interference to the clinical operation is to the radiologist's work routine. Because most of the historical examinations on the patients are on films, it is difficult to read previous examinations on films on an alternator, then turn around read the new films on a computer monitor. Because of the luminance level difference of the two displays, the eyes are constantly trying to adapt to the luminance levels. In addition, it is tiresome to switch back and forth from alternator to computer monitor. To resolve this problem, one may want to consider preloading the previous examinations into the PACS before the patient shows up for a new examination, so that the radiologists can read from only the PACS workstation from day one.

*What the UTSMS Did.* We planned the installation and configuration of the CT and MRI scanner over weekends and late evenings. We also rescheduled the inpatients while keeping scanners available with 30 min of notice for the emergency patient. We encountered no problems configuring the MRI scanner, which was already DICOM conformant. However, the CT scanner by the same vendor needed a DICOM interface box, which was problematic initially. It took us a while to troubleshoot this interface.

We preloaded the previous MRI/CT examinations onto the scanners then pushed them into the PACS workstation and archive the evening before the new examination was to occur, according to the patient's schedule. This is labor intensive but it makes the reading process much faster.

## 7.4  ACCEPTANCE TESTING

The acceptance testing must be defined before the installation and put into the contract. The responsible persons must all be satisfied with the PACS before the final acceptance is signed and the last payment paid. During the acceptance testing, the purchaser should at least check the following:

- PACS workstation software functionality.
- Optional software.
- Image file integrity.
- Image quality on the monitor.
- The speed of image transfer.
- Image printing and quality.
- Workflow configuration.
- Functionality of the archive and database management (preroutine, auto-routine, etc.).

## 7.5  POSTINSTALLATION MAINTENANCE

After installation, there may be some minor bugs and software glitches in the PACS that require service. Once these problems are resolved, the PACS usually runs smoothly.

Maintaining the system may require a reboot occasionally. The user should follow the instructions provided. There may also be some minor changes in the PACS configuration, such as autorouting images to a different location. The pretrained PACS administrator should be given the tools and training to make these changes. The PACS administrator should be trained by the vendor before installation. This PACS administrator can train new users within the organization. He or she is responsible for the regular maintenance of the PACS, including quality assurance (QA) and data integrity checkup. In addition, he or she will be responsible to maintain the quality control (QC) program on the PACS. The quality control program should at least include the monitors of the workstations, maintaining the archive device, and monitoring and testing the data integrity of the archive.

*What the UTSMS Did.* We hired one system administrator from our technologists. She is responsible for training the new users, and maintaining the PACS workstations and archive. We found it is efficient to do this. We are currently running a QC program on the workstation. This program will ensure image quality consistency across all the workstations of the same class. It is critical to control the image quality, because computer monitors vary greatly in sizes, quality, brightness, and color tones.

## 7.6   TELERADIOLOGY CONSIDERATIONS

PACS implementation within an organization is the first step to enable the institution to do teleradiology. In the past, teleradiology was often done by setting up a one-to-one connection between workstations and a film digitizer to a workstation via a dedicated line (often through a modem via telephone line). It had limited success partially because of the low speed of image transmission and image quality inconsistency among workstations. Some of the teleradiology systems were hardly used because of ill planning and lack of confidence in the users on the image quality obtained from the teleradiology system.

Similar to the planning of PACS, although much smaller in scale and complexity, implementing a teleradiology service requires equivalent analysis based on economical and technical common sense. One of the many reasons that a teleradiology system fails is because of economics. There may not be enough need for such a service in some area and it does not justify the cost of putting a dedicated workstation to a site with few patients. It probably does not make any economic sense. Another important factor is that the image quality from the old teleradiology system is poor. It was often done by digitizing a radiographic film, then sending the digitized image to the workstation. Not only were the images different from the original in spatial resolution but also the contrast of the images were poor owing to degradation. Because of these difficulties, some teleradiology systems have limited use, whereas some of the well-planned teleradiology services have been successful.

In the United States, another difficulty that teleradiology initiatives have to face is the legal issues of practicing medicine across state boundaries. Because of turf battles, technical difficulties, and some legitimate concerns about quality delivered by this technology, teleradiology as part of the telemedicine effort has not taken off as predicted by some analysts.

Putting the political and legal difficulties aside, the technical issues that a teleradiology service has to face are patient load and economical justification, the cost of converting to digital acquisition and receiving, and image quality assurance. It is crucial to implement a QA program on all the workstations and make sure that images are presented in a consistent manor and with optimal quality.

In conclusion, the successful implementation of PACS requires careful planning, teamwork, and cooperation from many parties, including vendor's project engineers. What the UTSMS did is not intended to be the only or the best way to implement a PACS. Our experience with PACS should only serve as an example of PACS implementation.

## 7.7 CHECKLISTS—FROM PLANNING TO ACCEPTANCE TESTING

### 7.7.1 Justification

1. What are the goals this PACS intend to accomplish?
   - Less film loss.
   - Film/chemical cost savings.
   - Fewer repeated examinations.
   - File room clerk reduction.
   - Imaging service to the floor.
   - Fast, simultaneous access to the images by radiology and clinical department.
   - Teleradiology service requirement.
   - Compete with other institutions in the area.
2. Why do you need a PACS now?
3. Which areas will this PACS be serving?
4. What are the benefits of implementing this PACS?
5. What will be the benchmarks to measure the success of PACS?
6. What is the cost to install a PACS? What will be the savings?

### 7.7.2 Planning

1. Who should be included in the steering group of planning?
2. Who should be included in the installation team?

3. What will be the phases of implementing PACS? What is included in each phase? Cost of each phase? Any infrastructure investment?

4. What is the workflow within the hospital? (Draw workflow diagrams.)

5. When should the image be archived into the patient folder? Should images Modified by clinicians also be achieved?

6. Based on the workflow, what is the estimated amount of data to be transferred during the peak hour?

7. What kind of network infrastructure exists for the institution? What does it take to upgrade it to meet the PACS requirements?

8. What is the archive capacity requirement? (Short term, long term.)

9. Do we have a RIS, HIS system? (If not, get a RIS system first.)

10. What is your purchasing leverage?

11. Is leasing the PACS an option? What about payment for certain amount image transferred/stored?

12. Selection of proper sites for visit. What are the issues found during the site visit that may potentially be a problem?

### 7.7.3  Technical Evaluation

1. File format compatibility and interfacing with other vendor's systems.
   - Is the system inherently DICOM conformant? Does it require gateways to communicate with other DICOM conformant devices?
   - What DICOM service classes does the workstation support? (Storage, query, retrieve, print, worklist management.)
   - What DICOM service classes does the archive support?
   - How does the PACS store CR image files? (Processed or raw?)
   - Any file compression used by the PACS? If there is, what kind? (Lossy or lossless.)

2. Network requirement.
   - What is the proposed configuration of the network?
   - What are the network infrastructure requirements for this PACS?
   - Speed of retrieving and archiving the files? (From the archive to the workstation, from workstation to workstation.)

3. Integration with RIS/HIS:
   - Does the PACS have an internal RIS function?
   - Can the PACS be interfaced with the existing RIS of the hospital?
   - What radiology information systems has the PACS has successfully interfaced with?

4. Database and storage system.
   - Is it a centralized or distributed archive? What is the expandability of the archive?

- What type of storage medium does it use? (Magnetic tape, magneto-optical disk, CD, DVD.)
- What are the data retrieval and write speeds?
- What is floor space it occupies, and what are the environmental requirements for the storage device?
- Can the PACS do scheduled data prefetching, prerouting?
- Is there any redundancy in the archive? What is the possible failure rate?
- Are the data stored compressed? If yes, how are they compressed? What is the average compression ratio?
- How accessible is the central storage system? What are the security measures?
- Does the PACS keep track of what files are currently presented on all the workstations on the network?

5. Hardcopy output capability.
   - Can it print out a hard copy? From which workstation(s)?
   - Does the PACS support DICOM print service class?
   - What is the dynamic range of the hard-copy display? What is the bit depth?

6. System QC.
   - Does the system perform self-check regularly? How often?
   - Does the PACS provide automatic warning if file loss is found?
   - What is included in the self-QC program?
   - How long does it take to do such a QC test?
   - Is there a QC program on the monitors of the workstations?
   - Does the system self-check the storage spaces available and provide appropriate warning?

7. Worklist management.
   - How is worklist management done with this PACS? (Auto data entry from RIS/HIS, bar code entry.)

8. Security issues.
   - Can the PACS administrator set user passwords and associated access privileges with it?
   - Does the PACS provide appropriate warning if attempts at unauthorized break-ins happen?
   - Are passwords updated regularly?
   - Does the PACS keep the user log-on record?
   - Does the PACS keep a record of access history to the patient image file?

9. Future software and hardware upgrade.

- What is the future software and hardware upgrade guaranty? Associated cost?

10. Downtime and uptime.
    - What is the average downtime of the system? What is the guaranteed uptime? Is there any emergency backup mechanism?
    - Will one workstation reboot affect the whole PACS system?

11. Configuration and user interface of the primary diagnosis workstation.
    - What kind of computer platform is it running on? What is the computer hardware configuration?
    - How many monitors can the system support? (Preferable four.)
    - Is the workstation intuitive to use? Are the icons for the tools intuitive?
    - Is there a graphical patient list?
    - Can the workstation show previous examinations and associated reports?
    - Can the patient database be sorted by name, date, clinical number, and type of examinations?
    - Is a short-cut keystroke function available?
    - How easy it is to query the archive and other servers?
    - How easy it is to add another image send or query destination?
    - Does an undo function exist? How many steps back?
    - What image-manipulation tool is available? (Edge enhancement, histogram analysis, 3-D surface rendering, MIP, magnifying, roaming, zooming, rotation, flip, measure distance, text notation, ROI measurement, etc.)
    - Is the magnification range adequate? Can the user zoom continuously by move of the mouse?
    - Is the speed of brining up an image acceptable?
    - Is the speed of roaming and moving the images adequate? (Not jerky or delayed.)
    - Are the window width and level setting displayed? (Can the user preset window and level?)
    - Is the workstation configurable to each reader's presettings?
    - Does the workstation keep each individual's customary setting by their logins?
    - Can it create teaching files in TIFF or GIF format? Then can the user send those files via ftp? By email?
    - Is the monitor cooling fan too noisy? How much heat does the workstation generate? Is additional climate control required?

12. Monitors.
    - What is the monitor line resolution? What is the number of scan lines per unit length?

- Is the display field sufficiently large? Is there obvious distortion over the entire display field?
- What is the line spread function at both vertical and horizontal direction on the monitor? Is the raster line visible from the normal viewing distance?
- What is the size of video card memory?
- What is the frame rate?
- What are the monitor maximum and minimum luminance levels? What is the displayed dynamic range of monitor $(I_{max} - I_{min})$? Is it uniform over the entire screen?
- What is the variation in luminance between the center and the edges of the monitor?
- What is the luminance consistency among multiple monitors?
- Does the high luminance level in one area significantly degrade the contrast in the adjacent low-luminance areas? (Spillover of the scan line or falloff distance.)
- Is the illuminant spectral distribution optimal for best achromatic vision?
- Is there any noticeable flicker of the monitor?
- Is there difference in resolution between the center and the edges of the display within the limits of acceptance?
- Is there any antireflection coating on the monitor? Any antiglare devices?
- Does the luminance of the monitor change with time? If so, how fast does it degrade?
- What is the lift expectancy of monitors?
- What is the LUT? Is it adjustable?
- Is the color of the monitor shell black or dark colored?

### 7.7.4 Installation, Acceptance Testing, and Training

1. User training.
   - How would the training of the users be handled? (Cost, Prerequisites.)
   - Who should be trained?
   - Who should be the PACS administrator?
2. Facility requirement for the PACS system.
   - What is the facility requirement for the workstation, archive? (Space, room remodeling, electrical power supply, special lighting for the reading room.)
   - Are there special ventilation and air-conditioning requirements?
   - Are all the work areas equipped with the appropriate network and communication ports?

3. Phases of installation and benchmarking of the installation.
   - When and what will be installed and be fully functioning?
   - What are the measurable deliverables and timelines?
   - What is required before the system installation and by when?
   - How long, if ever, will the installation interrupt the clinical operation?
   - When should training of users start?
4. Acceptance test.
   - What are the acceptance criteria?
   - Is the interface with HIS/RIS fully functioning?
   - Has staff training completed?
   - Are all DICOM interfaces between image acquisition devices and the PACS fully functioning?
   - What is the final sign-off procedure?
   - Are the image query, archive, and transfer speeds acceptable?
   - Are the prefetching and prerouting functions working?
   - Does every monitor meet its quality specification?

### 7.7.5  Contractual Issues

1. The vendor should guarantee to keep PACS software up-to-date for 3 years at no or minimal cost to the purchaser. The purchaser and the PACS vendor should agree on the definitions of software upgrade and new software release in advance.
2. As part of the service contract, the vendor should provide free system software reconfiguration such as adding another DICOM acquisition device (such as ultrasound, digital R/F, CR, and nuclear medicine).
3. The purchaser should specify system up time requirement and service response time.
4. The purchaser should negotiate the cost of expanding archive capacity in advance.

### 7.8  CURRENT STATUS OF DICOM CONFORMANCE OF IMAGE-ACQUISITION DEVICES IN RADIOLOGY

The status of DICOM conformance of all the image-acquisition modalities in radiology changes daily. Radiology equipment manufacturers are at different stages of implementing DICOM. The degree of DICOM conformance depends on the equipment vendor and type of equipment. For example, a latest MRI scanner may support DICOM storage class and some other DICOM service classes, whereas the latest CT scanner by the same manufacturer may not support any DICOM function at all. At the present, no single commercial equipment in the market fully supports all the DICOM functions. This is partially because the DICOM standard has been evolving until recently, and the vendors are playing catchup. It is foreseeable that the major vendors of radiology equipment will be DICOM conformant in some of the basic functions to make a PACS possible. These basic functions include storage, query/retrieve, worklist management, and DICOM print.

Currently, the major image-acquisition modalities in radiology are MRI, CT, ultrasound, nuclear medicine, radiography, mammography, fluoroscopy, and angiography. Most of the latest devices in these modalities acquire images in digital format. The image format varies from one modality to another. The image matrix size also varies. The DICOM conformance status varies also from vendor to vendor. In the following, I give a brief summary of the DICOM conformance status across modalities, without mentioning differences in DICOM conformance status among various vendors.

MRI images are inherently digital. Usually the image matrix size is $256 \times 256$. Depending on particular cases, each patient has about 100 to 300 images on average. Most of the latest MRI scanners sold today support DICOM storage. Some may support query and retrieve. Some claim that they do not intend to support query and retrieve at all because they are afraid of intrusion at the scanner. Some of them do support worklist management. Some support direct DICOM print class. Consequently, for most of the MRI scanners, images can only be sent out to the PACS via DICOM storage but can not be queried or retrieved.

CT images are also inherently digital. The image matrix size is usually $512 \times 512$ or smaller. Each patient has about 50 images on average. Most of the latest CT scanners support DICOM storage class. Few support query and retrieve for the reason mentioned above. Some support direct DICOM print, some support worklist management. As with the MRI scanner, CT images can be pushed out onto PACS workstations or data archive, but can not be queried and retrieved.

Ultrasound equipment has advanced rapidly in the past several years. Some of the latest high-end ultrasound scanners are inherent digital and support DICOM storage and DICOM print. However, many of the older ultrasound scanners still need an external video frame grabber to capture and convert the video signal into digital images. Then the digital images are converted into DICOM format and communicated to a PACS on a separate interface box. The ultrasound image matrix size is usually $256 \times 256$ or smaller, with 20 images per patient on average. In the next several years, however, I anticipate that most ultrasound vendors will support direct DICOM storage and DICOM print without the need for an interface box.

Most the latest nuclear medicine cameras acquire images in digital format. The image matrix size is usually $128 \times 128$, with 1 to 2 images per patient except for SPECT studies in which the number of images can be as high as 100 per patient. The majority of the latest nuclear medicine cameras support DICOM storage class. Some may support query and retrieve. Some vendors claim that additional functions such as DICOM print, and worklist management will be available soon.

Radiographic images are usually done with the conventional screen/film system. It is not digital without some kind of digital capture device such as CR or DR. CR is a relatively mature technology. It captures the radiographic image on a photo-stimulable phosphors plate and then uses a laser to read out the images out digitally. DR, on the other hand, uses microsemiconductor devices to convert radiographic image directly into digital signal. DR is not yet a fully mature product and is expensive. It has recently become commercially available. CR has been a commercial product for years. It is the primary tool to obtain a radiographic image in digital format. A typical CR radiographic image is approximately $2000 \times 2000$ in size. Thus the image size is usually around 8 MB to 10 MB per radiographic image. For a busy radiology department, several hundred examinations are taken each day. Therefore, to store all the CR images requires a large archive capacity. There are a limited number of vendors who manufacture CR. All of them claim that their CR products support DICOM storage class. Some support query and retrieve. They all have some ways to perform the worklist management function through a gateway interface to RIS/HIS.

There are two types of digital fluoroscopic images. One is the series of images taken at 15 to 30 frames per second (It is often called the scene image). Another is the digital spot image. As of today, some fluoroscopy units do not fully support DICOM storage class. A gateway computer is required to convert the proprietary image files into DICOM format. Most of the time, one can send out only the digital spot images but not the fluoroscopic cine images.

In summary, the recent development in DICOM conformance of radiology equipment makes it possible to directly send digital images to a PACS except for the fluoroscopic and DSA scene image. Consequently, it is possible to provide physicians instant access to the radiologic images as soon as they are acquired by using PACS. However, we have a long way to go before we can fully integrate the patient data (including laboratory results, patient history, and radiologic examination images) into a master database that contains the complete EMR for a patient. With the rapid development in PACS, computer technology, and network communication technology, a more efficient, computerized health-care system is foreseeable in the near future. PACS will become only a small part of that system.

# CHAPTER 8

# From Engineering to Surgery: The Harsh Realities of Virtual Reality

ROBERT JOHN STONE

Virtual Presence Ltd.
Sale, UK

With most new and exciting technologies, there is often an early tendency for the pioneers and proponents to become so engrossed with the novelty of the technology and so divorced from real-world applications that subsequent industrial uptake and technology "maturation" are painfully slow processes. So it was in the past with speech recognition, artificial intelligence, and neural networks. So it was—and, to some, extent still is—with virtual reality (VR).

Recently, there have been times when one could be forgiven for thinking that VR had outlived its usefulness (if, indeed, it had been used at all). It has been all too easy to stumble across Internet and newspaper reports of company closures, redundancies, downward-spiraling share prices, questionable accounting procedures—the list goes on and on. Fortunately for the survivors of what some might describe as a Darwinian process, this critical stage in the history of VR

*Information Technologies in Medicine, Volume II: Rehabilitation and Treatment,* Edited by Metin Akay and Andy Marsh.
ISBN 0-471-41492-1  © 2001 John Wiley & Sons, Inc.

looks set to end, with recent evidence suggesting that the markets for VR products and services are about to become buoyant again as the year 2000 approaches. Inevitably, one has to expect further casualties. A small number of these will be in the commercial VR arena. Notably, most will be probably be evident in the academic sector. Here the monotonous appearance of university-based "reality centers" or so-called centers of VR excellence has to come to an end soon, if only because, sooner or later, national and European funding bodies will recognize how much money has been spent on bricks, mortar, impressive projection theaters, and near-zero content. Exactly who, then, will survive?

> The VR companies that are succeeding today are those that have a customer base committed to VR product development ... The VR tools providers and full VR solution developers are succeeding relative to other companies, because the development community is increasing in size and ready for product to shorten development cycles in the process of creating VR applications (1).

This perceptive statement, emphasising market pull as opposed to technology push, is as true today as it was in 1994: a customer base committed to VR product development. The question is, how does one secure such a customer base and, just as important, how does one ensure that those same customers remain committed to developing the products further?

Since 1998, while observers of the VR arena might have wondered why the technology had died a sudden and somewhat quiet death, there has been, in fact, a period of considerable consolidation for the real-world users and developers of VR. With a few exceptions, the technology has, as a result, generally matured to such a level that affordable systems of impressive quality have become readily available. The once-pervasive childlike enthusiasm for VR has also matured, so much so that due concern is now (at last) being given by VR developers to the needs of the users and organizations into which they are selling their products and services. This is particularly evident in education, engineering, and medicine/surgery.

There is still much to do, however; and part of this chapter presents some observations on what can be done and is being done to help accelerate the uptake of VR technologies across numerous market sectors. Finally, returning to the medical relevance of this book, I conclude with a brief case study of one surgical training system, the development of which demonstrates some of the successes of adopting a user-driven approach to VR implementation and some of the consequences when such an approach is ignored.

## 8.1  SO WHAT HAPPENED IN 1996

In a market survey conducted for the UK government's Department of Trade and Industry (DTI) in 1996 (2), I attempted to develop a first-level business model, based on many years of experience of "selling" VR (solutions and turn-key systems) to commercial and industrial organizations. As the model was fine-tuned, it became apparent that the honeymoon period for VR was over.

The time when the technology was being investigated purely on the basis of its high-tech attractiveness had been and gone. Unfortunately, in 1996, VR technologies and services had not developed to the level at which they were capable of selling themselves or being sold with minimal effort. Part of the problem stemmed from the fact that VR was being heralded as a plug-and-play panacea for all future technological problems faced by (for example) engineering industries, educational bodies, heritage organizations, retail outlets, and medical practices. Among the main findings of the survey were the following issues:

1. The VR sales process had to be improved if adoption was to become more evident than it was then. No longer could VR companies trade solely on a short-term basis of hitting quarterly targets. Bullish sales into industry—where the annual costs of specialist technical and personnel support had been suppressed and postsales support had been minimal (this is still a problem today)—had not helped the growth of the VR community. VR users, be they from the engineering community, medical sector, or wherever, do not take kindly to being sold expensive and often risky IT solutions where the subsequent costs outweigh the initial aspiration to gain major savings by streamlining and enhancing their working practices.

2. The VR education process by which potential VR users are made aware of the benefits of VR to their organization was (and to some extent is still) weak, time-consuming, and costly, especially for the small VR companies. The publication of real case studies—*not* public relations announcements —was considered vital to the success of this process, as was the encouragement of short, low-cost, low-risk feasibility studies.

3. The education process must be mutual. In other words, the VR company must work hand in hand with the user company to understand the horizontal and vertical characteristics of the organization, no matter what its size or financial characteristics.

It may be of interest to note that since the publication of the DTI report, one of its recommendations, the establishment of a UK-VR forum, has actually happened. The forum is a body of VR users and developers (underpinned by the DTI). Since its launch, the forum has been increasing its education activities through the dissemination of case study material, staging workshops in such areas as heritage and manufacturing, and forming a dedicated Web site (www.vrforum.org.uk) with links to all key UK players.

## 8.2   A SIMPLE RECIPE FOR SUCCESS

Commercial and collaborative VR development projects carried out since 1992 by my team have been well documented elsewhere (3). Many of these, including the Rolls-Royce Trent 800 virtual prototype (Fig. 8.1), the GEC Marine virtual

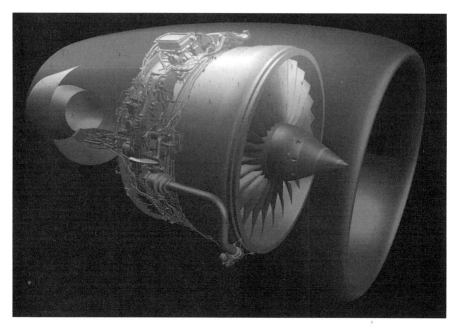

**Figure 8.1.** Virtual Rolls-Royce Trent 800 aero engine for maintenance verification and training.

submarine project (4), and the British Nuclear Fuels virtual control room for ergonomics and training (5) (Fig. 8.2) are prime examples of the importance of adopting a work ethic that fosters close coupling between VR developers and a customer base committed to VR product development. More recent examples, in which close interaction between developers and users was required, include consumer evaluation of virtual retail products (6) (Fig. 8.3); the *Crime Conquest* virtual societal trainer for schoolchildren, sponsored by the Greater Manchester Police Authority (7); and the development of a Windows NT-based VR system for interactive visualization of computational fluid dynamics databases (5).

The lessons learned during many of these projects are, today, regularly applied whenever an opportunity emerges for applications development effort or the introduction of a turnkey VR system. From an awareness perspective, they apply equally as well to the potential VR user organization as to the developer or researcher who is trying to provide a solution. The nine lesson are summarized as follows:

- *Lesson 1 (L1).* At the outset of a VR project opportunity, do not instantly offer solutions based on VR technologies *per se*; listen to what the organization or potential user wants. Also, as can quite easily happen, do not be influenced by the user's preoccupation with VR as his or her chosen solution. It is quite possible that a solution not based on VR or on a different form of VR from what is expected by the user will provide what the orga-

**Figure 8.2.** Virtual nuclear facility central control room for ergonomics assessment and operational training.

**Figure 8.3.** Virtual retail products for design, marketing, and consumer evaluation studies.

nization wants. Overenthusiastic technical presentations of VR as *the* solution to *all* IT problems will scare most users away. Others may well be quite happy to buy a solution based on technology push. However, experience shows that they expect considerably more than the deliverables they ultimately receive.

- *Lesson 2 (L2)*. Question the potential users about their organization's existing IT setup; their commitment to using IT; and any planned investments, working practices, personnel backgrounds (e.g., the characteristics of their future VR users), and organizational structure (both internally and in terms of their position in any commercial supply chain). All of these indicate how much the organization will want to invest in VR and integrate VR as a major operational tool.

- *Lesson 3 (L3)*. Once there is a good understanding of the potential user's problem and organization, describe VR in terms of what the user has already said, emphasizing such issues as reducing time and costs of concept to market, instant changes, reapplication (in other areas or departments), and reduced training costs.

- *Lesson 4 (L4)*. Identify and work closely with the organization's project champion(s).

- *Lesson 5 (L5)*. Recommend a short feasibility study (to include a user requirements or human factors analysis), addressing (among other issues) organizational (interdepartmental) communications, concurrent engineering/communication practices (intranet and Internet), recent and anticipated IT investments, personnel requirements (including skills base, training and ergonomics), and policies for the education and management of technological change.

- *Lesson 6 (L6)*. Ensure that a comprehensive and signed-off story board or requirements list form a major result from the feasibility study.

- *Lesson 7 (L7)*. Formally propose only what the story board or requirements list requires.

- *Lesson 8 (L8)*. Involve potential users in the evaluation trials (both during and at the end of the project).

- *Lesson 9 (L9)*. Involve the organization's own specialists in the project, e.g., for basic modeling and run-time training.

## 8.3   A SURGICAL EXAMPLE

Turning now to a more relevant, surgical VR project, focusing on minimally invasive therapy (laparoscopic cholecystectomy), the remainder of this chapter sets out to chart some of the successes and failures that can be attributed to following or ignoring the lessons or guidelines listed above. When a lesson was adhered to it will be indicated with a checkmark (e.g., L1✓). When it was ignored, it will be indicated by an ex (e.g., L1✗).

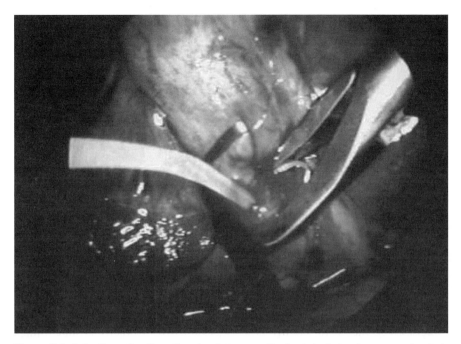

**Figure 8.4.** Injection of radioactive dye into a cystic duct during a laparoscopic cholecystectomy operation.

During the second half of 1994 and early in 1995, numerous articles appeared in the British press and on mainstream TV news programs that cast serious doubt on the future of keyhole surgery, specifically those practices in support of laparoscopic cholecystectomy (Fig. 8.4). The fact that patients had died or had been left in considerable pain, sometimes as a result of surgeon error, led to serious calls for action, especially in regard to improving the training of surgeons "graduating" from conventional, open surgery, onto these more remote techniques. In the UK, unlike the United States and some countries within continental Europe, live animal-based training is prohibited. As a result, primary laparoscopic experience is typically fostered through the remote handling of sweets/candy, grapes, raw chicken tissue, plastic tubing and foam-mounted balloons. This situation, coupled with increasing UK regulatory and certification pressures, meant that in 1994 the provision of even a basic simulator was seen as instrumental to the development of specific surgical skills.

Established in the spring of 1994, the North of England Wolfson Centre for Minimally Invasive Therapy commenced operations under grant support from the UK Wolfson Foundation and the British government's Department of Health. Today, as in 1994, the Manchester Centre revolves around a collaborative arrangement between three organizations; Virtual Presence Ltd., the Manchester Royal Infirmary, and the UK's North West Regional Health

Authority. The collaborators were, over a 2-year period, tasked with evaluating VR and related technologies, possibly progressing to a stage whereby a prototype British laparoscopic cholecystectomy simulator could be developed so that clinical and human factors evaluations could take place.

### 8.3.1   User Requirements

The first stage of the Wolfson Centre project involved a number of short in-theater observation and recording sessions (assisted by specialists at the Manchester Royal Infirmary), using video and digital endoscopy (L1✓, L4✓, L5✓). The aims of these task analyses was to obtain a clear understanding of the performance and ergonomic features of the surgeon's task and workplace and to evaluate a number of different forms of media for image capture (and subsequent digitizing for the anticipated anatomical texture mapping exercises [L1✗]). In addition, MRI surgeons provided practical demonstrations (L4✓) of current training practice and strictly supervised hands-on experience, to appreciate the physical properties of human anatomy, such as form, mass, compliance, and the extent of movement of the laparoscopic instruments. These exercises, together with lengthy briefing sessions from practising and trainee surgeons (L1✓, L2✓) produced the following main conclusions:

1. Any form of head-mounted display (HMD), be it for full or *partial* immersion (e.g., field sequential or polarization techniques) would not be acceptable to British surgeons, for image quality, in-theater communication, ergonomic, and hygiene reasons.
2. There was roughly a 50-50 split in opinions as to the need and value of stereoscopic viewing.
3. There was, it is interesting, a similar split in opinions regarding the importance of haptic feedback. Some surgeons claimed that vision was the overriding sense; others insisted that a simulator would have to include a reasonable representation of such features as elasticity, instrument constraints within the body cavity, and varying degrees of movement viscosity.
4. Surgeons wanted the VR simulator setup to be as close to that used in the operating theater, thereby enhancing transfer of training.

An early review of the U.S. market, which at first glance appeared to be rich in medical-simulation products, led to the conclusion that many of the hardware and software systems advertised in medical VR magazines and at trade shows were not as commercially available as their marketing collateral suggested. Consequently, and on the basis of the user requirements analysis, a decision was taken to execute a 2-year program of research, to develop the following (L6✓, L7✓):

An autostereoscopic (headset- and glasses-free) display system.

A suite of algorithms to simulate deformable virtual human tissue.

A prototype 3 degree-of-freedom (dof) haptic feedback system.

In general, these technical aspirations were successfully achieved by the time the Department of Health/Wolfson project was two-thirds through its planned timescale (8). A prototype, autostereoscopic display system, based on conventional LCDs combined with holographic optical elements (HOEs) had been developed by Richmond Holographics. A haptic feedback system, with simple graphics to demonstrate passive (elasticity and viscosity) and active (pulsing) organ/cavity conditions, had been designed and constructed by a postgraduate student from Manchester Metropolitan University. Students from Edinburgh University had collaborated in the development of software to demonstrate real-time, local geometric deformation of virtual tissue (at the point of instrument grasp) and force propagation through the virtual organs (Fig. 8.5). However, none of these developments was at a stage whereby it could be "productized" or even submitted to surgical specialists for clinical evaluation. Worse still, they existed as stand-alone systems—quite impressive demonstrators in their own right—but with limited scope for further development and integration into a single minimally invasive simulator.

With hindsight (a phrase used all too often in the VR community), it is obvious today that the initial direction taken by the North of England Wolfson

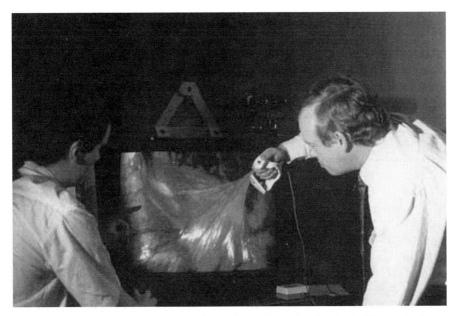

**Figure 8.5.** Early British deformable tissue simulation using Logitech Ultrasonic Space Tracker prototype.

Centre was not influenced by an unbiased ergonomics evaluation of the in-theater task analysis results. Rather the conclusions reached were very much influenced by the wishes of technology-enthusiastic surgeons (L1✗). In other words, the user the developers were trying to remember became the sole driving force behind the quest for, in this case, high simulator fidelity.

By the time the scale of the remaining development task facing the Wolfson Centre team had been quantified (with little hope of further national support), it was becoming obvious that more in-depth (and better resourced) visual and haptic simulation work was being carried out elsewhere, with toolkits and products gradually emerging from the United States (in particular). However, there was a more fundamental concern. The Wolfson Centre and other VR developers had targeted full-blown anatomic and physiologic simulations, all requiring the support of expensive, sophisticated graphics supercomputers. On revisiting the earlier user requirements data, it was concluded that what was actually required (especially for training within the British National Health system) was a simulator that represented an affordable and practical alternative to physical trainers and the high-fidelity VR packages.

### 8.3.2 MIST$_{VR}$

The specific result of taking a step back and revisiting the earlier task analyses with a more unbiased approach (L4✓, L5✓, L7✓) was the identification of an urgent need to develop a low-cost, PC-based laparoscopic cholecystectomy simulator. The end product of these further analyses was MIST$_{VR}$, a surgical psychomotor skills trainer, based on Immersion Corporation's instrumented laparoscopic interface, connected to an industry-standard PC (Fig. 8.6). Movements from the laparoscopic interface tools are translated into three-dimensional (3-D) computer graphics that accurately track and represent the movements of those tools within a virtual operating volume. Within this volume, simple geometric shapes are generated and subsequently manipulated using the interface tools (Fig. 8.7). The graphics have been intentionally kept simple so that high frame rates may be maintained on relatively low cost equipment and to preserve the validity and reliability of the simulations when used in applied experimental research.

The software was targeted to a low-end PC platform to keep costs to a minimum. The 3-D graphics were originally developed under Windows NT 3.51 using Sense8's *WorldToolKit* for OpenGL. The software ran on a 200 MHz Pentium Pro PC with 32 MB of RAM and a graphics card capable of accelerating OpenGL. With the advent of Direct 3D this specification has been revised downward. The software has been successfully ported to the Direct 3D libraries via *WorldToolKit* and runs under Windows '95. This solution provides acceptable frame rates running on a standard multimedia PC with a 200 MHz Pentium processor, 32 MB of RAM and a low-end Direct 3D graphics accelerator.

MIST$_{VR}$ features five general modes of operation: tutorial, training, examination, analysis, and configuration. Close analysis of the video records gen-

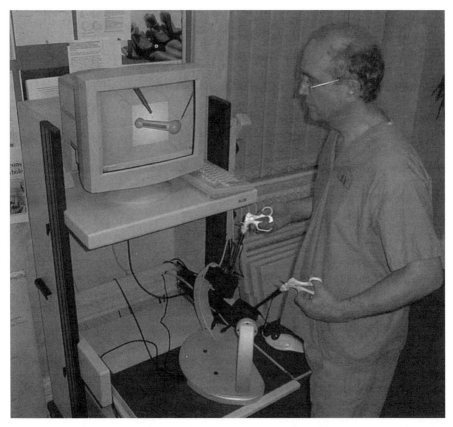

**Figure 8.6a.** The Latest Version of MISTVR, Showing Re-Engineered Instruments and One of Three New Gynaecological Tasks.

erated during the earlier in-theater observation sessions, together with iterative review sessions involving consultant surgeons and senior registrars drove the specification of six basic task modules for $MIST_{VR}$, including combinations of instrument approach, target acquisition, target manipulation and placement, transfer between instruments, target contact with optional diathermy, and controlled instrument withdrawal/replacement.

These tasks, described in more detail below, can be configured for varying degrees of difficulty and the configurations saved to a library for reuse. Specific task configurations can be assigned to individual students. In the examination mode, the supervisor can select the tasks and repetitions and is able to order and save to a specific file for that trainee. Progress can be assessed with optional performance playback of the training session or examination. Data analyses permit quantification of overall task performance (accuracy and errors, plus time to completion are logged during the tasks) and right/left hand perfor-

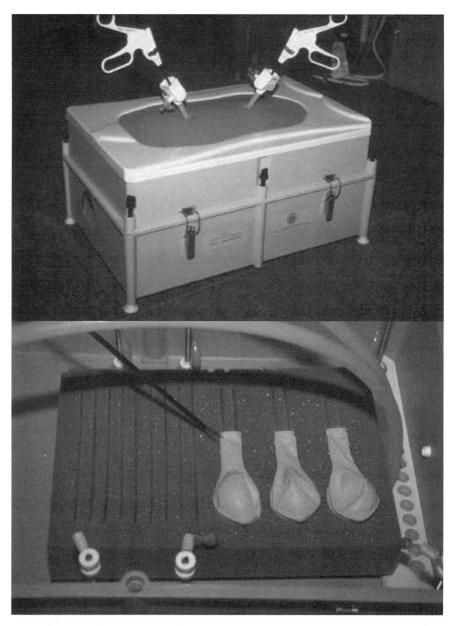

**Figure 8.6b.** A Conventional Physical Closed Box Endoscopic Trainer, Showing Synthetic Contents.

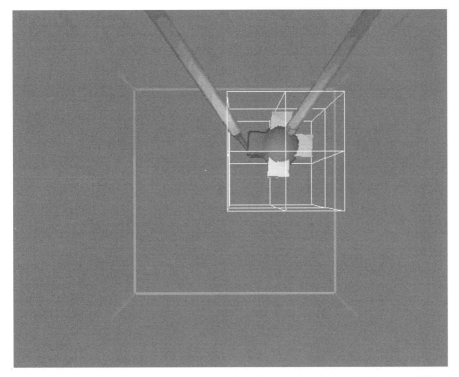

**Figure 8.7.** The typical MIST$_{VR}$ training screen format, showing Task 6 images (object manipulation and diathermy).

mances. The data are accessible in forms suitable for statistical analysis and significance testing.

### 8.3.3  The MIST$_{VR}$ Task Set

The main interface to MIST$_{VR}$ is quite simple. As well as the task setup, calibration, and help/text sections, the majority of the display is occupied by the interactive graphics window. In essence, this takes the form of a wireframe box that describes the effective operating volume in which target stimuli appear, are acquired, and can be manipulated by virtual representations of the laparoscopic instruments. In an earlier version of MIST$_{VR}$, concern was expressed that the predominantly perspective cue within the operational volume was insufficient to assist in the perception of depth and relative distance. However, when simple textures and grids were pasted onto the inside of the volume, it was felt that they cluttered the visual scene to an excessive degree and did not add any perceptual value. This research/experimental psychology issue is currently the subject of a university proposal to one of the UK's academic funding bodies.

For all tasks, a MIST$_{VR}$ training session starts when the subject manipulates the instruments to "touch" a simple start box located in the center of the operating volume. Once objects have been acquired, successful and erroneous acquisitions are color coded appropriately (and recorded).

### 8.3.3.1  Task 1: Simple Object Acquisition and Placement.

Task 1 tests the subject's ability to acquire an object with either hand and move it to a new 3-D location within the virtual operating volume. The task has relevance to such operative activities as clip placement, tissue removal, and gallstone recovery. The system generates a spherical target object at a random position within the operating volume. The subject moves the instrument tip to acquire the sphere. Once acquired, a small wireframe box appears at a random position within the operating volume, and the subject is required to position the sphere within the box. The task is repeated for a set number of repetitions.

### 8.3.3.2  Task 2: Between-Instrument Transfer.

Task 2 relates to a fundamental surgical requirement: the transfer of an object from one instrument to another. The task has relevance (for example) to the fundus of the gallbladder being passed between two grasping forceps before being retracted. A more advanced skill application would be passing a needle between two needle holders during suturing. The system generates a spherical target object at a random position within the operating volume. The subject moves the instrument tip to acquire the sphere. Once acquired, the subject is required to pass the sphere to the other instrument. Intersections with the sphere and parts of the instrument other than the tool tips result in deductions to the accuracy score. On successful transfer, a wireframe box appears at a random position within the operating volume, and the subject is required to position the sphere within the box. The task is repeated for a set number of repetitions.

### 8.3.3.3  Task 3: Target Traversal.

Task 3 focuses on sequential instrument-to-instrument transfer: the walking of instruments along vessels or structures to reach their extremities (e.g., the neck of the gallbladder, as seen at the start of a laparoscopic cholecystectomy). This task in effect combines the skills of tasks 1 and 2. The system generates a cylindrical target object at a random position within the operating volume. The cylinder is subdivided into a number of segments. The subject is required to grasp the top segment with either instrument, followed by the next segment along the cylinder with the remaining instrument. The procedure is repeated in a step-by-step fashion, alternating between instruments until all segments have been acquired. The task is repeated for a set number of repetitions.

### 8.3.3.4  Task 4: Tool Withdrawal and Insertion.

Changing from one instrument type to another and being able to reinsert the new instrument quickly and accurately is a key skill in laparoscopic surgery. In task 4, the system generates a spherical target object at a random position within the operating volume. The subject moves the instrument tip to acquire the sphere. Once acquired, the remaining instrument is brought into contact with the sphere. After contact has been made, it is then withdrawn completely from the operating volume. The same instrument is then reintroduced to make contact with the sphere. Unintentional collisions with the sphere and other instrument result in deductions to the accuracy score. The task is repeated for a set number of repetitions.

**8.3.3.5  *Task 5: Diathermy Procedures.*** Task 5 focuses on the accurate application of diathermy to specific bleeding points in the gallbladder bed. The task requires accurate 3-D location with activation of the diathermy instrument only when appropriate contact has been achieved. The system generates a spherical target object at a random position within the operating volume. In this case, the surface of the sphere possesses three small cubes that have to be accurately acquired with the appropriate instrument. Once acquisition of a cube has occurred, the application of diathermy is simulated via the depression of a foot pedal. The cube gradually changes color to reflect the amount of heating applied and vanishes when diathermy has been completed. All three cubes have to be removed. The task is repeated by switching the hands holding the grasping and diathermy instruments.

**8.3.3.6  *Task 6: Object Manipulation and Diathermy.*** The final task of the basic MIST$_{VR}$ trainer combines the skills acquired in tasks 4 and 5 and focuses on object acquisition, manipulation, and diathermy within a restrictive volume. An in-theater example might be accurate instrument replacement of dissecting forceps with a diathermy hook to control precisely a bleeding point on the gallbladder. As before, the system generates a spherical target object at a random position within the operating volume. The subject moves the appropriate instrument tip to acquire the sphere. The remaining instrument is then withdrawn completely from the operating volume. This triggers the system to endow the sphere with a preset number of small cubes. The previously withdrawn instrument is then reintroduced into the operating volume, and the subject is tasked to apply diathermy to the cubes, only this time the position of the sphere has to be maintained within a small bounding box as well (Fig. 8.7). The task is complete when the set number of cubes have been removed from the sphere. Any unintentional collisions with the sphere and other instrument result in deductions to the accuracy score. The task is repeated by switching the hands holding the grasping and diathermy instruments.

## 8.4  FUTURE DEVELOPMENTS

At the time of writing, MIST$_{VR}$ systems have been installed in a number of important research and surgical teaching organizations on a national and international level—e.g., Manchester Royal Infirmary, Queen's (Belfast), St

Mary's (London), and the European Surgical Institute (near Hamburg). The early results of experimental investigations using $MIST_{VR}$ are extremely encouraging and (again at the time of writing) are being compiled into papers for a number of important surgical journals. These results not only support the clinical use of $MIST_{VR}$ as a minimally invasive trainer but also serve to validate the initial selection of psychomotor tasks on the basis the revisited surgical task analyses.

Work is already under way to extend the surgical applications covered by $MIST_{VR}$; and to this end, in-theater and video-based analyses of gynaecologic operations have been undertaken (including ruptured ovarian cyst, ovarian removal, and vaginal prolapse). It has been encouraging to note that a fair proportion of the basic $MIST_{VR}$ task set can be reapplied in the gynaecology field (similar aspirations are held for cardiac and spinal intervention), although some unique activities (e.g., requiring $MIST_{VR}$ to support some form of simple deformable object) require the development of new modules to replace the original tasks not considered relevant.

## 8.5  CONCLUSION

The successful adoption of VR technologies into organizations, be it for commercial gain or for streamlining operational procedures is not just a case of trying to impress potential users with the capabilities of an exciting technology. Understanding the needs and characteristics of the individual user and his or her organization is essential to the future development of VR as a stable form of information technology. As was witnessed during the early stages of the UK Department of Health/Wolfson Foundation project described herein, it was all too easy (even for a qualified ergonomist) to fall into the trap of striving for visual excellence at the expense of usability and content, not to mention losing sight of the needs of the user organization (the British National Health Service):

> Many developers (especially in the human factors field) believe that one effect brought about by the existence of advanced [VR] hardware and software technologies has been a reduction in the application of scientific rigour to the design of human-system interfaces. Suddenly, reasonably user-friendly software tools have become readily available which have, in some cases, permitted the designers of information displays to "go to town" in their design approach. The result? "3D works of art"—visually impressive interface formats—but of questionable usability. The drive for visual impact appears to have over-shadowed the crucial issue of concentrating on the underpinning human factors issues surrounding the need for sophisticated 3D display formats (9).

It should always be borne in mind that VR should, first and foremost, be treated as a suite of technologies (2) capable of providing the human factors or ergonomics community with a toolkit for optimizing the design of some (but not all) human–system interfaces. Turning this argument around, ergonomics

—sometimes (ignorantly) underrated as a technological field of endeavor—also has a significant contribution to make to the development of VR in this millennium. Not just as a means of alerting VR users to health and safety issues of immersive VR (10) but as a means of helping the development of methodologies that will ensure that human-centered technologies are applied correctly and users' performances can be satisfactorily recorded and evaluated.

## REFERENCES

1. P. Glovsky, Interview. The red herring, July 1994:50.
2. R. J. Stone. A study of the virtual reality market [Ref. No. URN 96/994]. Department of Trade & Industry (Communications & Information Industries Directorate), 1996.
3. R. J. Stone. Virtual reality: definition, technology and selected engineering applications overview. Paper presented at Health and Safety Human Factors Seminar. BNFL, Risley, May 1998.
4. J. Martin. Design & Prototyping. Paper presented at Virtual Reality in Manufacturing. Coventry and Middlesborough, Mar–May, 1998.
5. N. Fell. Towards a virtual solution. Chem Eng 1998;660:18–19.
6. D. Hart. The virtues of virtual reality. Grocer July 11, 1998:50–51.
7. R. J. Stone and P. Gleave. Crime conquest: societal VR-based training for schoolchildren. Paper presented at Virtual Reality in Education & Training, VRET '98. London, July 8, 1998.
8. R. J. Stone and R. McCloy. Virtual environment training systems for laparoscopic surgery: activities at the UK's Wolfson Centre for Minimally Invasive Therapy. J Med VR 1996;1:42–51.
9. R. J. Stone. Report on 3D representations for tactical displays. Winds or, UK: DERA (Portsdown) Centre for Human Sciences, 1997.
10. E. M. Kolasinski. Simulator sickness in virtual environments [Report No. 1027]. U.S. Army Research Institute, 1995.

# CHAPTER 9

# Maxillofacial Virtual Surgery from 3-D CT Images

ALESSANDRO SARTI

University of California
Berkeley, CA
DEIS, University of Bologna
Bologna, Italy

ROBERTO GORI

DEIS, Bologna University
Bologna Italy

ALBERTO BIANCHI and CLAUDIO MARCHETTI

Bellaria Hospital
Bologna, Italy

CLAUDIO LAMBERTI

DEIS, University of Bologna
Bologna Italy

The history of scientific development is characterized by some key moments owing to the union of competences coming from far away research areas. Virtual

*Information Technologies in Medicine, Volume II: Rehabilitation and Treatment,* Edited by
Metin Akay and Andy Marsh.
ISBN 0-471-41492-1   © 2001 John Wiley & Sons, Inc.

surgery, a new discipline that recently appeared among the medical sciences, is an excellent example of contribution from medical and computational knowledges to health development and progress. Craniofacial surgery is a surgical branch regarding study and treatment of any kind of disease (malformations, trauma, and tumors) affecting the face. Peculiar to this surgery is that surgical procedures have not only functional but also a esthetical implications important for all patients' life. The anatomic and functional complexity of the face and skull, characterized by the presence of the eyes, ear, nose, mouth, facial nerves, and the proximity of important the brain and the respiratory system, make this area extremely hazardous for even skilled surgeons and a dangerous mine field for residents, fellows, and surgeons in training. Moreover, cadaver anatomic dissection, which in the past was the best way to learn surgery, is difficult to be performed on the face. For these scientific and teaching reasons, we planned a research project for craniofacial surgery simulation from 3-D CT images. Generally, the goal of computer-based surgery simulation is to enable a surgeon to experiment with different surgical procedures in an artificial environment. That leads to the following purpose statements:

1. To realize a real surgery simulation tool to predict the outcome of craniofacial surgery that considers the real soft tissue movements for each kind of surgery (osteotomies, graft, implants, etc.) using embedded boundary condition models that allow one to simulate the craniofacial surgery directly on a grid of 3-D CT images of the patient.
2. To create a multimedia teaching tool.

There are several key problems in the development of a surgical simulator (1). The first issue consists in the modeling of the target organ. The geometry is usually obtained from medical imaging device like CT and MR, and the mechanics of the soft tissues is determined by models of continuum biomechanics (2). Several methods for simulating the elastic nature of the soft tissues have been proposed. Terzopoulus (3), Platt (4) and Waters (5) use deformable models. Mass-spring models have been proposed to overcome computational complexity (6, 7). Finite elements schemes have been introduced to implement volumetric deformable models in virtual surgery (8). The problem of computing time reduction has been studied by using a condensation technique applied to finite element method (9). All these have trouble approximating the anatomic geometry with a computational mesh. The 3-D tesseletion of the geometric model into finite elements is indeed nontrivial for complex anatomic structures like bones and soft tissues of the head.

We propose a simulation method that allows one to deal with extremely complex anatomical geometries. The computational grid is the natural Cartesian grid in which the acquired 3-D image is defined. The rest of the chapter is discusses theoretical basis of the linear elastic problem with embedded Dirichlet boundary conditions, the numerical approximation scheme and the solution method, and the results obtained by the application of the method to a number of datasets. We show comparisons between virtual and real operations in real patients, and consider future work.

## 9.1 THEORY

The work presented here is focuses on the physically based modeling of soft tissue, in which displacements are constructed to obey continuum physics laws. A survey of soft tissue modeling can be found in the literature (10). We start from a linear elastic model for an isotropic, nonuniform, quasi-incompressible material that, despite limitations owing to the simplicity of the model, answers to the foundamental characteristics of the tissues that must be simulated (11).

Let a body occupy a space $S$. When the body is deformed, every particle takes up a new position. For example, a particle $P$ with original coordinates $P = P(a_i)$ is moved to the place $Q = Q(x_i)$ $(i = 1, 2, 3)$. The displacement vector $u$ is then defined as

$$u_i = x_i - a_i. \tag{8.1}$$

Owing to the impenetrability of matter the mapping $\mathcal{M} : \mathcal{A} \to \mathcal{X}$ is continuous and one to one; therefore, it has a unique inverse:

$$a_i = a_i(x_j); \quad i = 1, 2, 3; \quad j = 1, 2, 3; \tag{8.2}$$

in the whole domain, and the displacement can be rewritten as

$$u_i(x_j) = x_i - a_i(x_j). \tag{8.3}$$

Consider an infinitesimal line element connecting the point $P(a_i)$ to a point $P'(a_i + da_i)$. The square of the infinitesimal euclidean norm-2 between the points is given by

$$ds_0^2 = \delta_{ij} da_i da_j = \delta_{ij} \frac{\partial a_i}{\partial x_l} \frac{\partial a_j}{\partial x_m} dx_l dx_m \tag{8.4}$$

where $\delta_{ij}$ is the Kronecker delta. The difference between the deformed and the original Euclidean distance is then given by

$$ds^2 - ds_0^2 = \left( \delta_{ij} - \delta_{\alpha\beta} \frac{\partial a_\alpha}{\partial x_i} \frac{\partial a_\beta}{\partial x_j} \right) dx_i dx_j \tag{8.5}$$

and this allows us to define the Cauchy strain tensor

$$e_{ij} = \frac{1}{2}\left(\delta_{ij} - \delta_{\alpha\beta}\frac{\partial a_\alpha}{\partial x_i}\frac{\partial a_\beta}{\partial x_j}\right) \tag{8.6}$$

It is easy to check that the strain tensor (Eq. 8.6) can be explicited in terms of the displacement vector. After some manipulations it becomes

$$e_{ij} = \frac{1}{2}\left(\frac{\partial u_j}{\partial x_i} + \frac{\partial u_i}{\partial x_j} - \frac{\partial u_\alpha}{\partial x_i}\frac{\partial u_\alpha}{\partial x_j}\right) \tag{8.7}$$

If the displacement is very small, the square and products of partial derivatived of $u_i$ are negligible respect to the linear terms, and the strain tensor reduces to

$$e_{ij} = \frac{1}{2}\left(\frac{\partial u_j}{\partial x_i} + \frac{\partial u_i}{\partial x_j}\right) \tag{8.8}$$

The relationship between the strain and the related stress is a property of the material. It is described by a constitutive equation.

$$\sigma_{ij} = \Phi(e_{kl}) \tag{8.9}$$

If the stress tensor is linearly proportional to the strain tensor, the stress–strain relationship is given by the tensor of the elastic constant $C_{ij}$, which is a simmetric tensor with rank 4 and 81 elements ($3^4$). In this case, the constitutive equation takes the name of Hookean elastic solid equation

$$\sigma_{ij} = C_{ijkl}(e_{kl}) \tag{8.10}$$

If the material is isotropic, i.e., when the elastic properties are identical in all directions, the $\sigma$–$e$ relationship reduces to the simple form

$$\sigma_{ij} = \lambda e_{\alpha\alpha}\delta_{ij} + 2\mu(e_{ij}) \tag{8.11}$$

where the constants $\lambda$ and $\mu$ are called Lamé constants. By classical continuum mechanics results the equation of motion of a solid body with density $\rho$

$$\rho\frac{du_i}{dt} = \frac{\partial\sigma_{ij}}{\partial x_{ij}} + F_i \tag{8.12}$$

and it is obtained as a combination of the continuity equation, the momentum equation, and the Newton's law (11). The vector **F** represents the sum of the external forces acting on the body. The equation of motion for isotropic Hookean solids can be obtained by substituing in (Eq. 8.12) the corresponding stress–strain relationship (Eq. 8.11). If we consider small displacements, the strain is espressed in terms of the displacements by (Eq. 8.8), and finally we obtain

$$\rho \frac{du}{dt} = \mu \nabla^2 u + (\lambda + \mu)\nabla(\nabla u) + F \qquad (8.13)$$

Because we are interested in the steady state solution of (Eq. 8.12), we consider null the time derivatives and write the system of coupled equations of the static equilibrium for an isotropic elastic material in Cartesian coordinates

$$\mu \nabla^2 u + (\lambda + \mu)\nabla(\nabla(u, v, w)) + Fx = 0$$
$$\mu \nabla^2 v + (\lambda + \mu)\nabla(\nabla(u, v, w)) + Fy = 0 \qquad (8.14)$$
$$\mu \nabla^2 w + (\lambda + \mu)\nabla(\nabla(u, v, w)) + Fz = 0$$

where $u = u(x)$, $v = v(x)$, $w = w(x)$ are the displacements of the point $x = (x, y, z)$ in the $x$, $y$, $z$ directions.

In equation system 8.14, the forcing term **F** is considered as a known term, i.e., an input of the problem. It is easy to recognize that this term is unknown in surgery-simulation planning. In fact, during the planning of the operation, the surgeon thinks in terms of displacements to be applied to the bones of the patient and he or she can only roughly estimate the strength of the force to apply. The real input of the problem is the displacement field applied to the bones. Therefore, for each subset that corresponds to bones, we prescribe a known displacement field that acts as an embedded boundary condition subset. The resulting modified linear elasticity equations system for isotropic materials with embedded boundary conditions becomes:

$$\mu \nabla^2 u + (\lambda + \mu)\nabla(\nabla(u, v, w)) = 0$$
$$\mu \nabla^2 v + (\lambda + \mu)\nabla(\nabla(u, v, w)) = 0$$
$$\mu \nabla^2 w + (\lambda + \mu)\nabla(\nabla(u, v, w)) = 0$$

for $x \in \Omega_0 \subset \Omega$,

$$u = \tilde{u}$$
$$u = \tilde{u} \qquad (8.15)$$
$$w = \tilde{w}$$

for $x \in \Omega_1 \subset \Omega$,

$$\frac{\partial u}{\partial x} = 0$$
$$\frac{\partial v}{\partial y} = 0$$
$$\frac{\partial u}{\partial z} = 0$$

for $x \in \partial\Omega$. Where $\Omega_0$ is the subdomain of soft tissues, $\Omega_1$ is the subdomain of bones, $\tilde{u} = (\tilde{u}, \tilde{v}, \tilde{w})$ is the prescribed displacement, and Neumann boundary conditions have been considered on the boundary $\partial\Omega$. Because in the three-dimensional (3-D) image there is also a subdomain corresponding to air, to close the problem we have to add a set of equations to model this subvolume. We model this subset like an extremely compressible elastic material that does not significantly affect the solution in the soft tissue subdomain.

## 9.2 NUMERICAL SCHEME

This method allows to set a natural spatial discretization for equation 8.15 that coincides with the voxel structure of the 3-D medical images derived directly from the acquisition procedures. In fact the 3-D CT image defines a natural Euclidean embedding for the represented surfaces and volumes. In this way, it is possible to avoid a local parametrization of surfaces and volume, because the simple Euclidean metric with respect to the embedding is used and avoids re-parametrization and refining shapes after motion. The equation system 8.15 has been discretized by replacing first- and second-order differential operators with mask 3 centered differences. From the discretization procedure, a linear system of equations is obtained. The order of the system is given by the dimension of the grid multiplied by the number of unknown variables in the system, which are the three components of the displacement vectors. For CT and MRI volumes, the dimensions of the grid can vary significantly. We use $120 \times 120 \times 150$ voxel grids. Owing to the huge amount of data, it is necessary to use massively parallel computers to solve the equation system in short time.

The seven bands matrix can be preconditioned and solved with different resolution methods. Even if the preconditioning is not ever necessary, it still speed-up the convergence to the solution. Standard and ad hoc libraries have been used. The library of preconditioners and solvers of PETSC has been applied to invert the associated matrix The software has been develeloped in C and has been implemented both for sequential and distributed memory MIMD computers (in particular a CRAY T3E with 128 nodes).

The input data are given by a tridimensional matrix containing a segmentation and classification of the materials (soft tissues, still bones, moving bones, and embedding material), the dimensions of the grid, the embedded boundary conditions defined as Euclidean transformations applied to the subset of moving bones, the physical parameters of the model (Lamé constants), and the parameters related to the parallelization of the code. The output file contains the displacement field of the deformed tissues associated with each node of the grid. The program can be executed on one or more processors. When it is executed in the parallel version, each processor reads a block of rows of the associated matrix with the related set of elements of the known terms vector.

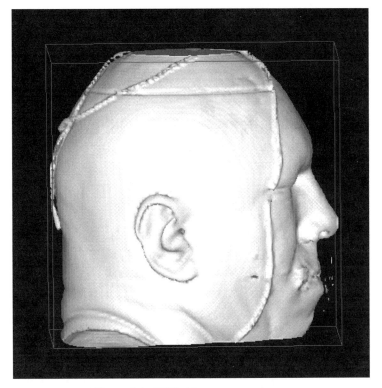

**Figure 9.1.** VHB skin reconstruction.

## 9.3 RESULTS

The application of this approach for modeling the elastic deformation of human tissue in response to movement of bones is demonstrated both on the Visible Human Dataset of the National Library of Medicine and the CT dataset of five real patients:

*Patient 0.* Visible Human Body face. We simulated a sagittal split mandibular ramus osteotomy with advancement (Figs. 9.1–9.4).

*Patient 1.* R.A., male. He had a class III malocclusion owing to maxillary hypoplasia; and underwent a Le Fort 1 maxillary advancement.

*Patient 2.* T.A., male. An orthognathic surgery patient who underwent a Le Fort I maxillary advancement.

*Patient 3.* K.A., male. A Crouzon patient who underwent a fronto-orbital advancement. It was possible to observe the good quality and the preci-

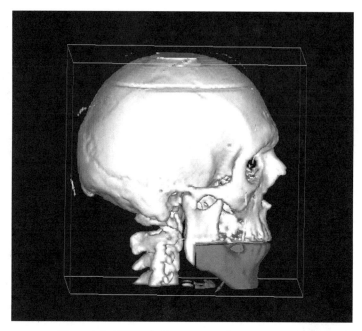

**Figure 9.2.** VHB skull reconstruction and cutting.

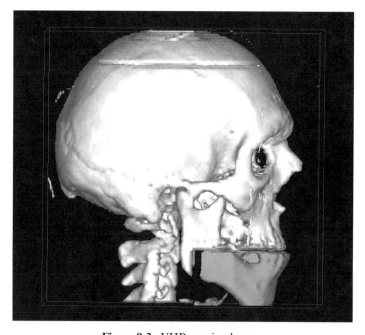

**Figure 9.3.** VHB moving bones.

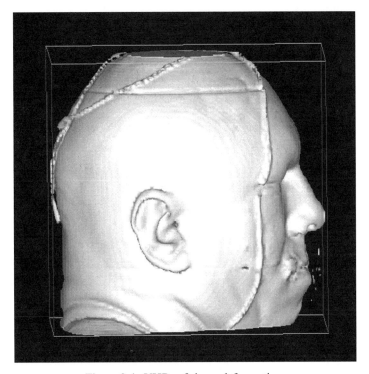

**Figure 9.4.** VHB soft issue deformation.

sion of the simulation compared to the surgical outcome. Some months later, we prepared a Le Fort III simulation; the surgical procedures were performed with a bone distraction procedure (Figs. 9.5–9.12).

*Patient 4.* M.R., female. She had a class III malocclusion owing to maxillary hypoplasia and underwent a Le Fort 1 maxillary advancement.

*Patient 5.* S.C., female. She had a class III malocclusion and mandibular deviation owing to maxillary hypoplasia and mandibular hyperplasia and underwent a Le Fort 1 high maxillary advancement that extended to the zigoma and a bilateral sagittal split mandibular ramus osteotomy.

All patients had studied with a 3-D CT scan. Patient 1 had been examined via a postoperative 3-D CT. Patients 2, 4, and 5 had been studied with only preoperative 3-D CT scans and with 3-D surgical VTO. Patient 3 underwent both stages of the surgery (fronto-orbital advancement and facial advancement) and the postoperative surgical outcome is known.

In the following we will consider the case of A.K., a 10-year-old Russian child who had a congenital malformation (Crouzon disease) characterized by craniofacialstenosys, which is a premature closing of the sutures and a resulting increase of the skull (Fig. 9.5). The operation was to widen the volume of the

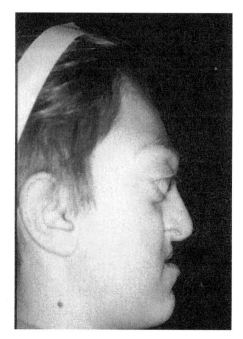

**Figure 9.5.** Presurgery.

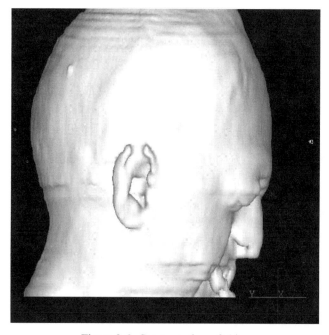

**Figure 9.6.** Segmentation of skin.

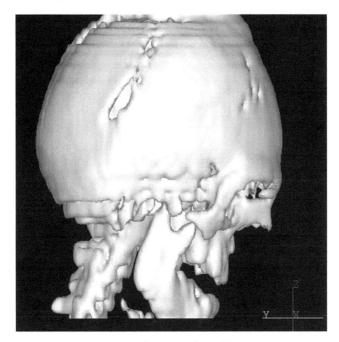

**Figure 9.7.** Segmentation of bones.

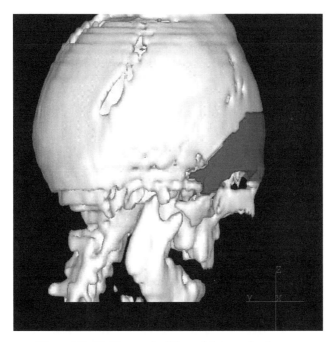

**Figure 9.8.** Cutting and editing of the moving bones.

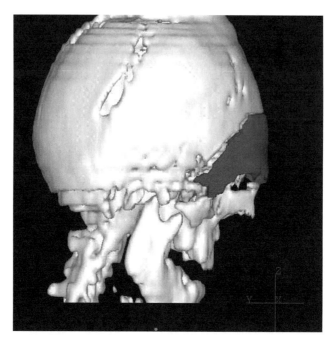

**Figure 9.9.** Fronto-orbital displacement of bones.

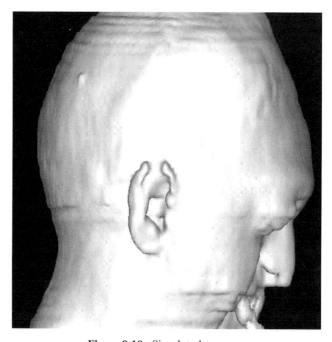

**Figure 9.10.** Simulated surgery.

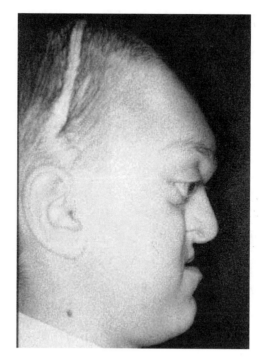

**Figure 9.11.** Real surgery.

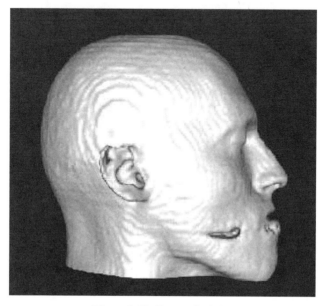

**Figure 9.12.** Presurgical CT.

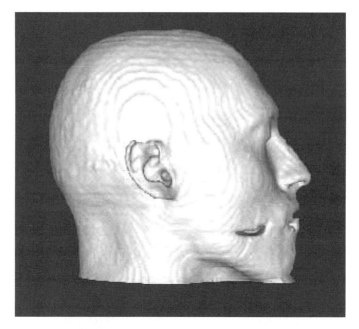

**Figure 9.13.** Surgical planning by numerical simulation.

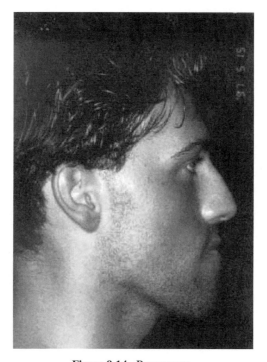

**Figure 9.14.** Presurgery.

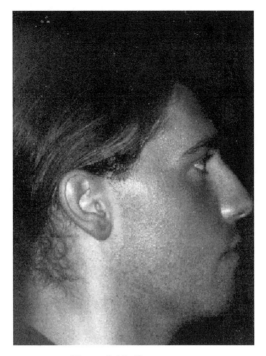

**Figure 9.15.**  Postsurgery.

cranial box through a fronto-orbital advance to give greater protection to the eyeballs and leave space for the brain to increase. The surgeon had to decide the entity and the modalities of the bones movements. For the planning of the surgery we demand a preoperative 3-D CT image of the patient, which allowed us to reconstruct the volume of the facial skin (Fig. 9.6) and the anatomic structures of the skull (Fig. 9.7). The interest of the surgeon was focused particularly on two types of tissues: hard tissues (the bones) that must be cut and moved and soft tissues that are consequently deformed. To simulate the cutting (Fig. 9.8) and moving of bones (Fig. 9.9), we built some AVS modules that allowed us to set the Euclidean transformation for each subset of bones. The entire application of editing was realized on a SGI ONIX2, with a real-time interaction on the 3-D geometries. For the fronto-orbital region the surgeon advanced the frontal direction by 8 mm and rotated it by $2.8°$. At this point, we have a tridimensional matrix containing a segmentation and classification of the materials and the embedded boundary conditions given by the Euclidean transformations applied to the subset of moving bones. We use these data as input for the resolution of the matrix associated to the equation system 8.15. In this case, the order of the matrix is about $10^7$, and we use parallel solvers implemented on the nodes of CRAY T3E. The result of the simulation, which is the vector field of the material displacements defined on each voxel, is then received and visualized on ONIX2. In Figure 9.10, the result of the entire virtual surgery session is shown. The result of the operation actually executed on the patient at the Bellaria Hospital of Bologna is shown in Figure 9.11.

## 9.5 CONCLUSION

A 3-D CT surgery simulation is a feasible tool, capable of being perfected, which could allow the surgeon to simulate the real (hard and soft tissues) outcome of craniofacial surgery procedures. The model will be tested with more cases to compare the final outcome with the preoperative simulation. The final goals of this research are to better understand for each kind of surgery (osteotomies, graft, implants, etc.) the true distribution of the soft tissue owing to the different modality of their incompressibility and, in this way, to improve the quality and likelihood of simulations.

## ACKNOWLEDGMENTS

The authors would like to acknowledge Giovanni Erbacci for the important discussions about parallelization methods and Antonella Guidazzoli and Luigi Calori for the support in medical volume visualization.

## REFERENCES

1. N. Ayache, S. Cotin, H. Delingette, et al. Simulation of endoscopic surgery. J Minimally Invas Ther Allied Technol, 1998;7:71–77.
2. Y. C. Fung. Biomechanics—mechanical properties of living tissues. 2nd ed. New York: Springer-Verlag, 1993.
3. D. Terzopoulos, J. Platt, A. Barr, and K. Fleisher. Elastically deformable models. Paper presented at SIGGRAPH '87. July 1997.
4. J. C. Platt and A. H. Barr. Constraint methods for flexible models. Paper presented at SIGGRAPH '88. 1988.
5. K. Waters. A physical model of facial tissue and muscle articulation derived from computer tomography data. Visualization in biomedical computing. Chapel Hill, NC: 1992.
6. R. Baumann and D. Glauser. Force feedback for virtual reality based minimally invasive surgery simulator. Paper presented at Medicine Meets Virtual Reality. San Diego, CA, 1996.
7. P. Meseure and C. Chaillou. Deformable body simulation with adaptive subdivision and cuttings. Paper presented at WSCG '97. 1997.
8. M. Bro-Nielsen. Medical image registration and surgery simulation. Ph.D. dissertation, IMM Technical University of Denmark, Lingby, Denmark, 1996.

9. M. Bro-Nielsen and S. Cotin. Real-time volumetric deformable models for surgery simulation using finite elements and condensation. Paper presented at Eurographics '96. 1996.

10. H. Delingette. Towards realistic soft tissue modeling in medical simulation. Proc IEEE 1998:512–523.

11. Y. C. Fung. A first course in continuum mechanics. Englewood Cliffs, NJ: Prentice-Hall, 1969.